The Special Theory of Relativity

David Bohm

ROUTLEDGE

London and New York

First published 1965 by W. A. Benjamin, Inc.

This edition published 1996
by Routledge
11 New Fetter Lane, London EC4P 4EE

Simultaneously published in the USA and Canada
by Routledge
29 West 35th Street, New York, NY 10001

© 1965, 1996 Sarah Bohm
Foreword © 1996 B. J. Hiley

Printed and bound in Great Britain by
T. J. Press (Padstow) Ltd, Padstow, Cornwall

British Library Cataloguing in Publication Data
A catalogue record for this book is available from
the British Library

Library of Congress Cataloguing in Publication Data
A catalogue record for this book has been requested

ISBN 0–415–14808–1 (hbk)
ISBN 0–415–14809–X (pbk)

Foreword

The final year undergraduate lectures on theoretical physics given by David Bohm at Birkbeck College were unique and inspiring. As they were attended by experimentalists and theoreticians, the lectures were not aimed at turning out students with a high level of manipulative skill in mathematics, but at exploring the conceptual structure and physical ideas that lay behind our theories. His lectures on special relativity form the content of this book.

This is not just another text on the subject. It goes deeply into the conceptual changes needed to make the transition from the classical world to the world of relativity. In order to appreciate the full nature of these radical changes, Bohm provides a unique appendix entitled "Physics and Perception" in which he shows how many of our "self-evident" notions of space and of time are, in fact, far from obvious and are actually learnt from experience. In this appendix he discusses how we develop our notions of space and of time in childhood, freely using the work of Jean Piaget, whose experiments pioneered our understanding of how children develop concepts in the first place.

Bohm also shows how, through perception and our activity in space, we become aware of the importance of the notion of *relationship* and the *order* in these relationships. Through the synthesis of these relationships, we abstract the notion of an object as an invariant feature within this activity which ultimately we assume to be permanent. It is through the relationship between objects that we arrive at our classical notion of space. Initially, these relations are essentially topological but eventually we begin to understand the importance of measure and the need to map the relationships of these objects on to a co-ordinate grid with time playing a unique role. His lucid account of how we arrive at our classical notions of space and absolute time is fascinating and forms the platform for the subsequent development of Einstein's relativity.

After presenting the difficulties with Newtonian mechanics and Maxwell's electrodynamics, he shows how the Michelson-Morley experiment can be understood in terms of a substantive view of the ether provided by Lorentz and Fitzgerald. The difficulties in this approach, which assumes actual contraction of material rods as they move through the ether, are discussed before a masterful account of Einstein's conception of space-time is presented. Bohm's clarity on this topic was no doubt helped by the many discussions he had with Einstein in his days at Princeton.

The principle of relativity is presented in terms of the notion of relationship and the order of relationship that were developed in the appendix and he argues that a general law of physics is merely a statement that certain relationships are invariant to the way we observe them. The application of this idea to observers in relative uniform motion immediately produces the Lorentz transformation and the laws of special relativity.

Interlaced with the chapters on the application of the Lorentz transformation, is a chapter on the general notion of the falsification of theories. Here he argues against the Popperian tradition that all that matters is mere experimental falsification. Although a preliminary explanation might fit the empirical data, it may ultimately lead to confusion and ambiguity and it is this that could also lead to its downfall and eventual abandonment in favour of another theory even though it contradicts no experiment. His final chapters on time and the twin paradox exhibit the clarity that runs throughout the book and makes this a unique presentation of special relativity.

B. J. HILEY

Preface

The general aim of this book is to present the theory of relativity as a unified whole, making clear the reasons which led to its adoption, explaining its basic meaning as far as possible in non-mathematical terms, and revealing the limited truth of some of the tacit "common sense" assumptions which make it difficult for us to appreciate its full implications. By thus showing that the concepts of this theory are interrelated to form a unified totality, which is very different from those of the older Newtonian theory, and by making clear the motivation for adopting such a different theory, we hope in some measure to supplement the view obtained in the many specialized courses included in the typical program of study, which tend to give the student a rather fragmentary impression of the logical and conceptual structure of physics as a whole.

The book begins with a brief review of prerelativistic physics and some of the main experimental facts which led physicists to question the older ideas of space and time that had held sway since Newton and before. Considerable emphasis is placed on some of the efforts to retain Newtonian concepts, especially those developed by Lorentz in terms of the ether theory. This procedure has the advantage, not only of helping the student to understand the history of this crucial phase of the development of physics better, but even more, of exhibiting very clearly the nature of the problems to which the older concepts gave rise. It is only against the background of these problems that one can fully appreciate the fact that Einstein's basic contribution was less in the proposal of new formulas than in the introduction of fundamental changes in our basic notions of space, time, matter, and movement.

To present such new ideas without relating them properly to previously held ideas gives the wrong impression that the theory of relativity is merely at a culminating point of earlier developments and does not properly bring out the fact that this theory is on a radically new line that contradicts Newtonian concepts in the very same step in which it extends physical law in new directions and into hitherto unexpected new domains. Therefore, in spite of the fact that the study of the basic concepts behind the ether theory occupies valuable time for which the student may be hard pressed by the demands of a broad range of subjects, the author feels that it is worthwhile to include in these lectures a brief summary of these notions.

Einstein's basically new step was in the adoption of a *relational* approach to physics. Instead of supposing that the task of physics is the study of an absolute underlying *substance* of the universe (such as the ether) he suggested that it is only in the study of *relationships* between various aspects of this universe, relationships that are in principle observable. It is important to realize in this connection that the earlier Newtonian concepts involve a mixture of these two approaches, such that while space and time were regarded as absolute, nevertheless they had been found to have a great many "relativistic" properties. In these lectures, a considerable effort is made to analyze the older concepts of space and time, along with those of "common sense" on which they are based, in order to reveal this mixture of relational and absolute points of view.

After bringing out some of the usually "hidden" assumptions behind common sense and Newtonian notions of space and time, assumptions which must be dropped if we are to understand the theory of relativity, we go on to Einstein's analysis of the concept of simultaneity, in which he regards time as a kind of "coordinate" expressing the relationship of an event to a concrete physical process in which this coordinate is measured. On the basis of the observed fact of the constancy of the actually measured velocity of light for all observers, one sees that observers moving at different speeds cannot agree on the time coordinate to be ascribed to distant events. From this conclusion, it also follows that they cannot agree on the lengths of objects or the rates of clocks. Thus, the essential implications of the theory of relativity are seen qualitatively, without the need for any formulas. The transformations of Lorentz are then shown to be the only ones that can express in precise quantitative form the same conclusions that were initially obtained without mathematics. In this way, it is hoped that the student will first see in general terms the significance of Einstein's notion of space and time, as well as the problems and facts that led him to adopt these notions, after which he can then go on to the finer-grained view that is supplied by the mathematics.

Some of the principal implications of the Lorentz transformation are then explained, not only with a view of exploring the meaning of this transformation, but also of leading in a natural way to a statement of the *principle of relativity*—that is, that the basic physical laws are the invariant *relationships*, the same for all observers. The principle of relativity is illustrated in a number of examples. It is then shown that this principle leads to Einstein's relativistic formulas, expressing the mass and momentum of a body in terms of its velocity. By means of an analysis of these formulas, one comes to Einstein's famous relationship, $E = mc^2$, between the energy of a body and its mass. The meaning of this relationship is developed in considerable detail, with special attention being given to the problem of "rest energy," and its explanation in terms of to-and-fro movements in the internal structure of the body, taking place at lower levels. In this connection, the author has found by experience that the relationship between mass and energy gives rise to many puzzles in the minds of students, largely because this relationship contradicts certain "hidden" assumptions concerning the general structure of the world, which are based on "common sense," and its development in Newtonian mechanics. It is therefore helpful to go into our implicit common sense assumptions about mass to show that they are not inevitable and to show in what way Einstein's notion of mass is different from these, so that it can be seen that there is no paradox involved in the equivalence of mass and energy.

Throughout the book, a great deal of attention is paid quite generally to the habitual tendency to regard older modes of thought

as inevitable, a tendency that has greatly impeded the development of new ideas on science. This tendency is seen to be based on
the tacit assumption that scientific laws constitute absolute truths.
The notion of absolute truth is analyzed in some detail in this book,
and it is shown to be in poor correspondence with the actual development of science. Instead, it is shown that scientific truths are
better regarded as relationships holding in some limited domain,
the extent of which can be delineated only with the aid of future
experimental and theoretical discoveries. While a given science
may have long periods in which a certain set of basic concepts is
developed and articulated, it also tends to come, from time to
time, into a critical phase, in which older concepts reveal ambiguity
and confusion. The resolution of such crises involves a radical
change of basic concepts, which contradicts older ideas, while in
some sense containing their correct features as special cases, limits,
or approximations. Thus, scientific research is not a process of
steady accumulation of absolute truths, which has culminated in
present theories, but rather a much more dynamic kind of process
in which there are no final theoretical concepts valid in unlimited
domains. The appreciation of this fact should be helpful not only
in physics but in other sciences where similar problems are involved.

The lectures on relativity end with a discussion of the Minkowski diagram. This is done in considerable detail, with a view to
illustrating the meaning of the principle of relativity in a graphical
way. In the course of this illustration, we introduce the K calculus,
which further brings out the meaning of Einstein's ideas on space
and time, as well as providing a comparison between the implications of these ideas and those of Newton. In this discussion, we
stress the role of the *event* and *process* as basic in relativistic physics, instead of that of the *object* and its *motion*, which are basic in
Newtonian theory. This leads us on to the (hyperbolic) geometry
of Minkowski space-time, with its invariant distinction of the
events inside of the past and future light cones from those outside.
On the basis of this distinction, it is made clear that the relativistic
failure of different observers to agree on simultaneity in no way
confuses the order of cause and effect, provided that no signals can
be transmitted faster than light.

We include in these lectures a thorough discussion of the two differently aging twins, one of whom remains on Earth while the other takes a trip on a rocket ship at a speed near to that of light. This discussion serves to illustrate the meaning of "proper-time" and brings out in some detail just how Einstein's notions of space and time leave room for two observers who separate to have experienced different intervals of "proper-time" when they meet again.

Finally, there is a concluding discussion of the relationship between the world and our various alternative conceptual maps of it, such as those afforded respectively by Newtonian physics and Einsteinian physics. This discussion is aimed at removing the confusion that results when one identifies a conceptual map with reality itself—a kind of confusion that is responsible for much of the difficulty that a student tends to meet when he is first confronted by the theory of relativity. In addition, this notion of relationship in terms of mapping is one that is basic in modern mathematics, so that an understanding of the Minkowski diagram as a map should help prepare the student for a broader kind of appreciation of the connection between physics and a great deal of mathematics.

The lectures proper are followed by an appendix, in which Einstein's notions of space, time, and matter are related to certain properties of ordinary perception. It is commonly believed that Newtonian concepts are in complete agreement with everyday perceptual experience. However, recent experimental and theoretical developments in the study of the actual process of perception make it clear that many of our "common sense" ideas are as inadequate and confused when applied to the field of our perceptions as they are in that of relativistic physics. Indeed, there seems to be a remarkable analogy between the relativistic notion of the universe as a structure of events and processes with its laws constituted by invariant relationships and the way in which we actually perceive the world through the abstraction of invariant relationships in the events and processes involved in our immediate contacts with this world. This analogy is developed in considerable detail in the appendix, in which we are finally led to suggest that science is *mainly* a way of extending our perceptual contact with the world, rather than of accumulating knowledge about it. In this way, one can understand the fact that scientific research does not lead to absolute truth, but rather (as happens in ordinary perception) an awareness and understanding of an ever-growing segment of the world with which we are in contact.

Although the appendix on perception is not part of the course, it should be helpful in calling the student's attention to certain aspects of everyday experience, in which he can appreciate intuitively relationships that are in *some* ways similar to those proposed by Einstein for physics. In addition, it may be hoped that the general approach to science will be clarified, if one regards it as a basically perceptual enterprise, rather than as an accumulation of knowledge.

DAVID BOHM

London, England
January, 1964

Contents

Foreword, v

Preface, vii

I.	*Introduction*	1
II.	*Pre-Einsteinian Notions of Relativity*	4
III.	*The Problem of the Relativity of the Laws of Electrodynamics*	10
IV.	*The Michelson-Morley Experiment*	14
V.	*Efforts to Save the Ether Hypothesis*	17
VI.	*The Lorentz Theory of the Electron*	23
VII.	*Further Development of the Lorentz Theory*	26
VIII.	*The Problem of Measuring Simultaneity in the Lorentz Theory*	31
IX.	*The Lorentz Transformation*	36
X.	*The Inherent Ambiguity in the Meanings of Space-Time Measurements, According to the Lorentz Theory*	40
XI.	*Analysis of Space and Time Concepts in Terms of Frames of Reference*	42
XII.	*"Common-Sense" Concepts of Space and Time*	48
XIII.	*Introduction to Einstein's Conceptions of Space and Time*	52
XIV.	*The Lorentz Transformation in Einstein's Point of View*	61

XV.	*Addition of Velocities*	66
XVI.	*The Principle of Relativity*	70
XVII.	*Some Applications of Relativity*	75
XVIII.	*Momentum and Mass in Relativity*	81
XIX.	*The Equivalence of Mass and Energy*	91
XX.	*The Relativistic Transformation Law for Energy and Momentum*	96
XXI.	*Charged Particles in an Electromagnetic Field*	100
XXII.	*Experimental Evidence for Special Relativity*	106
XXIII.	*More About the Equivalence of Mass and Energy*	110
XXIV.	*Toward a New Theory of Elementary Particles*	119
XXV.	*The Falsification of Theories*	123
XXVI.	*The Minkowski Diagram and the K Calculus*	131
XXVII.	*The Geometry of Events and the Space-Time Continuum*	146
XXVIII.	*The Question of Causality and the Maximum Speed of Propagation of Signals in Relativity Theory*	155
XXIX.	*Proper Time*	161
XXX.	*The "Paradox" of the Twins*	165
XXXI.	*The Significance of the Minkowski Diagram as a Reconstruction of the Past*	173

Appendix: *Physics and Perception,* 185

Index, 231

The Special Theory
of Relativity

I

Introduction

The theory of relativity is not merely a scientific development of great importance in its own right. It is even more significant as the first stage of a radical change in our basic concepts, which began in physics, and which is spreading into other fields of science, and indeed, even into a great deal of thinking outside of science. For as is well known, the modern trend is away from the notion of sure "absolute" truth (i.e., one which holds independently of all conditions, contexts, degrees, and types of approximation, etc.) and toward the idea that a given concept has significance only in relation to suitable broader forms of reference, within which that concept can be given its full meaning.

Just because of the very breadth of its implications, however, the theory of relativity has tended to lead to a certain kind of confusion in which truth is identified with nothing more than that which is convenient and useful. Thus it may be felt by some that since "everything is relative," it is entirely up to each person's choice to decide what he will say or think about any problem whatsoever. Such a tendency reflecting back into physics has often brought about something close to a sceptical and even cynical attitude to new developments. For the student is first trained to regard the older laws of Newton, Galileo, etc., as "eternal verities," and then suddenly, in the theory of relativity (and even more, in the quantum theory) he is told that this is all out of date and it is implied that he is now receiving a new set of "eternal verities" to replace the older ones. It is hardly surprising, then, that students may feel that a somewhat arbitrary game is being played by the physicists whose only goal is to obtain some convenient set of formulas that will predict the results of a number of experiments. The comparatively greater importance of mathematics in these new developments helps add to the impression, since the older conceptual understanding of the meaning of the laws of physics is now largely given up, and little is offered to take its place.

In these notes an effort will be made to provide a more easily understood account of the theory of relativity. To this end, we shall go in some detail into the background of problems out of which the theory of relativity emerged, not so much in the historical order of the problems as in an order that is designed to bring out the factors which induced scientists to change their concepts in so radical a way. As far as possible, we shall stress the understanding of the concepts of relativity in non-mathematical terms, similar to those used in elementary presentations of earlier Newtonian concepts. Nevertheless, we shall give the minimum of mathematics needed, without which the subject would be presented too vaguely to be appreciated properly. (For a more detailed mathematical treatment, it is suggested that the student refer to some of the many texts on the subject which are now available.)

To clarify the general problem of changing concepts in science we shall discuss fairly extensively several of the basic philosophical problems that are, as it were, interwoven into the very structure of the theory of relativity. These problems arise, in part, in the criticism of the older Lorentz theory of the ether and, in part, in Einstein's discovery of the equivalence of mass and energy. In addition, by replacing Newtonian mechanics after several centuries in which it had an undisputed reign, the theory of relativity raised important issues, to which we have already referred, of the kind of truth that scientific theories can have, if they are subject to fundamental revolutions from time to time. This question we shall discuss extensively in several chapters of the book.

In the Appendix we give an account of the role of perception in the development of our scientific thinking, which, it is hoped, will further clarify the general implication of a relational (or relativistic) point of view. In this account, the mode of development of our concepts of space and time as abstractions from everyday perception will be discussed; and in this discussion it will become evident that our notions of space and time have in fact been built up from common experience in a certain way. It therefore follows that such ideas are likely to be valid only in limited domains which are not too far from those in which they arise. When we come to new domains of experience, it is not surprising that new concepts are needed. But what is really interesting is that when the facts of the process of ordinary perception are studied scientifically, it is discovered that our customary way of looking at everyday experience (which with certain refinements is carried into Newtonian mechanics) is rather superficial and in many ways, very misleading. A more careful account of the process of perception then shows that the concepts needed to understand the actual facts of perception are closer to those of relativity than they are to those of Newtonian mechanics. In this way it may be possible to give relativity a certain kind of immediate intuitive significance, which tends to be lacking in a purely mathematical presentation. Since effective thinking in physics generally requires the integration of the intuitive with the mathematical sides, it is hoped that along these lines a deeper and more effective way of understanding relativity (and perhaps the quantum theory) may emerge.

II

Pre-Einsteinian Notions of Relativity

It is not commonly realized that the general trend to a relational (or relativistic) conception of the laws of physics began very early in the development of modern science. This trend arose in opposition to a still older Aristotelian tradition that dominated European thinking in the Middle Ages and continues to exert a strong but indirect influence even in modern times. Perhaps this tradition should not be ascribed so much to Aristotle as to the Medieval Scholastics, who rigidified and fixed certain notions that Aristotle himself probably proposed in a somewhat tentative way as a solution to various physical, cosmological, and philosophical problems that occupied Ancient Greek thinkers.

Aristotle's doctrines covered a very broad field, but, as far as our present discussion is concerned, it is his cosmological notion of the Earth as the center of the universe that interests us. He suggested that the whole universe is built in seven spheres with the Earth as the middle. In this theory, the *place* of an object in the universe plays a key role. Thus, each object was assumed to have a natural place, toward which it was striving, and which it approached, in so far as it was not impeded by obstacles. Movement was regarded as determined

4

by such "final causes," set into activity by "efficient causes." For example, an object was supposed to fall because of a tendency to try to reach its "natural place" at the center of the Earth, but some external "efficient" cause was needed to release the object, so that its internal striving "principle" could come into operation.

In many ways Aristotle's ideas gave a plausible explanation to the domain of phenomena known to the Ancient Greeks, although of course, as we know, they are not adequate in broader domains revealed in more modern scientific investigations. In particular, what has proved to be inadequate is the notion of an absolute hierarchial order of being, with each thing tending toward its appropriate place in this order. Thus, as we have seen, the whole of space was regarded as being organized into a kind of fixed hierarchy, in the form of the "seven crystal spheres," while time was later given an analogous organization by the Medieval Scholastics in the sense that a certain moment was taken as that of creation of the universe, which later was regarded as moving toward some goal as end. The development of such notions led to the idea that in the expressions of the laws of physics, certain places and times played a special or favored role, such that the properties of other places and times had to be referred to these special ones, in a unique way, if the laws of nature were to be properly understood. Similar ideas were carried into all fields of human endeavor, with the introduction of fixed categories, properties, etc., all organized into suitable hierarchies. In the total cosmological system, man was regarded as having a key role. For, in some sense, he was considered to be the central figure in the whole drama of existence, for whom all had been created, and on whose moral choices the fate of the universe turned.

A part of Aristotle's doctrine was that bodies in the Heavens (such as planets) being more perfect than Earthly matter, should move in an orbit which expresses the perfection of their natures. Since the circle was considered to be the most perfect geometrical figure, it was concluded that a planet must move in a circle around the Earth. When observations failed to disclose perfect circularity, this discrepancy was accommodated by the introduction of "epicycles," or of "circles within circles." In this way, the Ptolemaic theory was developed, which was able to "adjust" to any orbit whatsoever, by bringing in many epicycles in a very complicated way. Thus, Aristotelian principles were retained, and the appearances of the actual orbits were "saved."

The first big break in this scheme was due to Copernicus, who showed that the complicated and arbitrary system of epicycles could be avoided, if one assumed that the planets moved around the Sun and not around the Earth. This was really the beginning of a major change in the whole of human thought. For it showed that the Earth need not be at the center of things. Although Copernicus put the Sun at the center, it was not a very big step to see later that even the Sun might be only one star among many, so that there was no observable center at all. A similar idea about time developed very naturally, in which one regarded the universe as infinite and eternal, with no particular moment of creation, and no particular "end" to which it was moving.

The Copernican theory initiated a new revolution in human thought. For it eventually led to the notion that man is no longer to be regarded as a central figure in the cosmos. The somewhat shocking deflation of the role of man had enormous consequences in every phase of human life. But here we are concerned more with the scientific and philosophical implications of Copernican notions. These could be summed up by saying that they started an evolution of concepts leading eventually to the breakdown of the older notions of absolute space and time and the development of the notion that the significance of space and time is in relationship.

We shall explain this change at some length, because it brings us to the core of what is meant by the theory of relativity. Briefly, the main point is that since there are no favored places in space or moments of time, the laws of physics can equally well be referred to *any* point, taken as the center, and will give rise to the *same relationships*. In this regard, the situation is very different from that of the Aristotelian theory, which, for example, gave the center of the Earth a special role as the place toward which all matter was striving.

The trend toward relativity described above was carried further in the laws of Galileo and Newton. Galileo made a careful study of the laws of falling objects, in which he showed that while the velocity varies with time, the acceleration is constant. Before Galileo, a clear notion of acceleration had not been developed. This was perhaps one of the principal obstacles to the study of the movements of falling objects, because, without such a notion, it was not possible clearly to formulate the essential characteristics of their movements. What Galileo realized was, basically, that just as a uniform velocity is a constant rate of change of position, so one can conceive a uniform acceleration as a constant rate of change of velocity—i.e.,

$$\frac{v(t + \Delta t) - v(t)}{\Delta t} = a = \text{constant} \qquad (2\text{-}1)$$

where t is the time and Δt is a small increment of time. [$v(t)$ is, of course, the velocity at the time t, and $v(t + \Delta t)$ is the velocity of the time, $t + \Delta t$.] This means that a falling body is characterized by a certain *relationship* in its changing velocities, a relationship that does not refer to a special external fixed point but rather to the properties of the motion of the object itself.

Newton went still further, along these lines, in formulating his law of motion:

$$m\mathbf{a} = m\dot{\mathbf{v}} = \mathbf{F} \qquad (2\text{-}2)$$

where $\mathbf{a} = \dot{\mathbf{v}}$ is the acceleration of the body and $\mathbf{F}$ is the force on it. In these laws Newton comprehended Galileo's results through the fact that the force of gravity is constant near the surface of the Earth. At the same time he generalized the law to a relationship holding for any force, constant or variable. Implicit in Newton's equations of motion is also the *law of inertia*—that an object under no forces will move with constant velocity (or zero acceleration) and will continue to do so until some external force leads to a change in its velocity.

An important question raised by Newton's laws is that of the so-called "inertial frame" of coordinates, in which they apply. Indeed, it is clear that if these laws are valid in a given system S, they will not apply in an accelerated system S' without modification. For example, if one adopts a rotating frame, then one must add the centrifugal and Coriolis forces. As a first approximation, the surface of the Earth is taken as an inertial frame; but because it is rotating such an assumption is not exactly valid. Newton proposed that the distant "fixed stars" could be regarded as the basis of an exact frame, and this indeed proved to be feasible, since under this assumption the orbits of the planets were ultimately correctly calculated from Newton's laws.

Although the assumption of the "fixed stars" as an inertial frame worked well enough from a practical point of view, it suffered from a certain theoretical arbitrariness, which was contrary to the trend implicit in the development of mechanics, i.e., to express the laws of physics solely as internal relationships in the movement itself. For a "favored role" had, in effect, been transferred from the center of the Earth to the fixed stars.

Nevertheless, a significant gain had been made in "relativizing" the laws of physics, so as to make them cease to refer to special favored objects, places, times, etc. Not only was there no longer a special center in space and time but, also, *there was no favored velocity of the coordinate frame.* For example, suppose we have a given frame of coordinates **x** , referred to the fixed stars. Now imagine a rocket ship moving at a constant velocity, **u** relative to the original frame. The coordinates **x**′, *t*′, as measured relative to the rocket ship, are then assumed to be given by the *Galilean transformation,*[1]

$$\mathbf{x}' = \mathbf{x} - \mathbf{u}t$$
$$\mathbf{v}' = \mathbf{v} - \mathbf{u} \qquad\qquad (2\text{-}3)$$
$$t' = t$$

In other words, the velocities are taken to add linearly (which is in agreement with "common sense"). Note especially the third equation, $t' = t$, which asserts that clocks are not affected by relative motion.

Let us now look at the equations of motions in the new frame. Equation (2–2) becomes

$$m\mathbf{a}' = m\frac{d^2\mathbf{x}'}{dt'^2} = m\frac{d^2\mathbf{x}}{dt^2} = m\frac{d\mathbf{v}}{dt} = m\mathbf{a} = \mathbf{F} \qquad (2\text{-}4)$$

This means that one obtains the *same law* in the new frame as in the old frame. This is a limited principle of relativity. For the mechanical laws are the same relationship in all frames that are connected by a Galilean transformation.

Nevertheless, to make subsequent developments clear, it must be pointed out that Newton and those who followed him did not fully realize the relativistic implications of the dynamics that they developed. Indeed, the general attitude (of which that of Newton was typical) was that there is an *absolute space,* i.e., a space which exists in itself, as if it

---

[1] The Galilean transformation is, in fact, only an approximation, valid for velocities that are small compared with that of light. Further on we shall see that at higher velocities one must use the Lorentz transformation instead.

were a substance, with basic properties and qualities that are not dependent on its relationship to anything else whatsoever (e.g., the matter that is in this space). Likewise, he supposed that time "flowed" absolutely, uniformly, and evenly, without relationship to the actual events that happen as time passes. Moreover, he supposed that there is no essential relationship between space and time, i.e., that the properties of space are defined and determined independently of movement of objects and entities with the passage of time, and that the flow of time is independent of the spacial properties of such objects and entities. The inertial frame was, of course, identified with that of absolute space and time.

In a sense, it may be said that Newton continued, in a modified form, those aspects of the Aristotelian concept of absolute space that were compatible with physical facts available at the time. We shall see later, however, that further facts, which become available in the nineteenth century, were such as to make Newtonian notions of absolute space and time untenable, leading instead to Einstein's relativistic point of view.

III

The Problem of the Relativity of the Laws of Electrodynamics

We have seen that even in Newtonian mechanics there was a strong element of relativity. Einstein was therefore not the first to introduce relativistic notions into physics. What he did was to extend such notions to the phenomena of electrodynamics and optics, thus laying the foundation for the even more important step of bringing out explicitly and in a thoroughgoing manner the notion that all physical laws express invariant relationships which are to be found in the changes that are actually taking place in natural processes.

Why was it necessary to extend relativistic principles to the phenomena of electrodynamics and optics? The reason is basically that light has a finite velocity of propagation, $C \cong 3 \times 10^{10}$ cm per sec. Now, light was originally thought to be constituted of particles moving at this speed, but later, it was discovered to be a wave, with interference, diffraction properties, etc. Maxwell's equations for the electromagnetic field vectors $\mathscr{E}$ and $\mathscr{H}$ indeed predicted waves of this kind, in such a way that their speed was determined by the ratio of electrostatic and electromagnetic units. The calculated speed agreed with the observed speed of light, thus giving a strong indication that light was in fact a form of electromagnetic wave. The agreement of the observed polarization properties of light with those predicted by the electromagnetic theory provided further confirmation of this assumption. Light, infrared, and ultraviolet rays, as well as many other kinds of radiation, were then explained as electromagnetic radiations of very high frequency, emitted by electrons, atoms, etc., moving in heated and otherwise excited matter. Later, lower-frequency electromagnetic waves of the same kind (radiowaves) were produced in the laboratory. Gradually there emerged a whole spectrum of electromagnetic radiation, as shown in Figure 3–1.

Now, just as sound waves consist of vibrations of a material medium, air, it was postulated that electromagnetic waves are propagated in a rarefied, all-pervasive (space-filling) medium called "the ether," which was assumed to be so fine that planets pass through it without appreciable friction. The electromagnetic field was taken to be a certain kind of stress in the ether, somewhat similar to stresses that occur in ordinary solid, liquid, and gaseous materials that transmit waves of sound and mechanical strains (e.g., the ether was regarded as supporting Faraday's "tubes of electric and magnetic force").

If this assumption is true, then the Galilean relativity of mechanics cannot hold for electrodynamics, and particularly for light. For if light has a velocity C relative to the ether, then by Galileo's law (2–3) for addition of velocities, it will be $C' = C - U$, relative to a frame that is moving through the ether at a speed U. Maxwell's equations will then have to be different in different Galilean forms, in order to give different speeds of light. The laws of electrodynamics will have a "favored frame," i.e., that of the ether.

Figure 3–1

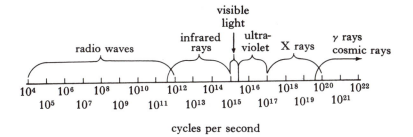

cycles per second

This is, of course, not an intrinsically unreasonable idea. Thus, sound waves do in fact move at a certain speed V_s, relative to the air. And relative to a train moving at a speed U, their velocity is $V_{s'} = V_s - U$. But here it must be recalled that whereas the air is a well-confirmed material medium, known to exist on many independent grounds, the ether is an unproved hypothesis, introduced only to explain the propagation of electromagnetic waves. It was therefore necessary to obtain some independent evidence of the existence and properties of the presumed ether.

One of the most obvious ideas for checking this point would have been to measure the velocity of light in a moving frame of reference, to see if its speed C', relative to the moving frame, is changed to $C' - U$, where U is the velocity of the frame. For example, consider Fizeau's experiment, diagrammed in Figure 3–2. Light is passed through a moving toothed wheel at A across the distance L and reflected back by a mirror. The speed of the wheel is adjusted so that the reflected light comes through a succeeding tooth. With the aid of a suitable clock, the speed of the wheel is measured; and from this, one knows the time T for one tooth to replace a previous one at a given angular position of the wheel. The speed of light is then given by

$$C = \frac{2L}{T} \qquad (3\text{–}1)$$

Now, we know that the Earth must be moving through the presumed ether at some variable but unknown velocity V. However, it is clear that this velocity will differ in summer and winter, for example, by

Figure 3–2

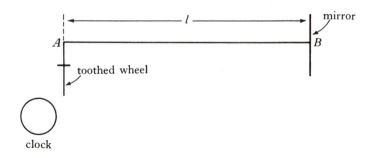

about 36 miles per sec. Let us now see if this difference would show up in the speed of light as observed in different seasons.

If C is the speed of light relative to the ether, it will be $C - V$ relative to the laboratory, while the light is going toward the mirror and $C + V$ while it is returning. The traversal time T is thus

$$T = \frac{L}{C + V} + \frac{L}{C - V} = \frac{2LC}{C^2 - V^2}$$

$$= \frac{2L}{C} \frac{1}{1 - (V^2/C^2)} \simeq \frac{2L}{C}\left(1 + \frac{V^2}{C^2} + \cdots\right) \quad (3\text{--}2)$$

where we have expanded the result as a series of powers of the small quantity V/C, retaining only up to second powers.

Note then that the observable effect is only of order V^2/C^2, which is of the order of 10^{-8}. At the same time when physicists began to study this problem seriously (toward the end of the nineteenth century) such an effect was too small to be detected, with the apparatus available (although now it can be done with Kerr cells, with results that will be discussed later).

IV

The Michelson–Morley Experiment

The main difficulty in checking the ether hypothesis was to obtain measurements of the speed of light with very great accuracy. Toward the end of the nineteenth century interferometers had been developed which were capable of quite high precision. Michelson and Morley made use of this fact to do an experiment that measured very accurately, not the velocity of light itself, but rather the ratio of the velocities of light in two perpendicular directions; which ratio would, as we shall see, also in principle serve as a means of testing the hypothesis of an ether.

The experimental arrangement is shown schematically in Figure 4–1. Light enters a half-silvered mirror at A. Part of the beam goes to a mirror at B, at a distance l_1 from A, which reflects it back. Another part goes to the mirror C at l_2, also to be reflected back. The two beams combine at A again to go on to D as indicated, giving rise to an interference pattern. By counting fringes it is possible to obtain very accurate measurements of the difference between the optical paths of the two beams.

If the Earth were at rest in the ether, and if l_1 were equal to l_2, there would be constructive interference at D. But suppose $l_1 \neq l_2$

14

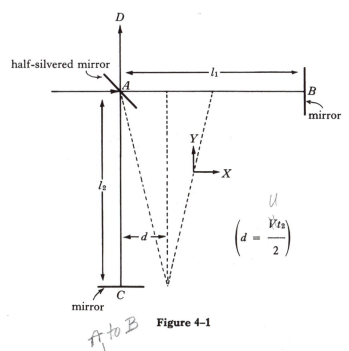

Figure 4-1

and that the Earth is moving at a speed U in the X direction. The time for light to go from B to C and back again is given (as in the Fizeau toothed-wheel experiment) Eq. (3–2):

$$t_1 = \frac{2l_1}{C} \frac{1}{1 - (V^2/C^2)} \cong \frac{2l_1}{C}\left(1 + \frac{U^2}{C^2} + \cdots\right) \qquad (4\text{–}1)$$

Let t_2 be the time for light to go from A to C and back. We note that while the light passes from A to C, the mirror at C moves relative to the ether through a distance $d = Ut_2/2$ in the X direction. Similarly, while the light is returning, the mirror A moves the same distance in the X direction. Then by the Pythagorean theorem, the total path length of the light ray is (back and forth)

$$L_2 = 2\sqrt{l_2^2 + \frac{U^2t_2^2}{4}} \qquad (4\text{–}2)$$

Since the speed of light in the ether is C, we have

$$t_2 = \frac{2}{C}\sqrt{l_2^2 + \frac{U^2 t_2^2}{4}} \tag{4.3}$$

$$t_2^2\left(1 - \frac{U^2}{C^2}\right) = \frac{4l_2^2}{C^2} \tag{4-4}$$

$$t_2 = \frac{2l_2}{C}\frac{1}{\sqrt{1 - U^2/C^2}} \simeq \frac{2l_2}{C}\left(1 + \frac{U^2}{2C^2} + \cdots\right) \tag{4-5}$$

The time difference is

$$\Delta t = t_1 - t_2 = \frac{2}{C}\left(\frac{l_1}{1 - (U^2/C^2)} - \frac{l_2}{\sqrt{1 - (U^2/C^2)}}\right) \tag{4-6}$$

If (as was the case in the actual experiment) $l_1 = l_2$, then

$$\Delta t \simeq \frac{2l}{C}\left(1 + \frac{U^2}{C^2} - 1 - \frac{U^2}{2C^2}\right) = \frac{l_1}{C}\frac{U^2}{C^2} \tag{4-7}$$

Δt is of course proportional to the fringe shift.

Now suppose that the apparatus is rotated through 90°. Then, the fringe pattern should be altered. So by rotating the apparatus, one should be able to observe a steadily changing fringe shift, with maximum and minimum indicating the direction of the Earth's velocity through the ether. From the magnitude of the fringe shift, one should be able to calculate the value U of the speed itself.

Of course, it might happen by accident that at the moment the experiment was done the Earth would be at rest in the ether, thus leading to no observable changes when the apparatus is rotated. But, by waiting 6 months, one could infer that the speed of the Earth must be about 36 miles per sec, so that a fringe shift could then be observed.

Because the predicted fringe shift is of order U^2/C^2, it should of course be very small. Yet, the apparatus of Michelson and Morley was sensitive enough to detect the predicted shifts. Nevertheless, when the experiment was done, *the result was negative* within the experimental accuracy. No fringe shifts were observed at any season of the year. Later, more accurate experiments of a similar kind continued to confirm the results of Michelson and Morley.

V

Efforts to Save the Ether Hypothesis

The Michelson–Morley experiment was doubtless one of the most crucial in modern physics. For it contradicts certain straightforward inferences of the hypothesis that light is carried by an ether. It ultimately led to the radical changes in our concepts of space and time brought in by the theory of relativity. Yet it must not be supposed that physicists immediately changed their ideas as a result of this experiment. Indeed, as was only natural, a long series of alternative hypotheses was tried, with the object either of saving the ether in one way or another, or at least of saving the "common-sense" notions of space and time that were behind Newton's laws of motion and their invariance under a Galilean transformation (2–3). Nevertheless, all of these attempts ultimately failed or else led to such confusion that physicists eventually felt it wiser not to proceed further along these lines.

We shall give here a summary of a few of the main accommodations and adjustments of ideas that were made in order to keep older ideas of space and time, while explaining the negative results of the Michelson–Morley experiment. [For a more thorough account of these efforts, see W. Panofsky and M. Phillips, *Classical Electricity and Magnetism*,

Addison–Wesley, Reading, Mass., 1955; also, C. Moller, *The Theory of Relativity*, Oxford, New York, 1952.]

One of the simplest of these was the suggestion that bodies such as the Earth drag the ether with them in their neighborhood, as a ball moving through air drags a layer of air near its surface. As a result, the measured velocity of light would not change with the seasons, because it would always be determined relative to the layer of ether that moves with the Earth.

Sir Oliver Lodge tried to test for such an effect by passing a beam of light near the edge of a rapidly spinning disk. If the disk had been dragging a layer of ether, observable effects on the light beam could have been expected. However, the results of this experiment were negative.

The idea arose quite naturally that while a small object does not drag a significant amount of ether, a larger body such as the Earth might still do so. But this explanation was ruled out by observations on the aberration of light.

To understand this problem let us temporarily reconsider the assumption that the Earth does not drag the ether with it. Suppose it to be moving relative to the ether at a velocity U in the X direction (see Figure 5–1) and that an astronomer was pointing his telescope

Figure 5–1

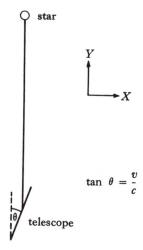

$$\tan \theta = \frac{v}{c}$$

at a distant star, which for the sake of simplicity we take to be in a direction perpendicular to that of motion of the Earth (i.e., Y). The light from the star propagates through the ether in the Y direction. However, because the telescope is moving with the Earth, it must be pointed at a certain angle, θ (usually very small), relative to the Y direction, such that $\tan\theta \cong \theta = V/C$. Since the Earth's velocity changes by 36 miles per sec between summer and winter, the angular position of the star should alter by about 2×10^{-4} rad, which is observable in a good telescope. And the shift is actually found.

Now, if the Earth dragged a layer of ether next to it, no such aberration (or shift) in the position of the star should be seen. The problem is very similar to that of sound waves incident on a moving railway train. To simplify the problem, let us again suppose the waves to be incident perpendicular to the side walls of the train from a very distant source, as indicated in Figure 5-2. These waves would set the walls and windows into vibration at the same frequency and these would in turn set the air inside the train in vibration. It is evident that since the incident sound is a plane wave, the walls of the train will emit corresponding plane waves in the same direction. Therefore, a variation of the speed of the train would produce no corresponding variation in the direction of the sound inside the train. And it is evident that in a similar way, plane light waves from a distant star incident on a moving layer of ether near the Earth's surface would not show any dependence of their direction on the speed of the Earth.

The experiment of Sir Oliver Lodge, along with observations on the aberration of light, seem fairly definitely to rule out the hypothesis of an ether drift, so that this cannot be used to explain the negative results of the Michelson–Morley experiment. Later, an alternative

[handwritten margin note: Why is the sun not moving in our galaxy and why is our galaxy not moving?]

Figure 5-2

sound waves from distant source

sound waves inside train   train $v \longrightarrow$

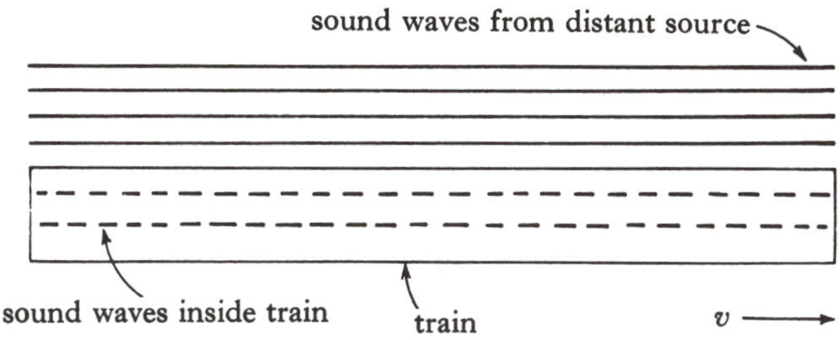

suggestion was tried—that perhaps the speed of light is determined as C not relative to some hypothetical ether but relative to the source of the light.

Of course the source of most of the light on the Earth is the Sun, but when this light is used it will have been reflected from bodies on the surface of the Earth. According to this theory, the last reflection would be the main factor determining the speed of light. So whether a lamp or reflected sunlight were used, one would expect the speed of light to be C relative to the Earth, thus explaining the negative result of the Michelson–Morley experiment.

This hypothesis was consistent with many of the facts available (including the observations on the aberration of light), but it ran into serious difficulties with regard to observations on double stars. To see what these difficulties are, let us assume, for the sake of simplicity, that there are (as shown in Figure 5–3) two stars, A and B, of equal mass moving on opposite sides of a circular orbit around their common center of mass C (similar results can easily be seen to follow for the more general case). Let us consider an observer P, at a very great distance d, from the center of the orbit of the stars, so that the angle subtended by their orbits is always very small. We consider only the light rays that are emitted in such a way as eventually to reach the point P. Let us begin with those rays which reach P after being emitted at the time t_1, when the diameter of the orbit is along the line PC (which is then the line of sight). By means of a little algebra (involving the Pythagorean theorem), we can see that because of the smallness of V/C (where V is the speed of rotation in the orbit), both rays can be regarded as traveling at the same speed along the direction of PC (neglecting terms of order V^2/C^2, which are small in relation to certain terms of order V/C that will be seen to be relevant in the subsequent

Figure 5–3

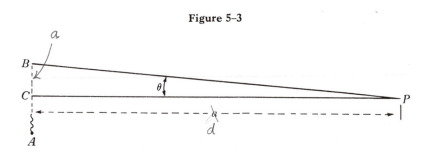

discussion). The time taken for light from the nearer star, A, to reach P will be

$$T_{1A} = \frac{d - a}{C\cdot} \qquad (5\text{-}1)$$

(where a is the radius of the orbit) and that light from the farther star, B, will be

$$T_{1B} = \frac{d + a}{C} \qquad (5\text{-}2)$$

As the orbits of the two stars develop (with the speed of light always being C relative to the emitting star), the rays reaching P from A and B will begin to have different velocities. Indeed, at the time t_2 when the diameter of the orbit is perpendicular to the line of sight, the light from A, which is receding from P, will have a velocity of $C - V$, while that from B, which is approaching P, will have a velocity of $C + V$. (We have here used the smallness of θ to neglect terms of order θ^2). The times taken for this light to reach P will be (in the approximations that we are using)

$$T_{2A} = \frac{d}{c - v} \qquad T_{2B} = \frac{d}{c + v} \qquad (5\text{-}3)$$

Finally, at the time t_3, when the orbits have turned through 180° (so that the diameter is once again along the line of sight), we shall have

$$T_{3A} = \frac{d + a}{C} \qquad T_{3B} = \frac{d - a}{C} \qquad (5\text{-}4)$$

Let us now compute

$$\Delta T = T_{2A} - T_{1A} = \frac{d}{c - v} - \frac{(d - a)}{C} \cong \frac{a}{c} - \frac{d\,v}{c\,c} \qquad (5\text{-}5)$$

This is a first-order quantity in v/c. Moreover, since d is an astronomical order of distance, it can easily happen that $(dv)/c^2 > a/c$. In such a case, the light emitted from star A at t_2 will arrive at P before the light emitted from this star at the time t_1. Hence there will have to be a corresponding period of time when no light from star A arrives at P (similar results follow, of course, for star B). This would produce a rather striking and easily observable kind of variation in the intensity of light from the double star, which has not in fact been found. We conclude, therefore, that the hypothesis that light is emitted at a velocity C relative to its source is not tenable.

VI

The Lorentz Theory of
the Electron

An entirely different way of trying to reconcile the ether hypothesis with the results of experiments (such as those cited in Chapters 4 and 5) was developed by Lorentz. The theory of Lorentz actually did lead, as we shall see, to such a reconciliation; but, in doing so, it brought up new problems of a much deeper order concerning the meaning of space and time measurements, which laid a foundation for Einstein's radically new concepts of space and time.

Even though the Lorentz theory is no longer generally accepted today, it is worthwhile to study it in some detail, not only because it helps to provide an appreciation of the historical context out of which the theory of relativity arose, but much more because it helps us to understand the essential content of Einstein's new approach to the problem. Indeed, a critical examination of the Lorentz theory leads one, on the basis of already familiar and accepted physical notions, to see clearly what is wrong with the Newtonian concepts of space and time, as well as to suggest a great many of the changes needed in order to avoid the difficulties to which these concepts lead.

Lorentz began by accepting the assumption of an ether. However, his basic new step was to study the dependence of the process of measurement of space and time on the relationship between the atomic constitution of matter and the movement of matter through the ether.

It was already known that matter was constituted of atoms, consisting of negatively charged particles, called electrons, and positively charged bodies (which were shown by Rutherford to be in the form of small nuclei) to which the electrons were attracted. The forces between atoms, responsible for binding them into molecules, and ultimately into macroscopic solid objects were, on plausible grounds, surmised to originate in the attractive forces between electrons and the positively charged part of an atom, and the repulsive forces between electrons and electrons. Consider, for example, a crystal lattice. The places where such electrical forces come to a balance would then determine the distance D between successive atoms in the lattice, so that, in the last analysis, the size of such a crystal containing a specified number of atomic steps in any given direction is determined in this way.

Lorentz assumed that the electrical forces were in essence states of stress and strain in the ether. From Maxwell's equations (assumed to hold in the reference frame in which the ether was at rest) it was possible to calculate the electromagnetic field surrounding a charged particle. For a particle at rest in the ether, it followed that this field was derivable from a potential ϕ, which was a spherically symmetric function of the distance R from the charge, i.e., $\phi = q/R$ (where q is the charge of the particle). When a similar calculation was done for a charge moving with a velocity $\mathbf{v}$ through the ether, it was found that the force field was no longer spherically symmetric. Rather its symmetry became that of an ellipse of revolution, having unchanged diameters in the directions perpendicular to the velocity, but shortened in the direction of motion in the ratio $\sqrt{1 - (v^2/c^2)}$. This shortening is evidently an effect of the movement of the electron through the ether.

Because the electrical potential due to all the atoms of the crystal is just the sum of the potentials due to each particle out of which it is constituted, it follows that the whole pattern of equipotentials is contracted in the direction of motion and left unaltered in a perpendicular direction, in just the same way as happens with the field of a single electron. Now the equilibrium positions of the atoms are at points of minimum potential (where the net force on them cancels out). It follows then that when the pattern of equipotentials is contracted in the direction of motion, there will be a corresponding contraction of the whole bar, in the same direction, so that it will be shortened in the ratio $\sqrt{1 - (v^2/c^2)}$. As a result, a measuring rod of length l_0 at rest will, when moving with a velocity v along the direction of its length, have the dimension

$$l = l_0\sqrt{1 - \frac{v^2}{c^2}} \tag{6-1}$$

But if the bar is perpendicular to the direction of motion, its length will of course not be altered.

Let us now return to the Michelson–Morley experiment. Since the arms of the interferometer are composed of atoms, we expect them to undergo the same shift as that given by Eq. (6–1). However, only the bar whose length is parallel to the direction of movement will be shortened; the other will not be changed in length. Since the two bars are assumed to be equal in length when they are at rest, we write in Eq. (4–6)

$$l_1 = l_0\sqrt{1 - (v^2/c^2)} \qquad l_2 = l_0 \tag{6-2}$$

and obtain

$$\Delta t = \frac{2l_0}{c}\left(\frac{1}{\sqrt{1 - (v^2/c^2)}} - \frac{1}{\sqrt{1 - (v^2/c^2)}} \right) = 0 \tag{6-3}$$

In this way we calculate that, independent of the velocity of the Earth, there will be *no fringe shift*, thus reconciling the ether theory with the results of the Michelson–Morley experiment. This reconciliation is of course directly a result of what has since been called the *Lorentz contraction* of an object moving through the ether.[1]

---

[1] Fitzgerald had earlier suggested a similar contraction on *ad hoc* grounds, but Lorentz was the first to justify it theoretically.

VII

Further Development of the Lorentz Theory

Although the result described in Chapter 6 is very suggestive, it does not by itself give a complete account of all the factors that are relevant in this problem. Thus, although the direct measurement of the velocity of light with the requisite accuracy was not possible in the time of Lorentz, it was evidently necessary for him to predict what would happen when such measurements became feasible (as they are now). For it might perhaps still be possible to measure the speed v of the Earth relative to the ether by a very exact Fizeau experiment, using the terms of order v^2/c^2 in Eq. (3–2) to calculate this speed.

To treat the problem Lorentz had to consider not only that rulers would contract when moving through the ether, but also that there might be some corresponding effect on clocks (since *both* a ruler *and* a clock are needed to measure the velocity of light in this way). This problem is rather a complicated one to analyze, so that we shall only sketch some of the principal factors involved.

A typical clock is a harmonic oscillator, satisfying the equation $M\ddot{X} = -KX$, where M is its mass and K is its force constant. Its period is

$$T = 2\pi \sqrt{\frac{M}{K}} \tag{7–1}$$

Now, let us first consider what happens to the mass of a moving electron. As we accelerate an electron, we create a magnetic field that is steadily increasing. As is well known, a changing magnetic field induces an electric field. And by Lenz's law, this electric field is such as to *oppose* the electromotive force that produced the increasing magnetic field in the first place. In other words, electromagnetic processes have a kind of inertia, or resistance to change, which shows up, for example, in the property of the inductance of a coil. With an electron this inertia appears as a resistance to acceleration. A detailed calculation (which is beyond the scope of this work) shows that if an electron is given the acceleration **a**, there is a "back force" given by

$$\mathbf{F}_l = -\lambda \mathbf{a} \tag{7-2}$$

where λ is a constant depending on the size and charge distribution of the electron. (For a slow-moving spherical-shell charge or radius r_0 and charge q, $\lambda \cong q^2/r_0$.) The equation of motion of the electron is then

$$m_m \mathbf{a} = -\lambda \mathbf{a} + \mathbf{F} \tag{7-3}$$

where m_m is the ordinary "mechanical" mass and **F** is the remainder of the applied force (over and above this reaction of the accelerating electron to the field produced by itself). This equation can be re-written as

$$(m_m + \lambda)\mathbf{a} = \mathbf{F} \quad or \quad m\mathbf{a} = \mathbf{F} \tag{7-4}$$

where $m = m_m + \lambda$. We note that in the actual equations of motion there is an *effective mass m*, which may also be called the *observed mass*. For it is this mass which is measured when we observe the force needed to accelerate the particle. On the other hand, λ is called the "electromagnetic mass," which evidently must be added to m_m to give the effective mass.

Such an effective mass is also found in hydrodynamics, where it is shown that a moving ball drags the fluid near it, so that it has a higher resistance to acceleration than such a ball in a vacuum. It may be said that the electromagnetic field near the electron contributes similarly to the inertia.

The above considerations show that the equations of mechanics are deeply bound with those of electrodynamics. This relationship would become especially significant if we could find some way of distinguishing

m_m and λ. According to Lorentz such a distinction should in principle, be possible. For a further calculation based on the Lorentz theory showed that the electromagnetic mass λ is a function of the velocity relative to the ether.

$$\lambda = \frac{\lambda_0}{\sqrt{1 - (v^2/c^2)}} \tag{7-5}$$

where λ_0 is the electromagnetic mass of an electron at rest in the ether. On the other hand, according to Newtonian concepts, the mechanical mass should be a constant, independent of the velocity. We therefore, write for the effective mass,

$$m = m_m + \frac{\lambda_0}{\sqrt{1 - (v^2/c^2)}} \tag{7-6}$$

By studies of the variation of effective mass with speed, one might then be able to distinguish the mechanical mass m_m from the electromagnetic mass $\lambda_0/\sqrt{1 - (v^2/c^2)}$. Such studies have in fact been made with cathode-ray measurements of e/m. These experiments disclose that the effective mass does in fact increase with the velocity and in the ratio $1/\sqrt{1 - (v^2/c^2)}$. Thus, it would seem either that *all* the mass is electromagnetic in origin or that, for unknown reason, the non-electromagnetic mass m_m is *also* proportional to $1/\sqrt{1 - (v^2/c^2)}$. As far as the laws of mechanics are concerned, both of these hypotheses lead to the same results, so that, in the present discussion, we need not concern ourselves further with the question of the origin of mass. For us it is sufficient to note that *in fact* we have

$$m = \frac{m_0}{\sqrt{1 - (v^2/c^2)}} \tag{7-7}$$

where m_0 is the observed mass of the particle at rest in the ether.

It is evident then that because every particle grows heavier in a clock moving through the ether, such a clock must oscillate more slowly. However, to calculate the period we would have to take into account not only the change of mass but also the change in force constant, K. This would require a rather detailed investigation of the effects of movement through the ether in the interatomic forces—a discussion too lengthy to record here.

Such a calculation would show that $K = K_0\sqrt{1 - (v^2/c^2)}$, with the result that

$$T = \frac{T_0}{\sqrt{1 - (v^2/c^2)}} \qquad (7\text{--}8)$$

where T_0 is the period of the clock at rest in the ether and T is the period of the corresponding clock as it moves through the ether. Thus clocks moving through the ether slow down in the ratio

$$\gamma = \frac{1}{\sqrt{1 - (v^2/c^2)}} \qquad (7\text{--}9)$$

Now the person who is moving with the laboratory is also constituted of atoms. Therefore, his body will be shortened in the same ratio as his rulers, so that he will not realize that there has been a change. Likewise, his physical-chemical processes will slow down in the same ratio as do his clocks. Presumably his mental processes will slow down in an equal ratio, so that he will not see that his clocks have altered. He will therefore attribute to his rulers the same length, l_0, that they would have if they were at rest in the ether, and likewise he will attribute the same period, T_0, to his clocks. In interpreting his experimental results, we must therefore take this into account.

Let us now return to the measurement of the velocity of light by the Fizeau method. Since the clocks and rulers of a laboratory moving with the surface of the Earth are altered, it is best to describe this experiment by imagining ourselves to be in a frame that is at rest relative to the ether. The velocity of light will then be c in this frame. Let a ray of light enter the toothed wheel at the time $t = 0$, as measured in the ether frame (see Figure 3–2). We suppose that the surface of the Earth (with the laboratory) is moving through the ether at the speed v. Let t_1 be the time taken for a light ray to go from A to the mirror at B, from which it will be reflected. Remembering the movement of the laboratory, we have

$$l + vt_1 = ct_1 \qquad \text{or} \qquad t_1 = \frac{l}{c - v} \qquad (7\text{--}10)$$

For the light ray on its way back, we similarly obtain

$$t_2 = \frac{l}{c + v} \quad \text{and} \quad T = t_1 + t_2 = \frac{2l}{c} \frac{1}{1 - (v^2/c^2)} \quad (7\text{--}11)$$

But now we recall that the actual length of the ruler is shortened to $l = l_0\sqrt{1 - (v^2/c^2)}$, while the period of the clock is increased so that $T = T_0/\sqrt{1 - (v^2/c^2)}$. Substitution of these values into Eq. (7–11) yields

$$\frac{T_0}{\sqrt{1 - (v^2/c^2)}} = \frac{2l_0}{c} \frac{1}{\sqrt{1 - (v^2/c^2)}} \quad \text{or} \quad T_0 = \frac{2l_0}{c} \quad (7\text{--}12)$$

This result is independent of the speed of the laboratory relative to the ether. But if the observer in the laboratory does not realize what is happening to his rulers and clocks, and measures the speed of light under the assumption that they are unaltered, he will, of course, calculate this speed as $2l_0/T_0$. We have thus proved that because of the Lorentz contraction and slowing down of moving clocks, *all observers will obtain the same measured speed of light by the Fizeau method*, if each one supposes his own instruments to be registering correctly. This means, of course, that *the Fizeau experiment cannot be used to find out the speed of the Earth relative to the ether*, because its result is independent of this speed.

VIII

The Problem of Measuring Simultaneity in the Lorentz Theory

The results of Chapters 6 and 7 show that *neither* the Michelson–Morley experiment nor the Fizeau experiment can provide us with knowledge of the speed of the Earth relative to the ether. Yet it is evident that this speed plays an essential role in the Lorentz theory. For, without knowing it, we cannot correct our rulers and clocks to find out how to measure the "true length" and the "true time," which would be indicated by rulers and clocks at rest relative to the ether.

As a further attempt to provide information on this question, let us consider yet another way of measuring the speed of light. Consider two points A and B, separated by a distance l_0, as measured in the laboratory frame. Suppose the laboratory to be moving at a speed v relative to the ether in the direction of the line $\overline{AB}$. Let us send a light signal from A to B and measure the time t_0 (as indicated by laboratory clocks) needed for the signal to pass from A to B. The measured speed of light would then be

$$C_m = \frac{l_0}{t_0} \tag{8-1}$$

If we could show that this measured speed depended in a calculable way on the speed of the laboratory relative to the ether, then we could solve our problem of finding this speed, thus permitting the correction of our rulers and clocks, so as to yield "true lengths" and "true times."

We could in principle do the experiment, if we could place equivalent clocks at A and B, which were accurately *synchronized*. The difference of readings of the clock at A on the departure of the signal and the clock at B on its arrival would then be equal to t_0. But how can we synchronize the clocks? A common way is to use radio signals. But this evidently will not do here, because the radio waves travel at the speed of light, which is, of course, just what we are trying to determine by the experiment. We shall therefore propose another purely mechanical way of synchronizing the clocks. Let us construct two similar clocks, place them side by side, and synchronize them. After we verify that they are running at the same rate, let us separate the clocks very slowly and gently, so as not to disturb the movements of their inner mechanisms by jolts and jarring accelerations. Then, at least according to the usually accepted principles of Newtonian mechanics, as well as of "common sense," the two clocks ought to continue to run at the same rates while being separated, so that they remain synchronous. To check on this we could bring them back together in a similar way and see if they continue to show the same readings.

Let us now see what would happen to these clocks, if they were in a laboratory moving at a speed v relative to the ether. Once again, we imagine ourselves to be observers at rest in the ether. While the clocks were initially together and being compared, we would see that they were running slower than similar clocks at rest in the ether, in the ratio $\sqrt{1 - (v^2/c^2)}$. Now, while clock A remains at the same place in the laboratory, clock B is moved. While it is moving, it has a velocity $v + \delta v$ relative to the ether. We assume that $\delta v \ll v$, in order to be sure that the movement is gentle and gradual. If l is the ultimate separation as measured in the ether frame, and τ is the time needed for separation (also as measured in the ether frame), we have

$$l = \delta v \tau \qquad (8\text{--}2)$$

While the clocks are separating, they will be running at slightly different rates. Indeed, if $\nu_0 = 1/T_0$ is the frequency of a clock when it is at rest in the ether, then the "true" frequency of clock A, as observed in the ether frame, will be

$$\nu_A = \nu_0 \sqrt{1 - \frac{v^2}{c^2}} \tag{8-3}$$

while that of clock B will be

$$\nu_B = \nu_0 \sqrt{1 - \frac{(v + \delta v)^2}{c^2}} \tag{8-4}$$

Expanding in powers of δv, and retaining only first powers of δv, we obtain

$$\nu_A - \nu_B \cong \frac{\delta v \nu_0 (v/c^2)}{\sqrt{1 - (v^2/c^2)}} = \frac{\delta v \nu_A (v/c^2)}{1 - (v^2/c^2)} \tag{8-5}$$

If a time τ is required to separate the clocks, then their phase differences will be

$$\Delta \phi = (\nu_A - \nu_B)\tau = \frac{\nu_A \tau \delta v (v/c^2)}{1 - (v^2/c^2)} = \frac{\nu_A l (v/c^2)}{1 - (v^2/c^2)} \tag{8-6}$$

The difference in time readings will be

$$t_A - t_B = \frac{\Delta \phi}{\nu_A} = \frac{l(v/c^2)}{1 - (v^2/c^2)} \tag{8-7}$$

Substitution of $l = l_0[1 - (v^2/c^2)]^{\frac{1}{2}}$ yields

$$t_A - t_B = \frac{l_0(v/c^2)}{\sqrt{1 - (v^2/c^2)}} \tag{8-8}$$

We see then that the clocks get out of phase by an amount proportional to their separation, l_0 and to v. Even if δv is small, so that the two clocks run at nearly the same rate while they are separating, the time interval, $\tau = l/\delta v$, increases correspondingly, so that the total relative phase shift is independent of δv. Note also that by a similar argument it can be shown that if the two clocks are brought back together again, they will come back into phase and show the same readings.

Of course, when δv is large, the expansion in power of δv must be carried further, and the phase difference between the clocks becomes a rather complicated function, which is no longer given by Eqs. (8–6) to (8–8). We shall later show (see Chapter 28) that when δv approaches C, the two clocks will indeed not show the same reading if separated and then brought together again. But for the present we restrict ourselves to small δv, so that (8–6) to (8–8) will hold.

The above discussion demonstrates that even if two clocks are equivalently constructed and run at the same rate while side by side, they will get out of synchronism and read different times on being separated, although they will return to synchronous readings when they are brought back together again (provided that their relative velocity, δv, is never very great). On the other hand, the observer in the laboratory frame (which is generally moving relative to the ether), who does not realize the existence of this phase shift, will call two events simultaneous when his two clocks A and B give the same readings. Thus, he will make a mistake about what is simultaneous and what is not.

Let us try to find the relationship between the times ascribed by a laboratory observer and the "true" times, as measured by clocks at rest in the ether [note that according to (8–8), when $v = 0$, displaced clocks remain synchronous, so that such clocks at rest in the ether do measure "true" time even if they are in different places]. Now the laboratory clock reading must not only be corrected according to the formula $t' = t_0/\sqrt{1 - (v^2/c^2)}$, but it must have the error in simultaneity removed; from Eq. (8–8) we see that the displaced clock reads *less* than the undisplaced one, so that (8–8) must be *added* to t'. This gives

$$ t = \frac{t_0 + vl_0/c^2}{\sqrt{1 - (v^2/c^2)}} \qquad (8\text{–}9) $$

Let us now return to the problem of measuring the velocity of light by emitting a flash at A and finding the time needed for light to go a measured distance to be received at B. Let us suppose that the distance and time measured with the aid of the laboratory equipment are, respectively, l_0 and t_0, yielding a *measured* velocity of light, $c_m = l_0/t_0$. Let us further suppose that the laboratory is moving at a velocity v relative to the ether, in the direction of the line AB. We let l be the "true" distance between A and B. But because the laboratory is moving, the light must travel a distance $l' = l + vt$, where t is the "true" time taken by light to go from A to B. Since $l' = ct$, we have

$$l = (c - v)t$$

But using (8–9), and with $l = l_0\sqrt{1 - (v^2/c^2)}$, we arrive at

$$\sqrt{1 - \frac{v^2}{c^2}}\,l_0 = \frac{(c - v)(t_0 + vl_0/c^2)}{\sqrt{1 - (v^2/c^2)}}$$

$$l_0 = ct_0 \tag{8-10}$$

Comparing with (8–1) we see that the moving observer will always obtain the same *measured* velocity for light ($C_m = C$), independent of his speed through the ether.

Or:

Let l_0, t_0 be the "true" length and time as measured at rest in the ether. Then

$$l_0/t_0 = c$$

An observer at rest in the ether knows that in the lab. the light speed is not $C_\ell = l/t$ but rather:

$$C_\ell t = l + vt$$
$$l/t = (C_\ell - v)$$

As measured by two synchronized clocks attached to the ends of the rod in the lab.

from:

$$l = l_0/\gamma, \quad t = \gamma(t_0 + vl_0/c^2), \quad \gamma = 1/(1 - v^2/c^2)^{1/2}$$

ie,

$$(C_\ell - v) = l/t = \frac{l_0}{\gamma^2(t_0 + vt_0/c^2)} = \frac{l_0}{t_0}\frac{(1 - v^2/c^2)}{(1 + v/c)}$$

$$= (C - v) \ ; \quad C_\ell = C.$$

IX

The Lorentz Transformation

We have seen in Chapters 6, 7, and 8 that the Lorentz theory implies that several natural methods of observing the speed of light relative to the ether (the Michelson–Morley experiment, the Fizeau toothed-wheel experiment, and the direct measurement of the time needed for a signal to propagate between two points) lead to results that are independent of the speed of the laboratory instruments. The question then arises as to whether there exists *any experiment at all* where results would depend on this speed, and thus permit its being measured. In this chapter we shall show that according to the Lorentz theory no such experiment is in fact possible.

We shall begin by finding the relationship between the coordinates x', y', z' of an event with its time t', as measured by instruments moving through the ether with the laboratory, and the "true" coordinates x, y, z with the "true" time t, as measured by corresponding instruments at rest in the ether (see Figure 9–1).

For the sake of convenience let us consider coordinate frames in which an event with coordinates $x' = y' = z' = t' = 0$ corresponds to one with $x = y = z = t = 0$. We suppose that the laboratory has a speed v in the z direction. If we consider a measuring rod fixed in the laboratory frame, whose rear edge is at $z' = 0$ while its front edge is at $z' = l_0$, then Eq. (8–9) already gives us the proper expression

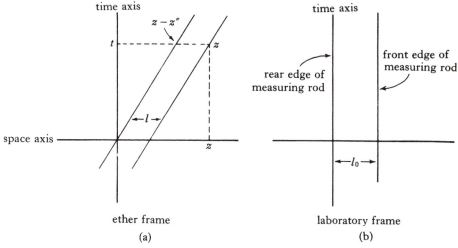

Figure 9-1

for the time t corresponding to $z' = l_0$. With $z' = l_0$ we obtain

$$t = \frac{t' + vz'/c^2}{\sqrt{1 - (v^2/c^2)}} \qquad (9\text{--}1)$$

Since x and y are unchanged by motions in the z direction, we have

$$x = x' \qquad y = y' \qquad (9\text{--}2)$$

There remains only the problem of finding a corresponding expression for z in terms of z' and t'. Actually, it is easier to begin by solving for z' in terms of z and t, rather than the other way round. To do this, we first recall that in the ether frame the ruler is moving with velocity v along the direction of its length. To simplify the problem, suppose that at $t = 0$ the rear edge of the ruler passes $z = 0$. In accordance with our choice of the origins of coordinates in the two frames, this will correspond to $z' = 0$, $t' = 0$ in the laboratory frame. Then, if the front edge of the ruler reaches the point z at the time t (corresponding to z', t' in the laboratory frame), the actual length of the ruler will be $z'' = z - vt$ (to take into account its movement).

From the Lorentz contraction, we have $z'' = z'\sqrt{1 - (v^2/c^2)}$, or

$$z' = \frac{z - vt}{\sqrt{1 - (v^2/c^2)}} \tag{9-3}$$

Substituting (9–1) for t in the above, we obtain

$$z' = -\frac{v^2}{c^2}\frac{z'}{1 - (v^2/c^2)} - \frac{vt'}{1 - (v^2/c^2)} + \frac{z}{\sqrt{1 - (v^2/c^2)}} \tag{9-4}$$

A little algebra yields

$$z = \frac{z' + vt'}{\sqrt{1 - (v^2/c^2)}} \tag{9-5}$$

Equations (9–1), (9–2) and (9–5) express x, y, z, t as functions of x', y', z', t', thus defining a transformation between the "true" coordinates and those that are measured by an observer moving relative to the ether with velocity V in the direction. This is called the *Lorentz transformation*.

Alternatively, we could have eliminated z from (9–1), obtaining

$$t' = \frac{t - vz/c^2}{\sqrt{1 - (v^2/c^2)}} \tag{9-6}$$

Equations (9–3), (9–6) and (9–2) now express x', y', z', t' as functions of x, y, z, t. This is the *inverse* Lorentz transformation from x, y, z, t to x, y', z', t'. The direction and inverse forms of the transformation are of course equivalent, because one can be derived from the other.

Let us now consider a light wave emitted from the origin ($x = y = z = 0$) at $t = 0$. A light wave will be propagated through the ether at speed C, so that the wave front is defined by the surface

$$c^2t^2 - x^2 - y^2 - z^2 = 0 \tag{9-7}$$

Let us now express this in terms of x', y', z', t'. Using Eqs. (9–1), (9–2), and (9–5) we obtain

$$c^2t'^2 - x'^2 - y'^2 - z'^2 = 0 \tag{9-8}$$

We see from Eq. (9–8) that the front will also be a sphere in the x', y', z', t' frame representing a wave propagated at the "measured velocity" C. This result shows that because of the changes of rulers and clocks resulting from the motion through the ether, the Lorentz theory implies that *all uniformly moving observers will ascribe the same velocity C to light, independent of their speed of motion through the ether.* In this way we generalize the results of Chapters 6, 7, and 8, where we have seen how particular ways of measuring the speed of light give values that do not depend on the speed of the laboratory frame.

X

The Inherent Ambiguity in the Meanings of Space–Time Measurements, According to the Lorentz Theory

Chapters 6, 7, 8, and 9 show that according to the Lorentz theory every measurement of the velocity of light will lead to the same result, independent of the speed of the laboratory relative to the ether. Nevertheless, this theory formulates all its laws and equations in terms of "true" distances and times, measured by rulers and clocks that are supposed to be at rest in the ether. Therefore, the measured distances ought to be corrected, to take into account the effect of the movement of the instruments before we can know what they really mean. But if the Lorentz theory is right, there can be no way thus to correct observed distances and times. The "true" distances and times are therefore inherently ambiguous, because they drop out of all observable relationships that can be found in actual measurements and experiments.

What then can be the status of these "true" distances and times that are supposed to be measured by rulers and clocks at rest in the ether? If we recall that the ether is in any case a purely hypothetical entity, not proved on the basis of any other independent evidence, the problem becomes even sharper. Do these "true" distances and times really mean anything at all? Or are they not just purely conceptual inventions, like dotted lines that we sometimes draw in our imaginations, when we apply geometrical theorems, in order to draw conclusions concerning real objects?

The problem is not just a purely theoretical one, which arises only as a result of the analysis of Lorentz's theory. It is also a factual problem. For the Michelson–Morley experiment actually gave results that were independent of the speed of the Earth, in accordance with what the Lorentz theory says. In Lorentz's time, the Fizeau toothed-wheel experiment was not feasible with the accuracy needed to test the theory, but since then, electrical methods of timing pulses of light have been developed which do have the requisite accuracy, and these experiments also give a measured speed of light that is independent of the speed of the Earth. Moreover, as we shall see later, Einstein's theory of relativity, which is based on the assumption that all observers will obtain the same measured velocity of light, has been found to be correct in so many different kinds of experiments that one can regard this fundamental assumption as very well confirmed indeed. Therefore, the consideration of the experimental evidence available leads to just the same problem as that to which the Lorentz theory gives rise: "How can one measure the 'true' distances and 'times' that refer to the frame of the ether?"

In this connection it is perhaps worth noting parenthetically that a *direct* measurement of the speed of propagation of light between two points has not yet been done, probably because of technical difficulties in synchronizing clocks in different places without using electrical signals. With the new, very accurate cesium clocks that are now available, it should perhaps soon be possible to do such an experiment. But considering the enormous amount of evidence on this point that has already been accumulated in other experiments, there seems to be little reason to suppose that this experiment would not also fail to depend on the velocity of the laboratory relative to the presumed ether.

XI

Analysis of Space and Time Concepts in Terms of Frames of Reference

In the preceding chapter we saw that both theoretically and experimentally, the older concepts of space and time lead to a critical problem, which is very deep in the sense that it goes to the root of basic notions that are at the foundation of physics, as well as of a large part of our everyday, technical, and industrial activities. This problem is of a novel kind. For the difficulty was not that the Lorentz theory disagreed with experiment. On the contrary, it was in accord with all that had been observed at the time of Lorentz, and in fact, it is also in accord with all that has been observed since then. The problem was rather that the *fundamental concepts* entering into the Lorentz theory, i.e., the "true" time and "true" space coordinates as measured by apparatus that would be at rest in the ether, were in fact *completely ambiguous*. For, as we have seen, it was deduced on the basis of the Lorentz theory itself that no means at all could ever be found to correct the readings of laboratory instruments to give the values of the "true" coordinates and times. Indeed, since these properties of the "ether" frame of coordinates cancel out of all observable results, *it makes no difference whether we assume that there is such a frame or not.*

Of course, if some properties of the ether had turned out to be observable, then the ether would have had a further physical significance. But if *none* of its properties are observable, it can be said to have only the role of serving as a vehicle for the notions of absolute space and time which are basic in Newtonian mechanics. Moreover, the attempt to adjust these notions to the observed facts had, as we have seen, led to a state of confusion in which it was no longer clear what was meant by our basic space and time concepts or what could be done with them.

It seems evident that what is needed here is a fresh approach to this problem, starting not from inherently untestable hypothesis concerning the ether, but as far as possible from facts that are known and further basic hypotheses that can at least in *principle* be tested by experiment. In order to help lay the foundation for such an approach, we shall begin by giving a preliminary analysis of some of the main facts underlying our use of space and time ccordinates.

The first relevant fact in this problem is that space and time co-ordinates consist of *relationships* of objects and events to some kinds of measuring instruments, set up by the physicist himself. For example, to measure the length of something we can use a sufficiently rigid ruler, and find (approximately) the numbers on the ruler to which the two ends of our object correspond. Or alternatively, we can observe its ends with a telescope, measuring the angle subtended by the object, assuming that light travels in straight lines. From observations made at several points separated by known distances, we can then calculate the length of our object, with the aid of Euclidian geometry. With regard to time, we need, of course, some kind of clock, which may consist of a pendulum or a harmonic oscillator. Alternatively, we can use some regular natural process as a clock, for example, the period of rotation of the Earth as the half-life of certain radioactive elements.

Of course it is not enough to consider only the results of individual measurements in isolation. The real significance of our measurements arises in the fact that we can observe distances and time intervals in many ways, with many different kinds of instruments and procedures, and yet obtain equivalent results. For example, measurements of length made with different rulers yield the same value, within a certain experimental imprecision or error, that is characteristic of the ruler. And if we use triangulation with the aid of light rays, or still another method, we can obtain essentially the same value for the length of an object. This result may seem obvious and even trivial, but it is a *fact* of extraordinary importance, not only for science but for the whole of our lives. For example, the possibility of making machines with interchangeable parts depends on the fact that the measurements determining the size of one part will yield a length that is equivalent to that given by measurements determining the size of another part, into which, for example, the first part must fit. We can easily *imagine* a world in which there are no quasi-rigid objects, in which case such measurements would of course mean almost nothing. But, in fact, in the world in which we actually live, there is a wide-enough distribution of quasi-rigid objects to make the results of such measurements quite significant.

In measuring time the problem is very similar. In order that such measurements shall have their usual significance it is necessary that different instruments and procedures be able to yield equivalent results when applied to the same sets of events. For example, two people with good watches may agree to meet at a certain place; and if they follow the readings on their watches they will *in fact* meet, in the sense of reaching that place in such a manner that one does not have to wait for the other. Likewise, one can follow one's watch in catching a train that is scheduled to leave at a certain time, and generally one will actually meet the train. Or with regard to natural phenomena, one can plan to do a certain amount of work before sunset, and if one manages to arrange the order of work according to the clock, one can actually do the work before it is made impossible by darkness. It is hardly necessary to emphasize the importance of a common measure of time in ordering, arranging, and organizing our lives, both in relation to society and in relation to natural phenomena.

The regularity and order in the properties of space can be summed up in the notion of a *frame of reference*. This is essentially a regular grid of coordinates, set up to make possible the expression of the results of different measurements in a common language, and thus to facilitate the establishment of relationships between these measurements. For example, one can imagine a set of parallel regularly spaced lines, say at intervals of 1 cm. Three similar sets of this kind are required for three-dimensional space. They are usually taken perpendicular to each other, although nonorthogonal systems of lines are also sometimes used. A point, P, is specified by giving it three *coordinates*, x, y, z, which are in essence, the number of unit steps needed along each of the three sets of lines in order to reach that point from some origin, O (which can be chosen arbitrarily according to convenience). If we need a higher accuracy of specification, we can in principle always divide up the grid into intervals of the necessary degree of fineness.

It is important to emphasize that these coordinates do not actually exist in space but are a purely conceptual invention, an abstraction introduced by us for our own convenience. Nevertheless, they do have a certain objective content, because it is possible for any number of different observers using various kinds of measurements to agree on these coordinates. This possibility of agreement is an extremely important *fact* representing the results of countless tests over many generations of men. (Recall that in a world where there were no quasi-rigid objects, our current measurement procedures would not yield such systematic agreement.)

There is, of course, some arbitrariness in the choice of a coordinate frame, so that, for example, one observer may choose a nonorthogonal frame, while another chooses an orthogonal frame. Even if both choose orthogonal frames, they may have *different origins* as well as *different orientations*. But here the important fact is that there exists a set of transformations between different systems of coordinates, which enables us to know how the coordinates of the *same point* in any specified system are related to those in another system. For example, let the coordinates of a point P be x_0, y_0, z_0, in system A. In system B, which is parallel to A, but whose origin is displaced by a vector with components a, b, c, the coordinates of the *same point* will be

$$x = x_0 - a \qquad y = y_0 - b \qquad z = z_0 - c \qquad (11\text{--}1)$$

Similarly, if we have two coordinate frames with the same origin, such that frame B is rotated through an angle θ about the Z axis relative to A, the coordinates of the same point P in these two frames are related by the equations

$$x = x_0 \cos \theta + y_0 \sin \theta \qquad y = y_0 \cos \theta - x_0 \sin \theta \qquad (11\text{--}2)$$

In both these transformations it is easily shown that the distance between any two points, P and Q, is an *invariant function*; i.e., it is the same function of its arguments in every coordinate frame related by these transformations (displacement and rotation). We need not give the proof (which is essentially based on the Pythagorean theorem) but merely state the result.

If x_1, y_1, z_1 and x_2, y_2, z_2 are the coordinates in the frame B of the points P and Q respectively, while (x_1', y_1', z_1') and (x_2', y_2', z_2') represent the coordinate of the corresponding points in frame A, we have

$$(x_1 - x_2)^2 + (y_1 - y_2)^2 + (z_1 - z_2)^2 = (x_1' - x_2')^2$$
$$+ (y_1' - y_2')^2 + (z_1' - z_2')^2 = \text{constant} = \text{invariant function}$$
$$(11\text{-}3)$$

It is, of course, also possible to find transformations between orthogonal and nonorthogonal systems of coordinates, but, of course, in nonorthogonal frames Eq. (11–3) no longer yields an invariant function. There do, however, exist more general invariant functions, which apply to nonorthogonal frames as well as to orthogonal frames. These are significant for Einstein's *general* theory of relativity. But for his special theory of relativity, which we are discussing here, it is adequate to consider only orthogonal frames, so that we shall not hereafter refer to nonorthogonal systems of space coordinates.

There also exists a *time frame of reference*. But as far as Newtonian mechanics is concerned, this is much simpler than the space frame. With the aid of a clock, one can of course mark off regular intervals of time, which are in principle as fine as are needed in any particular problem. The number of such intervals between a given event and an arbitrary origin is equal (on a suitably chosen scale) to the time coordinate of that event. But with regard to time, it is assumed that there is in essence only one system of time coordinates (except for the possibility of a change of scale and of a displacement that shifts the origin to any desired moment). This implies that given any event with time coordinate t, as measured by an accurate clock, there exists a potentially infinite set of events, all co-present with the first mentioned event. As a result, no observer who carries out proper procedures for time measurement will ever find that any one of this set of events is before or after another. If this is the case, then it makes sense to ascribe the same time coordinate t to all these events, and to say that they are *simultaneous*.

Of course, this assumption has been tested by means of a tremendous range of observations, both in common experience and in scientific observations. Thus, in actual fact it is common for people in different places to agree to do things at the same time, as measured by their watches. Then, even if they are in different places, they can see each other performing the planned action, if they are in each other's line sight. Or else, they can use radio or electrical signals to let each other know what is happening (e.g., two people on opposite sides of the world can agree to call each other up when their watches have the same reading, in terms of Greenwich mean time, and they will in fact discover that when one of them calls, the other is ready, waiting to listen).

Of course, all this experience depends on the circumstance that the speed of light, radio waves, etc., is so great that on the ordinary scale of time and distance, the time taken for a signal to travel from one place to another can be neglected. This is equivalent to assuming an infinite speed of light. When the finite speed of light is taken into account, new problems do in fact arise, which will be discussed later. But for the present, we are, of course, concerned only with the notions of pre-relativistic physics, with the object of making clear the background of ideas that have to be taken into account, in order to come to more clear notions of space and time than those which had developed by the end of the nineteenth century.

XII

"Common-Sense" Notions of Space and Time

In the previous chapter we saw that certain notions of space and time have been built up in physics. These notions are founded on a tremendous amount of general experience, observation, and experiment over many generations. They are summed up in the idea of a space-and-time *frame of reference*, specified by suitable coordinates x, y, z, and t, which have been found to be capable of being put into a unique (i.e., one-one) correspondence with a very wide variety of actual events and objects, as observed and measured by any qualified observer, and in many different possible ways. By thus using coordinates associated to frames of reference, we comprehend the essential content of the *facts* behind the notions of space and time that are used in physics. Actually, however, these facts are seen to be based on a tremendous totality of observed *relationships* between a very wide variety of phenomena and various kinds of measuring apparatus, the whole of which set of relationships is such that it can be ordered, organized, and integrated into a structure capable of being described accurately in terms of such frames of reference.

If all the facts consist of observed relationships of the kind described above, what then is the origin of the Newtonian idea of an absolute space and time, supposed to be like a self-existent and flowing substance, essentially independent of all relationships? Evidently it does not come primarily from experiment and observation, but rather, as was suggested in Chapter 2, probably from the continuation in modified form of certain aspects of the older Aristotelian notions of space. And if we ask where Aristotle found his ideas, the answer is not far to seek. For Aristotle was merely expressing in a systematic, organized, and somewhat speculative form a set of notions that has in essence probably been held by everybody for many ages before the time of the Ancient Greeks, and is still our "common-sense" view of space. In this view, space is regarded as a kind of receptacle, inside which each thing has a certain place, size, and form. Thus space is in effect "substantialized" and taken as an absolute.

We shall discuss the problem in some detail in the Appendix where we shall show that there is a great deal of evidence demonstrating that the notion of space described above has been built up and learned in the early years of each person's life. Since then the use of this concept has become a habit, further reinforced by the structure of the common language, in such a way that it is very difficult even to think or to say something that is intended to deny or contradict it. Of course, such a procedure is probably to a large extent inevitable, and it is not our intention to suggest that in everyday life we could do without "common-sense" notions of space. However, a very serious problem arises, because we are not ordinarily aware of this process of learning our concept of space and reinforcing it through habit and through the structure of our language. As a result, we tend to think of it as necessary and inevitable, something that cannot be otherwise. Then scientists incorporate such ideas into their theories, which now apparently provide scientific confirmation of the inescapability of these concepts. But the fact is that these concepts are the outcome of a long process that, in effect, conditions us to believe in their inevitability in all *possible* contexts and modes of existence of everything, and not merely to use them as tentative and therefore dispensable hypotheses when we enter new domains of study. Out of this kind of conditioning has arisen what is perhaps the principal problem that modern physics has had to face in new domains such as those of relativity and the quantum theory—i.e., the difficulty of entertaining new concepts which clash with older ones that we have held habitually since childhood in such a way that to go beyond such ideas seems inconceivable.

With regard to the concept of time, the problem of conditioning is perhaps even more serious than it is for that of space. Indeed, just as we are in the habit of conceiving an absolute space, which we suppose to represent the real place, size, and form of objects, we are also in the habit from the time of childhood onward of conceptualizing the flux of process, both in nature and in our own "inward" psychological experiences, as ordered in a unique and absolute time sequence. The basis of this ordering is evident. At any moment we see the whole of our environment, as what is co-present in our perceptions—optical, aural, tactile, etc. At the moment when we are experiencing this totality of what we perceive, we refer to it as "now." Because the speed of light is so great, we can of course neglect the time needed for light to reach us, at least as far as objects in our immediate environment are concerned, while for most purposes even the time needed for sound to reach us can also be neglected.

Within a certain limited domain we have found that it is indeed possible to ascribe a single, universal, well-defined time order to events, as is implicit in the notions described above. Within this domain, many different observers, using different instruments and procedures, all agree within an appropriate experimental error which events are co-present, which are before others, and which are after. In other words, there is a good factual basis for the assumption of the *chronological order* of a unique past, present, and future, the same for all events of every kind, regardless of where they take place and how they are observed.

As in the case of our ideas about space, the problem with our common concept of time is evidently not that it is *totally wrong*. If it were, then nobody would be foolish enough to try to hold onto it. The difficulty arises because it is adequate in a limited domain, but inappropriate, as we shall see when extended beyond this domain. But as a result of the fact that this domain of adequacy includes a tremendous amount of common experience beginning with childhood, and because this experience has been incorporated into the structure of the language, we find it very hard to get out of the habit of regarding our ordinary concept of time as inevitable. Indeed, this sense of inevitability extends so far that we perceive the world only through this concept of time. As a result, we do not seem to be able actually to imagine that things could happen differently than in a unique and absolute time order, the same for the whole universe. Nevertheless, as we shall see presently, the theory of relativity demands that just such a notion is what we have to consider. We must do this only abstractly and conceptually at first, even if it contradicts "common-sense" notions. Later perhaps, as we become familiar with such ideas, we may begin to grasp them in a more "intuitive" fashion.

To sum up, then, the concepts of absolute space and time are based only on the continuation of certain modes of perceiving, conceiving, experiencing, etc., arising in the domain of everyday life, which are now habitual but which we once learned as children. These habits seem to be adequate in their proper domain, but there do not exist any well-confirmed *facts* supporting the notion that such concepts are inevitable. Indeed, as we have seen, the physical facts concerning space and time coordinates consists only of sets of *relationships* between observed phenomena and instruments, in which no absolute space and time is ever to be seen. Likewise, as we shall show in the Appendix, the *facts* concerning perception in common experience show that this also is always concerned with relationships, and that here, too, there is in reality no absolute space and time. This means that both in the field of physics *and* in that of everyday experience, it may be necessary to set aside the notions of absolute space and time, if we are to understand what has been discovered in broader domains.

XIII

Introduction to Einstein's Conceptions of Space and Time

As soon as we come to a domain in which the time taken for light to propagate between different points cannot be ignored, then ordinary ideas in time and space begin to lead to difficulties and problems that cannot be resolved within their limited framework. We have already seen, in the study of the Lorentz theory, for example, that when equivalent clocks running together synchronously are separated by a distance l_0, their relative readings of time will change by $(l_0 v/c^2)/\sqrt{1 - (v^2/c^2)}$, where v is the velocity of the clocks relative to the hypothetical ether. But because there is no way to measure this velocity, we can never *know* precisely how much clocks which show the same time at different places actually deviate from being "truly" synchronous. In ordinary experience, such effects are of course so small that they can be neglected. In very accurate measurements, however, we have seen that they play a crucial role.

Even at the level of immediate experience, the ambiguity in what is meant by simultaneity will become significant, when very long distances are involved. Consider, for example, the problem of radio-television communication that will arise when astronauts succeed in reaching Mars. Suppose that a man on the Earth asks his friend on Mars what is happening "now." Because of the time needed for the signals to reach Mars and the signals from Mars to come to the Earth, the reply will not come for 10 minutes or more. By the time the answer is received, the information will refer, not to what is happening "now," but to what *was* happening when the signal left Mars. So we will not know what is happening "now" on Mars.

One might perhaps wish at least to know at what time this event *did happen*. To do this, one might look at the television image of a clock carried by the astronaut, a clock that was equivalently constructed to one in the laboratory, and which was so made that it ought to keep time properly even while it was subject to the acceleration of the rocket ship. But, according to the Lorentz theory, this clock would measure time differently from the one on the Earth, and be out of synchronism with the one on the Earth by $(l_0 v/c^2)/\sqrt{1 - (v^2/c^2)}$, where l_0 is the distance to Mars and v is the velocity of the clock relative to the ether. Since v is unknown, the "true" time of this event on Mars would, for us, be ambiguous.

We might perhaps try to correct the time of the event on Mars, not by referring to the television image of a clock in the space ship, but by "correcting" directly for the time interval needed for light to reach us. But to make the right correction, we should have, according to the Lorentz theory, to know the "true" distance l, as well as the true velocity v, of the Earth *relative* to the ether to yield the correction, $\Delta t = l/(c - v)$. Once again, we encounter essentially the same ambiguity in the attempt to find out precisely when an event happens on Mars.

It is clear then that our ordinary ideas of what is the meaning of simultaneity become ambiguous when they are extended too far beyond the domains in which they arose. As we saw in Chapter 11, these ideas are based on the intuitive notion that all that is co-present in a given moment of what we perceive with our senses is actually happening at the same time, "now." But as soon as we come to distant events, such as those taking place on Mars, we see that even when we use the fastest means of communication available to us (radio waves or light), what we perceive, for example in the television image, is *not* happening at the same time, but rather the more distant the event, the earlier it has happened. Indeed, we know that light now visible in telescopes was emitted by stars as much as a thousand million years ago. Thus it is clear that for long distances, co-presence to our sense perceptions no longer means the same thing as simultaneity. And in accurate measurements involving shorter distances, essentially the same conclusion follows, in the sense that the events detected as co-present in a given instrument (e.g., what appears in a given photograph) are also not necessarily all simultaneous.

What is even more significant than the nonequivalence of co-presence and simultaneity described above is the fact that there is, as we have seen, no unique way to ascribe a given event unambiguously to a well-defined time in the past. It follows, then, that the whole of our intuitive notion of what is meant by "now," as well as of past and future, no longer refers clearly to what we can actually observe, perceive, experience, or measure.

In view of this deep and fundamental ambiguity that has developed in the application of intuitive notions of time beyond their proper domain, our approach must be, as we remarked earlier, to set aside this whole mode of thinking and to begin afresh. Instead of referring to a suppositious moment of simultaneity that could be observed only if we knew what cannot be known, i.e., our own speed relative to an intrinsically unobservable ether, we begin our inquiry by basing ourselves as far as possible on the facts of the case and on hypotheses that are in principle testable. What are these facts? In Chapter 10 we have already discussed one aspect of the relevant facts, viz., that all our actual knowledge of space and time coordinates of real events is based on, at least in principle, observable *relationships* of physical phenomena to suitable measuring instruments. In order to avoid ambiguity in our fundamental notions of space and time, it is therefore necessary to express the whole content of physical law in terms of such relationships, and not in terms of an ether with intrinsically untestable properties that are inherently ambiguous.

We are now ready to consider what was, in essence, Einstein's point of departure—i.e., that in terms of actually measurable coordinates of the kind described above, all uniformly moving (that is, unaccelerated) observers obtain the same measured velocity of light, independent of their own speeds, if each uses equivalently constructed instruments and follows equivalent measurement procedures in relation to the reference frame of his own laboratory. (*Special* relativity restricts itself to relationships holding for uniformly moving observers; to deal with accelerated observers, one must use the *general* theory of relativity, which is beyond the scope of the present discussion.)

Einstein did not regard the above result as a deduction from the Lorentz theory, but as a *basic hypothesis* which was evidently subject to experimental tests and which had in fact already been confirmed in many experiments at the time Einstein first developed his theory (having since then been confirmed in a much wider variety of experimental contexts, and never yet having been refuted).

To see more clearly what this hypothesis implied with regard to the meaning of the notions of simultaneity in physics, Einstein considered a simple experiment. It is only an *imagined* experiment in the sense that we do not, at least for the present, possess instruments sensitive enough to do what is called for. Yet this experiment is in *principle* possible; and it has the advantage that reflection on it brings out clearly the essential difficulty in older notions of what constitutes simultaneity of two separated events.

Consider a train moving on a railway embankment with a velocity v. Let us suppose that there is an observer fixed on the embankment at the point O, more or less adjoining the middle of the train. This observer has two colleagues situated at A and B, possessing well-synchronized clocks in relation to the embankment, as shown in Figure 13–1. A and B are assumed to be the same distance, l, from O, as measured by rulers at rest relative to the embankment. Suppose that O's colleagues at A and B set off flashes of light, and that these flashes reach O at the same time. From the fact of their being seen together, it evidently does not necessarily follow that they originated at the same time. Indeed, O must correct, taking into account the time for light to reach him from A and from B. Since the distances are the same, and since the speed of light is the same in both directions, it follows that in this case O will calculate that the flashes occurred at the same time.

Figure 13–1

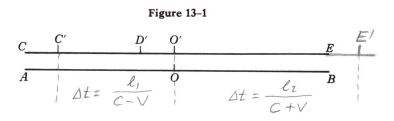

Now consider an observer O' on the moving train. Suppose that O' happens to be opposite to O when O receives the two flashes from A and B. Of course, O' will also see the two flashes at the same time. But he too must calculate the times at which they started. To do this, he must measure the distance between him and the sources of light, as shown by *his* rulers, which move with the train. He can accomplish this conveniently with the aid of several of his own colleagues, in different parts of the train.

Suppose that one of these colleagues happens to be at A when the flash is emitted there. This observer will then proceed to record the reading, C, on his ruler, for the point corresponding to A, at the moment that A passes him. Now, the light passes from C to O' (or equivalently from A to O), taking some time to do so. Considering the process from the point of view of an embankment observer, we see that when the flash is first emitted, the original train observer, who will later be opposite to O, cannot yet have reached O' but will have attained only a point D', to the left of O', such that the distance $D'O'$ will be covered while the light is moving from A to O (or alternatively from C to O'). When this observer reaches O' and sees the flash, the point C will have, according to the embankment observer, moved over to C', a distance equal to $D'O'$. Since the train observer O' regards himself as at rest, he does not take this movement into account when he comes to record the distance between himself and the origin of the light flash. Rather, he assigns the distance as $C'O'$, which is less than the distance AO assigned by the embankment observer. In a similar way, he will assign a distance EO', for the light to travel from E to O', which is greater than the distance BO assigned by the embankment observer.

Now, if Newtonian mechanics were valid, this different assignment of distances by the two observers would be compensated, because the train observer would assign a lower speed of light $(c - v)$ to the flash coming from c, and a higher speed $(c + v)$ to the flash coming from E. As a result, he would, in agreement with the embankment observer (as well as with what "common sense" leads us to expect), calculate that the flashes at C and E were emitted at the same time.

In fact, however, all observers must assign the same speed to light, since as we have seen, experiments show this to be the case. Therefore the train observer can no longer agree that the two flashes are simultaneous, because they cover different distances at the same speed.

This is a major break with older ideas, because different observers do not agree on what is the same time for events that are far away. It must be emphasized, however, that for distant events the establishment of simultaneity is based only on an *indirect deduction*, the result of a calculation, which expresses the correction for the time needed by a light (or radio) signal to pass from the observed point to the point where the observation actually takes place. Simultaneity is therefore no longer an *immediate fact* corresponding to co-presence in our everyday experience. For it is now seen to depend, to a large extent, on a purely *conventional* means of taking into account the time of passage of a signal. This convention seems natural and inevitable to our "common sense," but it leads to unambiguous results, the same for all observers, only under conditions in which the Galilean law for the addition of velocities is a good approximation. When the velocity of light can no longer be regarded as effectively infinite, then the experimental facts of physics make it clear that the results will depend on the speed of the observer's instruments.

It follows from the above discussion that simultaneity is not an *absolute* quality of events, whose significance is independent of state of movement of the measuring apparatus. Rather, the meaning of simultaneity must be understood as being *relative* to the observing instruments, in the sense that observers carrying out equivalent procedures with equivalently constructed instruments moving at different speeds will ascribe the property of simultaneity to different sets of events.

If there were some way to obtain an instantaneous signal from one event to another, then no corrections for the time of propagation would be needed, and the above-described relativity of simultaneity need not arise. But there is no *known* signal that can go faster than light. Moreover, as we shall see later, the theory of relativity implies that *such a signal is not possible*, in the sense that the assumption that such a signal is possible leads to a contradiction with the theory of relativity. Therefore, at least as far as we now know, and as far as the present theories of physics are concerned, a correction must always be made in order to calculate the times of distant events, in a conventional way that depends on taking into account the time needed for light signals to propagate between different points, and using the fact that all observers measure the same velocity for light. Under these conditions, the relativity of simultaneity will be an inescapable necessity.

Once we admit that simultaneity is relative to the speed of the observer, it immediately follows that the measurements of length and time intervals must have a corresponding relativity. To demonstrate this with regard to length, let us return to our example of the two observers, one fixed on the railway embankment and one moving with the train. Suppose that the observer on the embankment has laid out a ruler from A to B and sets up clocks at A and B, synchronized by light flashes, corrected by the rule $t' = t - (l/c)$. The observer on the train follows the same procedure in his moving frame of reference, setting up a corresponding ruler and clocks, synchronized by light flashes, corrected by the formula $t_0{}^A = t_0 - (l_0{}^A/c)$ and $t_0{}^B = t_0 - (l_0{}^B/c)$, where $l_0{}^A$ and $l_0{}^B$ are the respective distances from O to A and O to B as measured by rulers moving with the train.

Now, as long as a rod is not moving in relation to an observer, he can measure its length without regard to time measurements. Thus, he can consider one end, A, "now" and the other end, B, "a bit later," and this will not affect the result that he gets. But if a rod is moving in relation to an observer, he *defines* its lengths as the distance between its end points *at the same time*. (Thus, if the observer in the embankment measured the position of the rear of the train at one moment and the front an hour later, he could ascribe a length of 60 miles or more to the train, evidently an absurd result.)

Now, let us suppose that the colleagues of O at A and B set off flashes, at the same time, *as measured by their clocks*, at rest on the embankment, and that this is just the moment when the ends of the train are passing A and B, respectively. Suppose likewise that corresponding moving observers at A' and B' at the two ends of the train set off flashes when *their* clocks showed the same reading. According to our discussions of simultaneity, it follows that observers on the embankment would conclude that the flashes said to be simultaneous by the moving observers actually occur at different times, as calculated by embankment observers. Vice versa, the observers on the train would calculate that the flashes said by the embankment observers to be simultaneous actually occur at different times.

Let us say that the flashes regarded as simultaneous by the observer on the train have, for the embankment observer, a time difference of δt. In this time the train moves a distance $v\delta t$. The embankment observer therefore concludes that the train observer is not really measuring the "true" length of the train, but is adding in the effects of the displacement due to its motion during the interval δt. It is therefore not surprising that he comes to a different result. In a similar way, the train observer concludes that the observer on the embankment is not measuring the "true" length of the trains, so that he too is not surprised at the difference of the results of the two observers. But we in the analysis of the results of *both* observers can see more, i.e., that since the conventions of the two observers for determining simultaneity do not have the same meaning, it follows that there is a similar problem with regard to the conventions for defining length. In other words, although each observer goes through the same procedure in relation to *his* reference frame, using equivalently constructed instruments, the two are not *in fact* referring to the *same set of events* when they are talking about the length of something.

A similar problem arises in the measurement of time intervals. To see these, let us consider again our example in which the front end of the train passes A and the rear end B at what are shown by O's clocks at A and B to be the same time. (This fact could, for example, be noted by O's colleagues at A and B.) Now, consider a clock on the train, which showed the time t_1', when the front of the train passed A and t_2' when it passed B. An observer on the train would say then that a time interval $\Delta t' = t_2' - t_1'$ was needed for the front end of the train to go from A to B. On the other hand, the observers on the embankment would measure the time for this to happen by means of two of their own "synchronized" clocks at A and B. If t_A were the time at which the front end of the train was seen by an observer at A to pass this point, and t_B were the time at which a corresponding observer saw it passing B, then the observers on the embankment would conclude that the time interval is $\Delta t = t_B - t_A$. However, as we have seen, the observers on the train would regard the clocks at A and B as *not* synchronous; so that they would argue that the embankment observers were not really measuring the "true" time interval for the train to go from A to B. And by a similar argument the embankment observers would argue that those on the train were likewise not measuring the "true" time interval properly. But, as in the case of length measurements, it is clear that where moving clocks are concerned, the relativity of simultaneity implies that the definition of time intervals also has a certain *conventional* aspect; as a result there is no absolute significance to time intervals, but rather, their meaning is relative to the speed of the instruments with the aid of which time is measured.

We see then that there is a close interrelationship of the definitions of *simultaneity, length, and time interval,* and that the *fact* that all observers obtain the same measured velocity for light implies that all three of these concepts must be considered not as absolutes but rather as having a meaning only in relationship to a frame of reference.

XIV

The Lorentz Transformation in Einstein's Point of view

The essentially relational character of space and time coordinates as described in the previous chapter may be compared to a similar characteristic that is already familiar in the measurement of space coordinates alone. In such a measurement each observer is able to orient his apparatus in a different direction, so that all observers do not obtain the same value for the x coordinate of the same point. That is to say, the x coordinate is not an "absolute" property of a point but rather specifies a *relationship* between that point and a certain frame of reference. Similarly observers moving at different speeds do not obtain the same values for the "time coordinates" of a given event, so that this coordinate must also correspond to some relationship to a frame of reference and not to an "absolute" property of the event in question.

Now, in the geometry of space, it has been found that in spite of this "relativity" in the meanings of coordinates, there are certain transformations, such as translations (11–1) and rotations (11–2), which enable us to know when we are dealing with the same point, even though measurements are carried out on the basis of differently oriented and centered reference frames. Are there similar transformations in the space and time coordinates taken together?

In Chapter 2 we saw that in Newtonian mechanics there is the Galilean transformation, Eq. (2–3), which does in fact enable us to relate the space and time coordinates of the same event when measurements are carried out in frames of reference that are moving with respect to each other. However, as we have seen, the Galilean law of addition of velocities implies that the speed of light should vary with the speed of the observing equipment. Since this predicted variation is contrary to fact, the Galilean transformation evidently cannot be the correct one (except as an approximation holding under conditions in which the speed of light can be regarded as effectively infinite).

What we are seeking is a transformation between the set of space coordinates x, y, z and time t of an event, as measured in a given frame of reference A and a corresponding set x', y', z', t' belonging to the same event, as measured in another frame of reference B, moving in relation to the frame A. To simplify the argument, let us suppose that the velocity of B relative to A is v, in the direction z (generalization to arbitrary directions will be seen to be quite straightforward).

This transformation must be compatible with the fact that the measured velocity of light is c, the same in all uniformly moving frames of reference. To express the fact, choose our origin of space and time coordinates, O, for both frames, as the event corresponding to the emission of a given light ray. Then, in the frame A, the light ray must after a time t have reached a spherical surface given by

$$c^2t^2 - x^2 - y^2 - z^2 = 0 \qquad (14\text{--}1)$$

while in frame B it will also have reached the spherical surface

$$c^2t'^2 - x'^2 - y'^2 - z'^2 = 0 \qquad (14\text{--}2)$$

We therefore need a transformation which leaves the above relationship expressing the spherical propagation of a light wave invariant.

In Chapter 9 we have already shown that there does exist a transformation leaving the speed of light invariant, viz., the *Lorentz transformation*. To this we may evidently add an arbitrary *rotation in space*, since this leaves invariant the function $x^2 + y^2 + z^2 = x'^2 + y'^2 + z'^2$, while it also leaves the time invariant ($t' = t$), with the result that the function $c^2t^2 - x^2 - y^2 - z^2$, is also left invariant. Besides that, there are the reflections in space and in time, such as $x = -x'$, $t = -t'$, etc., which evidently also leave the speed of light invariant.

The question then naturally arises as to whether there are any other transformations that leave the speed of light invariant. The answer is that if we make the physically reasonable requirement that the transformation possesses no singular points (so that it is everywhere regular and continuous) then it can be shown that the Lorentz transformations plus rotations plus reflections are the only ones that are possible.

It cannot be emphasized too strongly that in Einstein's approach one does not deduce the Lorentz transformation as a consequence of the changes in observing instruments as they move through a hypothetical ether, and, from this, infer that all observers will obtain the same measured velocity, independent of their speeds. Rather, as we have already indicated in earlier chapters, one begins with the experimentally well-confirmed hypothesis of the invariance of the velocity of light, as *actually measured.* This needs no explanation (e.g., in terms of changes of instruments in an assumed ether), but is just our basic starting point in further work (as in Newtonian mechanics, we start from Newton's laws as a well-confirmed hypothesis, and in electrodynamics we start with Faraday's and Ampère's laws). With this starting point, Einstein then goes on to show in the manner described above that the Lorentz transformation is the only physically allowable one that is compatible with our basic starting hypothesis. $(c = constant)$

Let us now write down the Lorentz transformation (which expresses coordinates in system B in terms of those in system A) once again [see Eqs. (9–1), (9–2), (9–3), and (9–5)]:

$$z' = \frac{z - vt}{\sqrt{1 - (v^2/c^2)}} \qquad t' = \frac{t - vz/c^2}{\sqrt{1 - (v^2/c^2)}}$$

$$x' = x \qquad y' = y \qquad (14\text{--}3)$$

The inverse transformation (expressing coordinates in system A in terms of those of system B) is

$$z = \frac{z' + v t'}{\sqrt{1 - (v^2/c^2)}} \qquad t = \frac{t' + vz/c^2}{\sqrt{1 - (v^2/c^2)}}$$

$$x = x' \qquad y = y' \qquad (14\text{--}4)$$

Note that the inverse transformation is obtained from the original one by replacing v by $-v$. This is, of course, to be expected, since if the velocity of B relative to A is v, the velocity of A relative to B is $-v$. Therefore, one is in reality using the *same function* of the actual velocity when one transforms B to A as when one transforms A to B.

Note also that as $v/c \to 0$ (which is equivalent to letting $c \to \infty$), the Lorentz transformation reduces to

$$z' = z - vt \qquad t' = t$$
$$x' = x \qquad y' = y \qquad (14\text{--}5)$$

which is just the Galilean transformation. In this way we see definitively that the older concepts of space and time are contained in those of Einstein, as special limiting cases, applicable when v/c is not too large.

It is evident that the Lorentz transformation implies the relativity of simultaneity, length, and time intervals, as described in the previous chapter. For example, if we consider a set of events which observer B described as simultaneous, so that $t' = 0$ for all of them, then according to Eq. (14–4) observer A will say that for these events $t = vz/c^2$; such events are evidently not simultaneous. Likewise, if observer A is measuring the length of an object moving in the z direction with velocity v, he must consider the two ends at the same time, as measured in his frame (say $t = 0$). From Eq. (14–3) we obtain $z' = z/\sqrt{1 - (v^2/c^2)}$, or $z = \sqrt{1 - (v^2/c^2)}z'$. Since we have chosen v as the speed of the object, it is clear that z' is the length of the object in a frame in which it is at rest, so that we have obtained the Lorentz contraction.

To study the change in rates of clocks, let us begin by regarding B as the frame in which the clock is at rest (say at $z' = 0$). Let its period be t'. Then by (14–4) we obtain $t = t'/\sqrt{1 - (v^2/c^2)}$, which is just the formula for the slowing down of moving clocks.

Because the transformation between B and A is the same one as between A and B, with v replaced by $-v$, it follows that the conclusions that A draws about the change of the relationship of B's instruments to what is actually being measured will be drawn also by B in relation to A's instruments. Thus, for example, A says that he sees B's rulers as contracted, while B says that he sees A's rulers as contracted.

How is it possible for each to see a contraction of the same kind in the rulers of the other? That is, if A says that B's rulers are shorter, why does not B say that A's rulers are longer? The answer is, as we have already seen, that A and B do not refer to the same set of *events* when they measure the length of an object. Because they disagree on simultaneity, A says that B is allowing the ruler to move while making his measurements, and thus he is measuring something different from the real length, while B says the same about A.

One may perhaps compare this situation to what happens when two people A and B separate, while still in each other's line of sight. A says that B seems to be getting smaller, while B says that A seems to be getting smaller. Why then does not B say that A seems to be getting larger? The answer is that each is seeing *something different*, i.e., the image of the world on *his* retina. There is no paradox in the fact that the image of A on B's retina gets smaller at the same time that the image of B on A's retina gets smaller. Similarly, there is no paradox in saying that A will ascribe a contraction to B's ruler, while B ascribes a contraction to A's, simply because each is referring to *something different* when he talks about the length of an object.

XV

Addition of Velocities

Earlier we saw that the Galilean transformation between coordinates x', y', z', t' in a frame B moving at velocity v in the z direction and a resting frame A, with coordinates x, y, z, t is

$$z' = z - vt \qquad x = x', \ y = y', \ t = t' \qquad (15\text{--}1)$$

If an observer in the frame A is watching an object moving in the X direction with velocity u, he will see this object moving in the line given by $z = ut + z_0$. For simplicity, let us suppose $z_0 = 0$. Then he will obtain $u = z/t$. To calculate what is seen by observer B, we apply the Galilean transformation, which yields

$$z' = z - vt = (u - v)t = (u - v)t' \qquad (15\text{--}2)$$

The observer B will therefore ascribe to the moving object the velocity

$$w = z'/t' = u - v \qquad (15\text{--}3)$$

This is of course, just the well-known Galilean law of addition of velocities, given in Eq. (2–3), which we have derived again in more detail, in order to facilitate comparison with what is done in Einstein's approach.

If the correct transformation between A and B is that of Lorentz rather than that of Galileo, then we begin with the expression (14–3) for B's coordinates in terms of those of A:

$$z' = \frac{z - vt}{\sqrt{1 - (v^2/c^2)}} \qquad (15\text{–}4)$$

As in the case of the Galilean transformation, one writes $z = ut$ as the equation of the trajectory of the moving object, expressed in A's frame. This yields

$$z' = \frac{(u - v)t}{\sqrt{1 - (u^2/c^2)}} \qquad (15\text{–}5)$$

From (14–3) we also obtain

$$t' = \frac{t - (vz/c^2)}{\sqrt{1 - (v^2/c^2)}} = \frac{t[1 - (uv/c^2)]}{\sqrt{1 - (u^2/c^2)}} \qquad (15\text{-}6)$$

and

$$w = \frac{z'}{t'} = \frac{u - v}{1 - (uv/c^2)} \qquad (15\text{–}7)$$

This is the relativistic law for addition of velocities. Note that as v/c approaches zero it approaches the Galilean law, $w = u - v$. More generally, however, it is evidently quite different from the Galilean law. Indeed, as can easily be seen, it is impossible by adding velocities that are less than c ever to exceed the speed c. To prove this, let us consider a case in which we transform, not between A and B, but between B and A. As seen from Eqs. (14–3) and (14–4) this involves only the replacement of v by $-v$. A little reflection shows that our argument on the addition of velocities would then yield

$$W = \frac{u + v}{1 + (uv/c^2)} \qquad (15\text{–}8)$$

where we are using a capital letter as a symbol in order to distinguish (15–8) from (15–7).

It is clear then that if u and v are positive, $W < u + v$, so that if we take an object with velocity u, and then regard it from a frame with velocity $-v$, the object will not have what "common sense" leads us to expect, i.e., the sum of the two velocities. As v/c approaches unity, the new effects become more and more evident. To see what this leads to, consider the quantity

$$c^2 - w^2 = c^2 - \frac{(u + v)^2}{[1 + (uv/c^2)]^2} = \frac{c^2[1 - (u^2/c^2)][1 - (v^2/c^2)]}{[1 + (uv/c^2)]^2}$$

$$(15\text{--}9)$$

As long as $u^2/c^2 < 1$, $v^2/c^2 < 1$, then $c^2 - w^2$ is positive and $|w| < c$. Therefore, it is impossible by adding two velocities less than c to obtain a velocity equal to that of light. (For example, let $u = 0.9c$, $v = 0.9c$; then $w/c = 1.8/(1 + 0.9 \times 0.9) = 1.8/1.81 < 1$.) On the other hand, if $u = c$ we have $w = (v + c)/[1 + (v/c)] = c$, so that we verify that the velocity of light is the same in the new frame as it was in the old one.

The above discussion implies that the speed of light is a limit that material objects can approach but never reach or exceed. Thus, consider a rocket ship. Suppose that a series of bursts were fired, such that *in the frame of the rocket ship* each burst would lead to a change, Δv, in the velocity. From the relativistic law for the addition of velocities it follows that no matter how long the ship continued to be accelerated in this manner, it would never reach the speed of light, i.e., by the burning of any finite amount, however large, of fuel. (In a later chapter we shall arrive at the same result by a different method, showing that the ship cannot reach the speed of light because its mass would approach infinity, so that it would become harder and harder to accelerate it as it approached the speed of light.)

Thus far we have discussed the addition of velocities only when they are parallel, so that the problem reduces to the one-dimensional case. But it is quite easy to extend the results to three dimensions. Thus, suppose that in frame A an object has a velocity with components u_x, u_y, u_z, so that its trajectory is given by $x = u_x t$, $y = u_y t$, $z = u_z t$. Suppose that a Lorentz transformation is made with a velocity v (which can always be taken to be in the z direction, if we assume that our coordinate systems are suitably oriented). Then we have

$$u'_z = \frac{z'}{t'} = \frac{u_z - v}{1 - (u_z v/c^2)}$$

$$u'_x = \frac{x'}{t'} = \frac{\sqrt{1 - (u^2/c^2)}u_x}{1 - (u_z v/c^2)} \qquad u_y = \frac{y'}{t'} = \frac{\sqrt{1 - (v^2/c^2)}u_y}{1 - (u_z v/c^2)}$$

$$(15\text{-}10)$$

In vector notation, this can be written conveniently as

$$\mathbf{u}' = \frac{\sqrt{1 - (v^2/c^2)}}{1 - (\mathbf{u}\cdot\mathbf{v}/c^2)}(\mathbf{u} - (\mathbf{u}\cdot\hat{v})\hat{v}) + \frac{(\mathbf{u}\cdot v)v}{1 - (\mathbf{u}\cdot\mathbf{v}/c^2)}$$

$$(15\text{-}11)$$

where $\hat{v}$ is a unit vector in the direction $\mathbf{v}$.

It is also sometimes convenient to write the Lorentz transformation itself in vector notation. This yields

$$\mathbf{x}' = x - (\hat{v}\cdot\mathbf{x})\hat{v} + \frac{(\hat{v}\cdot\mathbf{x})\hat{v} - \mathbf{v}t}{\sqrt{1 - (u^2/c^2)}}$$

$$t' = \frac{t - \mathbf{v}\cdot\mathbf{x}/c^2}{\sqrt{1 - (v^2/c^2)}}$$

$$(15\text{-}12)$$

XVI

The Principle of Relativity

Since the time of Aristotle and the Medieval Scholastics, physics has been developing toward a more relational or "relativistic" point of view. Thus, Copernicus laid the foundation for dropping the notion that there are special places in space and moments in time, which have an absolute significance, in the sense that they must be given a unique role for privileged position in the expression of the laws of physics. Along with this went, of course, the realization that there is no favored "absolute direction" in space, so that the laws of physics take the same form, no matter how the coordinate system is rotated. Then came the discovery that the laws of mechanics are invariant to a Galilean transformation, so that Newton's equations express relationships of the *same form*, independent of the speed of the frame of reference.

This development toward a relational point of view encountered difficulties and new problems, when the properties of light and the phenomena of electrodynamics were investigated. For because light had a finite speed, c, it was clear, according to the Galilean transformation, that its speed relative to an observer ought to depend on his reference frame. Likewise, Maxwell's equations for the electromagnetic field, which explained the propagation of light and other electromagnetic radiation, as well as their polarization properties, were also seen to be evidently not invariant in form under a Galilean transformation. In other words, there must exist a favored frame in which Maxwell's equations apply exactly, and in which the speed of light is c in every direction. Nineteenth-century physicists then postulated an ether, an idea which had in effect the function of suggesting a physical reason why such a favored frame ought to exist.

When subsequent experiments, such as that of Michelson and Morley, failed to confirm the predictions of the simple ether theory concerning such a favored frame, Lorentz proposed an alternative theory, explaining these negative results as a consequence of changes in the observing instruments as they moved through the ether. This theory led however to the difficulty that the exact values of the "true" distances and times referring to a frame at rest in the ether became ambiguous and unknowable.

The essence of Einstein's approach was to drop the notion of an absolute space and time, as embodied in the ether hypothesis, and instead to carry the relational approach into the phenomena of electrodynamics and the propagation of electromagnetic radiation. As Newton's laws of motion were seen to constitute the *same relationships* in every uniformly moving frame related by a Galilean transformation, the law of the invariance of the observed velocity of light is seen to constitute the *same relationship* in every uniformly moving frame related by a Lorentz transformation. And as a more detailed study shows, Maxwell's equations are likewise invariant under a Lorentz transformation, in the sense that these equations take the same form when expressed in any set of frames related by this transformation (we shall discuss this further in Chapter 21). So up to this point Einstein was merely summing up what are the evident facts, that electromagnetic radiation is observed quantitatively by means of suitable relationships between electromagnetic phenomena and certain instruments, and that the laws of electrodynamics are known by experiment to imply *invariant* relationships among the quantities thus observed. By this *invariance* of the relationships that constitute the laws of electrodynamics (i.e., Maxwell's equations) one refers to their taking the same form independent of the place or time at which electromagnetic phenomena are observed, and of the origin, orientation, and speed of the reference frames (which latter are related to each other by displacements, rotations, and Lorentz transformations).

But now it is evident that if Newton's laws are invariant to a Galilean transformation, they cannot also be invariant to a Lorentz transformation. To see this in detail, let us first write down Newton's equations $m(du'/dt') = \mathbf{F}$ in a given frame of reference B moving at a velocity $\mathbf{v}$ relative to another reference frame A. We consider a particle that is moving only in the z direction, which is also taken to be the direction of the velocity $\mathbf{v}$. Then if B and A are related by a Lorentz transformation, Eq. (15–7) yields $u' = (u - v)/[1 - (uv/c^2)]$. Moreover, dt' is just a time interval, as measured in reference frame B, being the amount of time needed for the particle to move the distance $dz' = u'\,dt'$. According to Eq. (14–4) the corresponding time interval dt, as measured in frame A, will be

$$\frac{dt' + v\,dz'/c^2}{\sqrt{1 - (v^2/c^2)}} = \frac{dt'[1 + (u'v/c^2)]}{\sqrt{(1 - (v/c^2)}}$$

$$= \frac{dt'}{\sqrt{1 - (v^2/c^2)}}\left[\frac{1 + (uv/c^2) - (v^2/c^2)}{1 - (uv/c^2)}\right] = dt'\frac{\sqrt{1 - (v^2/c^2)}}{1 - (uv/c^2)}$$

$$(16\text{–}1)$$

Newton's laws of motion then become (noting that $dv/dt = 0$)

$$\frac{m[1 - (uv/c^2)]}{\sqrt{1 - (v^2/c^2)}}\frac{d}{dt}\left[\frac{(u - v)}{1 - (uv/c^2)}\right]$$

$$= \frac{m}{\sqrt{1 - v^2/c^2}}\frac{1 - (uv/c^2) - (u^2/c^2)}{1 - (uv/c^2)}\frac{du}{dt} = F$$

$$(16\text{–}2)$$

It is clear that the form of Newton's laws of motion is *not* invariant under a Lorentz transformation. And since the experimental facts that have been discussed (as well as others) make it evident that the actual transformation between coordinate frames must be that of Lorentz and not that of Galileo, as well as that the laws of mechanics are indeed invariant to a change of velocity of the reference frame, it follows that Newton's laws *cannot* be the correct laws of mechanics, (except as an approximation holding in the limiting case as v/c approaches zero).

Einstein's approach to this problem was again based on a careful consideration of the meanings of all these facts. Now, by definition, a *law* of physics must be a relationship that holds without exception. If it has exceptions, then we need a broader law, which specifies when there will be exceptions, and why they are to be expected, or else we cannot rely on the law at all (e.g., if it could fail to hold in arbitrary places, times, or conditions). In other words, a *general* law of physics is merely a statement that certain *relationships* in what can in principle be observed in nature are invariant, regardless of the place, time, frames of reference, or other conditions (e.g., temperature, pressure, etc.) under which they may be tested.

Now, if the correct transformation between different frames of reference is that of Lorentz, it follows that the question of what are actually the laws of mechanics will have to be considered afresh, in a new light. In doing this, we shall have to be guided by what Einstein called *the principle of relativity*, which states in essence just what has been said above, i.e., that the laws of physics must satisfy the requirement of being *relationships of the same form*, in every frame of reference. This principle has two forms, that of *restricted* or *special* relativity, which refers only to frames with a uniform velocity, and that of *general* relativity, which refers to *any* frame (which may, for example, be accelerated). In this work we will, of course, be concerned with the restricted principle of relativity.

The principle of relativity may be summed up in terms of more intuitive notions, by considering a rocket ship moving through empty space with no windows or other contacts with the external environment. According to the principle of relativity the phenomena observed by an observer *within such a ship* should not depend at all on the speed of the ship. Evidently, the ether theory would not satisfy this requirement, because, according to it, light would move at a speed c relative to the ether, so that the observed speed of light would depend on the speed of the ship. More generally all electromagnetic phenomena (determined by Maxwell's equations valid only in the ether frame) would vary according to the speed of the ship.

The principle of relativity has had an enormous *heuristic value*. That is, it has been indispensible in helping suggest new laws and relationships, not only in the field of mechanics but also in many other problems. Indeed, whenever we know of a relationship that holds in some limited set of frames of reference, the principle of relativity can usually lead us to a generalization that holds independent of the frames of reference and that has a new content in this broader set of frames, which can then be tested by further experiments. In the next few chapters we shall illustrate this heuristic value of the principle of relativity in a number of special applications.

XVII

Some Applications of Relativity

In order to bring out the meaning of the principle of relativity in a more concrete form, we shall now give a few applications in which this principle demonstrates its power to lead to new results arising from the invariant generalization of relationships that were previously known in some more limited contexts.

First, we consider the measurement of the velocity of light in running water.[1] For a long time this question was a key one that had to be faced by prerelativistic physics, which led in fact to many ambiguities and unclear points, such as, for example, that of the extent to which the moving water dragged the surrounding ether with it. (See C. C. Moller, *The Theory of Relativity*, for a further discussion.)

If n is the index of refraction for light in a fluid medium at rest, the phase velocity of light in this medium is $u_0 = c/n$. The problem is to calculate the phase velocity u when the fluid is moving with velocity v. It is evident that the principle of relativity provides a direct and unambiguous answer to this question, without the need

---

[1] Only the velocity of light *in a vacuum* is equal to the universal constant C, while in a material medium the velocity of light will in general differ from C.

for any further assumptions. For, according to this principle, the properties of the fluid as observed in *the frame in which it is at rest* must be independent of the speed of this frame relative to the laboratory. Therefore, all that we need to do, in order to calculate what will be observed in the laboratory frame, is to make a Lorentz transformation on what is observed in the frame that moves with the fluid. So, if the phase velocity of light in the frame of the fluid is c/n, we can use the relativistic law for the addition of velocities [Eq. (15–8)] (which follows from the Lorentz transformation). This gives

$$u = \frac{u_0 + v}{1 + (u_0 v/c^2)} = \frac{(c/n) + v}{1 + (v/cn)} \cong \left(\frac{c}{n} + v\right)\left(1 - \frac{v}{cn} + \frac{v^2}{c^2 n^2} + 0\right)$$

$$(17\text{–}1)$$

We see that the water effectively "drags" the light to some extent but that it does not add the full velocity v of the water to the phase velocity c/n of the light.

This formula is, in fact, in accord with all experiments that have thus far been done. Such experiments may be said, in effect, to confirm the relativistic formula for addition of velocities.

The second experiment that we shall consider is the decay of mesons. As is well known, mesons are unstable particles, discovered to be created when cosmic rays or high-energy particles accelerated in the laboratory are allowed to bombard blocks of matter. These particles all decay, transforming into other particles. There is a statistical distribution of decay times for an ensemble of particles, but the average time of decay τ of a particular kind of meson can be measured, and, depending on the kind of particle, it may be from 10^{-6} to 10^{-10} sec or less.

Now let τ_0 be the mean time for a meson at rest (or with a low velocity) to decay. Then one can calculate the mean time τ for a particle of velocity v to decay. For, according to the principle of relativity, the decay time in the frame in which the meson is at rest is independent of the speed of the meson relative to the laboratory. In this case, the result of the Lorentz transformation to the laboratory frame is very easy to calculate, because the decay time τ_0 in effect serves as a kind of clock or natural measure of time. The decay time in the laboratory system is then given by the well-known formula relating the periods of clocks in the two frames,

$$\tau = \frac{\tau_0}{\sqrt{1 - (v^2/c^2)}} \qquad (17\text{--}2)$$

As a result, moving mesons should take more time to decay than resting ones, in the ratio $\sqrt{1 - (v^2/c^2)}$. This prediction has been tested, both for mesons produced in the laboratory and for those produced by cosmic rays. In all cases the predicted slowing down of the rate of meson decay is confirmed. For some cosmic-ray mesons v comes very close to c, so that the ratio $1/\sqrt{1 - (v^2/c^2)}$ becomes as large as 1000; and even in this extreme case, the relativistic formula is verified. Thus the relativistic prediction of the different rates of clocks moving at different speeds is verified quite well.

Finally, we wish to consider the Doppler shift of light emitted by a moving body (along with the aberration in its direction, to which it is intimately related). As in the previous cases, we begin in the frame in which the body is at rest, in which case we know by experiment what will happen, and then we make a Lorentz transformation to see what will happen from the point of view of the laboratory frame.

Now, consider a body at rest, to be emitting light in some direction θ_0, relative to the z_0 axis. Let the frequency of the light be ν_0. We know that the speed of light is c, so that the wavelength is $\lambda_0 = c/\nu_0$.

Now, let the body move in the z direction with the velocity v, and let us observe its light from the laboratory frame. According to the principle of relativity, what is observed in the frame in which the atom is at rest is independent of the speed of this frame relative to the laboratory, so that we need only make a Lorentz transformation to find out what will be observed in the laboratory frame.

Now, we have already seen that in a Lorentz transformation the speed of light will be the same in both frames. But the *direction* and the *frequency* of the light ray will generally be different in the two frames.

To calculate the direction of the light ray, as observed from the laboratory frame, let us suppose that a light ray passes through the point O, which we take to be the origin of our coordinate system. Then if, for example, the ray is in the $x_0 - z_0$ plane, it will in the time t_0 reach the point $z_0 = \cos \theta_0\, ct_0$, $x_0 = \sin \theta_0\, ct_0$, $y_0 = 0$. To see what this ray will look like in the laboratory frame, we apply the Lorentz transformation given in Eq. (14–4), obtaining

$$z = \frac{\cos \theta_0 \, ct_0 + vt_0}{\sqrt{1 - (u^2/c^2)}} = \frac{ct_0[\cos \theta_0 + (v/c)]}{\sqrt{1 - (u^2/c^2)}}$$

$$x = \sin \theta_0 \, ct_0$$

$$t = \frac{t_0 + (v/c) \cos \theta_0 \, t_0}{\sqrt{1 - (u^2/c^2)}} = \frac{t_0}{\sqrt{1 - (u^2/c^2)}}\left(1 + \frac{v}{c} \cos \theta_0\right)$$

$$(17\text{–}3)$$

The direction of the light ray in the laboratory frame is then given by

$$\tan \theta = \frac{x}{z} = \frac{\sin \theta_0 \sqrt{1 - (v^2/c^2)}}{\cos \theta_0 + (v/c)} \qquad (17\text{–}4)$$

This formula implies that for $\theta_0 \lessgtr \pi/2$ the angle in the laboratory is always smaller than it is in the original system. When v/c approaches unity [so that $\sqrt{1 - (v^2/c^2)}$ approaches zero], this effect becomes particularly important. Indeed, with cosmic rays, there are some particles so energetic that when they collide with others, v/c is very close to unity for the center-of-mass system of the two particles. Then, although the distribution of particles over the angle θ_0 of collision may be fairly uniform in the center-of-mass system, it is transformed into a narrow cone in the laboratory system [of width of the order of $\sqrt{1 - (v^2/c^2)}$]. Such narrow cones are observed in certain very high energy cosmic-ray showers originating in collisions of single particles with nuclei. [Although the outgoing particles do not have the speed of light, they come very close to this speed, and, as can be shown, Eq. (17–4) will apply to such particles as a good approximation.]

The observed widths of these cones is actually in good agreement with what would be calculated according to the above argument, from the velocity of the center-of-mass system, which can be obtained from the energy of the incident particle, observable by independent means. It can thus be said that (17–4) is fairly well verified by experiment.

We shall now calculate the wavelength of the light as observed in the laboratory frame. This is obtained basically from the formula for the phase of the plane wave in the direction θ_0.

$$\Phi = 2\pi\left(\nu_0 t_0 - \frac{\cos\theta_0\, z_0 + \sin\theta_0\, x_0}{\lambda_0}\right) \qquad (17\text{–}5)$$

with $\lambda_0\nu_0 = c$. If we apply the Lorentz transformation (14–3) we obtain

$$\Phi = \frac{2\pi}{\sqrt{1-(v^2/c^2)}}\left[\nu_0\left(t - \frac{vz}{c^2}\right) - \frac{\cos\theta_0}{\lambda_0}(z - vt) - \frac{\sin\theta_0}{\lambda_0}x\right] \qquad (17\text{–}6)$$

Now, in the laboratory frame, the formula for the phase of the corresponding plane wave is

$$\Phi = 2\pi\left(\nu t - \frac{\cos\theta}{\lambda}z - \frac{\sin\theta}{\lambda}x\right) \qquad (17\text{–}7)$$

with $\lambda\nu = c$.

Comparing (17–3) with (17–6) we see that

$$\nu = \frac{\nu_0}{\sqrt{1-(v^2/c^2)}} + \frac{v}{\lambda_0}\frac{\cos\theta_0}{\sqrt{1-(v^2/c^2)}} = \frac{\nu_0}{\sqrt{1-(v^2/c^2)}}\left(1 + \frac{v}{c}\cos\theta_0\right) \qquad (17\text{–}8)$$

$$\frac{\cos\theta}{\lambda} = \frac{\cos\theta_0}{\lambda_0\sqrt{1-(v^2/c^2)}} + \frac{v}{c^2}\frac{\nu_0}{\sqrt{1-(v^2/c^2)}} \qquad (17\text{–}9)$$

$$\frac{\sin\theta_0}{\lambda_0} = \frac{\sin\theta}{\lambda} \qquad (17\text{–}10)$$

Using $\lambda_0\nu_0 = c = \lambda\nu$ we obtain

$$\frac{\sin\theta}{\sin\theta_0} = \frac{\nu_0}{\nu} \qquad \cos\theta = \frac{\nu_0}{\nu\sqrt{1-(v^2/c^2)}}\left(\cos\theta_0 + \frac{v}{c}\right) \qquad (17\text{–}11)$$

$$\tan\theta = \frac{\sin\theta_0\sqrt{1-(v^2/c^2)}}{\cos\theta_0 + (v/c)}$$

The above is, of course, the same as (17–4), obtained by considering the directions of the light *rays* (which are normal to the wave fronts).

Evidently, the two points of view lead to equivalent results concerning the direction of the light, as they must, since the rays' directions are determined as the normals to the wave fronts (surfaces of constant phase Φ).

From (17–11) and (17–18) we obtain

$$\cos\theta_0 = -\frac{v}{c} + \frac{v}{v_0}\cos\theta\,\sqrt{1 - v^2/c^2}$$

$$\nu = \frac{\nu_0}{\sqrt{1 - (v^2/c^2)}}\left(1 + \frac{v}{c}\,\sqrt{1 - \frac{v^2}{c^2}}\cos\theta\right)$$

$$\frac{\nu}{\nu_0} = \frac{\sqrt{1 - (v^2/c^2)}}{1 - (v/c)\cos\theta} \tag{17–12}$$

As v/c approaches zero, the above evidently approaches the well-known nonrelativistic formula for the Doppler shift,

$$\frac{\nu}{\nu_0} = \frac{1}{1 - (v/c)\cos\theta}$$

More generally, however, there is evidently a further relativistic correction of order $\sqrt{1 - (v^2/c^2)}$. In the case that the light ray is perpendicular to the direction of motion of the body emitting it (as measured in the laboratory frame), this formula reduces to

$$\frac{\nu}{\nu_0} = \sqrt{1 - (v^2/c^2)} \quad\text{or}\quad \frac{T}{T_0} = \frac{1}{\sqrt{1 - (v^2/c^2)}} \tag{17–13}$$

where T is the period of oscillation of the light wave.

For perpendicular incidence, the Doppler shift vanishes in the nonrelativistic theory. The reason that it does not vanish in the relativistic theory is basically that the period of light can be regarded as a kind of "clock," so that in the change from one reference frame to another moving at a speed v, relative to the first, there remains an increase of this period in the ratio $1/\sqrt{1 - (v^2/c^2)}$.

Experiments on the Doppler shift from moving radiating atoms at perpendicular incidence verify the relativistic formula and may thus be regarded as a further confirmation of the relativistic prediction of the change of rate of clocks, when observed in a system relative to which the clocks are in motion.

XVIII

Momentum and Mass in Relativity

We have already seen from Eq. (16–2) that Newton's laws of motion are not invariant to a Lorentz transformation, and that the principle of relativity therefore implies that (except in the limit as v/c approaches zero), these cannot be the correct laws of mechanics. In accordance with the notion discussed in Chapters 15 and 16, our first problem with regard to these laws is therefore to generalize them so as to obtain a new set of equations that is invariant to a Lorentz transformation.

In carrying out the generalization described above, it will be convenient to write Newton's laws in terms of the momentum **p** of the body. These laws then take the form

$$\frac{d\mathbf{p}}{dt} = \mathbf{F} \tag{18–1}$$

$$\mathbf{p} = m\mathbf{v} \tag{18–2}$$

$$\frac{dm}{dt} = 0 \qquad \text{(so that the mass is a constant)} \tag{18–3}$$

In a system of bodies, the *total* momentum **P** and the total mass M are given by

$$\mathbf{P} = \sum_{i=1}^{N} m_i v_i \qquad M = \sum_{i=1}^{N} m_i \tag{18-4}$$

when m_i is the mass of the ith particle and v_i is its velocity. The velocity of the center of mass is

$$\mathbf{V} = \frac{\mathbf{P}}{M} \tag{18-5}$$

It is a well-known theorem in Newtonian mechanics that for an isolated system the total momentum satisfies the equation $d\mathbf{P}/dt = 0$ and $\mathbf{P} =$ a constant vector. Similarly, it follows from (18–3) that in such a system the total mass is also a constant.

These laws, viz., the conservation of momentum and the conservation of mass, are evidently much simpler in form than are Newton's equations, and should therefore be correspondingly easier to generalize. After doing this, we shall then go on in Chapter 21 to generalize Newton's laws themselves.

The basic idea behind our procedure is that it is essential in physical theories to be able to analyze a whole system into parts or components. Thus in a theory of a continuous medium, such as hydrodynamics, we regard the fluid as being constituted out of small elements of volume, and, in a theory which explains matter as having a discrete atomic structure, a whole system is likewise regarded as constituted out of small elements, now taken to be the atoms. In both kinds of theories we can treat the *total momentum* of a system as the sum of the momenta of its parts, likewise with the total mass and the total energy. Moreover, at least in the domain where Newtonian theory applies, such systems are known by experiment (as well as from the theory) to satisfy the laws of conservation of momentum, conservation of mass, and conservation of energy.

Because of these conservation laws, the entire momentum and mass (and also the energy) of a system can be regarded not only as sums of the corresponding properties of the set of its parts but also as an *integral whole* with values of these total quantities that remain constant, as long as the system is isolated. Indeed, such total values are evidently independent of the changes that are going on in each of the parts, as they engage in very complex interactions. It is this fact that is at the basis of the possibility of treating a block of matter as a single macroscopic entity, ignoring the unknown and indescribably complicated details of the motions of its molecules.

It is clear that the property possessed by bulk matter—being capable alternatively of analysis into parts or treatment as a single whole—is a general feature of the world. This feature must therefore be implied by any proposed set of laws of mechanics, if they are to be fully adequate to *all* the experimental facts that are available.

The characteristics described above were first achieved in non-relativistic theories. But, according to the principle of relativity, the basic physical properties of a system do not depend on its speed relative to an observer. Therefore, it is necessary that a system should continue thus to be capable alternatively of being treated as a whole or by analysis into parts, with the same conservation laws applying, even if it is moving at a high speed relative to the laboratory. We shall see that this requirement, plus that of a Lorentz transformation between different frames, is sufficient to determine the proper relativistic formulas for momentum, mass, and energy.

To embody the above-described notions in terms of a mathematical theory we first point out that if v_i is the velocity of the ith particle in a system of N particles, and if m_i is its mass, the ideas discussed in the previous paragraphs imply that the total momentum of the system $\mathbf{P}$ is the sum of the momenta $p_i = m_i v_i$ of its constituent particles:

$$\mathbf{P} = \sum_{i=1}^{N} m_i \mathbf{v}_i \qquad (18\text{--}6)$$

The total mass is, of course,

$$M = \sum_{i=1}^{N} m_i \qquad (18\text{--}7)$$

If we are to be able to continue to carry out the procedure of regarding any collection of particles as forming a single over-all unit, it is necessary that this unit have a general "system velocity," which we denote by **V**, and that its total momentum be expressible as $\mathbf{P} = M\mathbf{V}$, so that

$$V = \frac{\mathbf{P}}{M} = \frac{\displaystyle\sum_{i=1}^{N} m_i v_i}{\displaystyle\sum_{i=1}^{N} m_i} \tag{18–8}$$

evidently corresponds to an average velocity, with each particle contributing to this average according to its mass.

In nonrelativistic mechanics **V** is *also* the velocity of the center of mass. It turns out, however, that in relativity the notion of center of mass is a rather complicated one, not having such a direct physical significance as it has nonrelativistically (essentially because in relativity there is no unique "center-of-mass point," which latter depends in fact on the frame of reference[1]). Nevertheless, it is clear from the above definition of **V** as a suitable weighted average that it will still have the appropriate properties to represent a general system velocity.

We shall now begin the deduction of the relativistic formulas for mass and momentum as functions of the velocity. This can conveniently be done by considering a system of two particles assumed to be first observed in the frame B in which their general system velocity is zero. For the present we restrict ourselves to the one-dimensional case (generalization to three dimensions will be discussed later). If m_1 and m_2 are the masses of these particles, and v_1 and v_2 are their velocities, then we have, for the total momentum of the system,

$$P = m_1 v_1 + m_2 v_2 = 0 \tag{18–9}$$

The total mass is, of course,

$$M = m_1 + m_2 \tag{18–10}$$

while the general system velocity is, of course, by definition,

$$V = \frac{P}{M} = 0 \tag{18–11}$$

[1] This point has been discussed by C. C. Moller, *Ann. Inst. Henri Poincaré*, **11**, 251 (1949).

Let us now view this system of two particles from another frame A, such that in this frame, the general system velocity is V' (also in the z direction). Let m'_1 and m'_2 be the masses of the two particles in this new frame and v'_1 and v'_2 their velocities. Then by our principle of relativity, which requires the analyzability of the system into component parts in frame A as well as in frame B, the total momentum of the particles must be capable of being written as a sum.

$$P' = m'_1 v'_1 + m'_2 v'_2 \qquad (18\text{-}12)$$

Likewise, we must be able to express the total mass as a sum

$$M' = m'_1 + m'_2 \qquad (18\text{-}13)$$

But since in the frame B, in which the general system velocity is zero, we can equally well regard the system as a single whole with mass $M = m_1 + m_2$ and the general system velocity V (in this case, zero), it follows from the principle of relativity that the same possibility should exist when the system is viewed from the frame A. Therefore, we must have

$$P' = M'V' \qquad (18\text{-}14)$$

From (18–9) we obtain

$$\frac{m_1}{m_2} = -\frac{v_2}{v_1} \qquad (18\text{-}15)$$

From (18–12), (18–13), and (18–14) it follows that

$$m'_1 v'_1 + m'_2 v'_2 = (m'_1 + m'_2)V' \qquad (18\text{-}16)$$

and

$$\frac{m'_1}{m'_2} = -\frac{(V' - v'_2)}{(V' - v'_1)} \qquad (18\text{-}17)$$

We now refer to the relativistic law (15–8) for the addition of velocities, which gives

$$v'_1 = \frac{v_1 + V'}{1 + (v_1 V'/c^2)} \qquad v'_2 = \frac{v_2 + V'}{1 + (v_2 V'/c^2)} \qquad (18\text{-}18)$$

When these are substituted into (18–17) one obtains (after a little algebra)

$$\frac{m_1'}{m_2'} = -\frac{1 + (v_1V'/c^2)}{1 + (v_2V'/c^2)}\frac{v^2}{v}\left(\frac{v_2}{v_1}\right) \qquad (18\text{–}19)$$

and with the aid of (18–15) this reduces to

$$\frac{m_1'}{m_2'} = \frac{1 + (v_1V'/c^2)}{1 + (v_2V'/c^2)}\frac{m_1}{m_2} \qquad (18\text{–}20)$$

The above can be expressed more conveniently as

$$\frac{m_1'/m_1}{m_2'/m_2} = \frac{1 + (v_1V'/c^2)}{1 + (v_2V'/c^2)} \qquad (18\text{–}21)$$

But now, we can easily obtain another expression for the right-hand side of the above equation. To do this, let us first find out how the quantity $\beta = \sqrt{1 - (v_1'^2/c^2)}$ transforms. To do this we write

$$\beta = \sqrt{1 - \frac{v_1'^2}{c^2}} = \sqrt{1 - \frac{(v_1 + V')^2}{c^2[1 + (v_1V'/c^2)]^2}}$$

$$= \frac{\sqrt{1 - (V'^2/c^2)}\sqrt{1 - (v_1^2/c^2)}}{1 + (v_1V'/c^2)} \qquad (18\text{–}22)$$

We then obtain

$$\frac{m_1'/m_1}{m_2'/m_2} = \frac{\sqrt{1 - (v_1^2/c^2)}/\sqrt{1 - (v_1'^2/c^2)}}{\sqrt{1 - (v_2^2/c^2)}/\sqrt{1 - (v_2'^2/c^2)}} = \frac{R(v_1v_1')}{R(v_2, v_2')} \qquad (18\text{–}23)$$

where

$$R(v_1, v_1') = \frac{\sqrt{1 - (v_1^2/c^2)}}{\sqrt{1 - (v_1'^2/c^2)}} \qquad R(v_2, v_2') = \frac{\sqrt{1 - (v_2^2/c^2)}}{\sqrt{1 - (v_2'^2/c^2)}} \qquad (18\text{–}24)$$

Now (18–23) must hold for *arbitrary* v_1, v_2, v_1, and v_2. To see what this implies, take the logarithm of both sides:

$$\ln\left(\frac{m_1'}{m_1}\right) - \ln\left(\frac{m_2'}{m_2}\right) = \ln R(v_1, v_1') - \ln R(v_2, v_2')$$

or

$$\ln\left(\frac{m_1'}{m_1}\right) - \ln R(v_1, v_1') = \ln\left(\frac{m_2'}{m_2}\right) - \ln R(v_2, v_2') \qquad (18\text{–}25)$$

On one side of the above equation appear only quantities referring to the first particle, while on the other side there appear only quantities referring to the second particle. Because the velocities of the two particles can be altered arbitrarily in relation to each other, Eq. (18–25) can have a solution only if both sides are equal to a constant α independent of all the quantities in the equations. It follows then that

$$\ln\left(\frac{m_1'}{m_1}\right) - \ln R(v_1, v_1') = \alpha$$

$$\ln\left(\frac{m_2'}{m_2}\right) - \ln R(v_2, v_2') = \alpha \qquad (18\text{--}26)$$

Taking the exponential of the above equations with $l^\alpha = K$, we obtain

$$\frac{m_1'}{m_1} = KR(v_1, v_1') = \frac{K\sqrt{1 - (v_1^2/c^2)}}{\sqrt{1 - (v_1'^2/c^2)}}$$

$$\frac{m_2'}{m_2} = KR(v_2, v_2') = \frac{K\sqrt{1 - (v_2^2/c^2)}}{\sqrt{1 - (v_2'^2/c^2)}} \qquad (18\text{--}27)$$

Consider now the special case in which $v_1 = 0$. We then obtain

$$\frac{m_1'}{m_1} = \frac{K}{\sqrt{1 - (v_1'^2/c^2)}} \qquad (18\text{--}28)$$

In this case m_1 is the mass of the particle when it is at rest. This is, however, just the ordinary mass that appears nonrelativistically in Newton's equations of motion (which apply, of course, in the limit as v/c approaches zero). Let us denote this rest mass by $m_{1,0}$. We therefore have

$$m_1' = \frac{Km_{1,0}}{\sqrt{1 - (v_1'^2/c^2)}} \qquad (18\text{--}29)$$

Let us go now to the still more special case in which $v_1' = 0$. Here, we must have $m_1' = m_{1,0}$ from which it follows that $K = 1$. A similar result evidently holds for the second particle. Therefore, we can write a formula, valid for both particles,

$$m(v) = \frac{m_0}{\sqrt{1 - (v^2/c^2)}} \qquad (18\text{--}30)$$

The momentum is then

$$p = mv = \frac{m_0 v}{\sqrt{1 - (v^2/c^2)}} \qquad (18\text{-}31)$$

The above are the relativistic formulas for mass and momentum, respectively. Note that the mass depends on the velocity and is no longer a constant as it is in the Newtonian theory.

These results can easily be extended to a system of N particles. For we can first apply them to any two, and then regard these two as a whole system, with total mass $M = m_1 + m_2$, total momentum $P = p_1 + p_2$, and general system velocity $V = P/M$. This whole system can then be treated as a single particle, and it can be regarded in combination with the third particle, to form a new pair, to which all the conclusions that we have derived in this chapter will apply. We can then regard the three particles as a single whole and go in this way, by induction, till we have included all the particles in the system. It is not difficult in this way to show that if the Eqs. (18–30) and (18–31) are taken as holding for each particle, then the system can be analyzed into any desired sets of parts in a relativistically invariant way, i.e., so that the same analysis will hold in all frames of reference connected by a Lorentz transformation.

From this it follows that in *every* such frame we have the same functional relationships for the total mass and the total momentum.

$$M = \sum_{i=1}^{N} \frac{m_{0i}}{\sqrt{1 - (v_i^2/c^2)}} \qquad P = \sum_{i=1}^{N} \frac{m_{0i} v_i}{\sqrt{1 - (v_i^2/c^2)}} \qquad (18\text{-}32)$$

If the particles are allowed to interact, the momenta and masses of each of the particles taken individually will in general change. Now, as we have seen in nonrelativistic mechanics, the *total* momentum of the system and its *total* mass are conserved, even when these properties of the various parts alter as a result of such interactions. It can easily be seen that these properties can be generalized relativistically, in the sense that if the total mass and total momenta are conserved in any one Lorentz frame, they will be conserved in every other frame of this kind. To demonstrate this, we refer to Eq. (18–22) and write for the mass of the ith particle in the "primed" system of coordinates

$$m'_i = \frac{m_{0i}}{\sqrt{1 - (v_i{}^2/c^2)}} = \frac{m_{0i}(1 + v_i V'/c^2)}{\sqrt{1 - (v_i{}^2/c^2)}\sqrt{1 - (V'^2/c^2)}} \quad (18.22)$$

$(v_i{}')^2$ (18.30)

$$= \frac{m_i + p_i V'/c^2}{\sqrt{1 - (V'^2/c^2)}} \quad (18\text{-}33)$$

$$M' = \sum_i m'_i = \frac{1}{\sqrt{1 - (V'^2/c^2)}} \sum_i (m_i + p_i V'/c^2)$$

where m_i is the mass of the ith particle in the "unprimed" system of coordinates and p_i is its momentum. If the total mass $\Sigma_i m_i$ and the total momentum $\Sigma_i p_i$ are conserved in the unprimed system, then (since V' is a constant), it follows that the total mass $\Sigma_i m'_i$ is conserved in the "primed" system. And from Eq. (18–14) it follows that the total momentum $P' = M'V'$ is also conserved in the latter system.

To see in more detail what the relativistic conservation laws mean, let us consider, as an example, the collision of two particles. Let $m_1{}^A$, $m_2{}^A$, $v_1{}^A$, $v_2{}^A$ refer to the masses and velocities of the two particles before collision, $m_1{}^B$, $m_2{}^B$, $v_1{}^B$, $v_2{}^B$ after collision. If the particles are so slow that nonrelativistic theory can be applied, we know that

$$m_1{}^A v_1{}^A + m_2{}^A v_2{}^A = m_1{}^B v_1{}^B + m_2{}^B v_2{}^B \quad (18\text{-}34)$$

(conservation of total momentum)

$$m_1{}^A = m_1{}^B \qquad m_2{}^A = m_2{}^B \quad (18\text{-}35)$$

(constancy of mass of each particle)

Now, if this collision is viewed from another frame in which the general system velocity of the two atoms is high, the results of this chapter show that the conservation law (18–34) for the total momentum will still hold in the new frame, provided that Eqs. (18–30) and (18–31) are adopted for the mass and momentum of the particles in the new system. However, instead of (18–35), which expresses the constancy of mass of each particle, we shall have

$$m_1{}^A + m_2{}^A = m_1{}^B + m_2{}^B \quad (18\text{-}36)$$

which implies that only the *total mass* of the system is conserved, while that of its separate particles will in general change [as it must, according to (18–30), because this mass depends on the velocity of the particle, which does in fact alter in a collision].

Thus far we have derived our results under the assumption that all movement is in one direction, that of z. When the problem is considered in three dimensions, however, essentially the same properties are obtained, as can easily be shown by a more detailed calculation that we shall not give here. The mass is still given by an equation similar to (18–30), except that we must regard v as the absolute value of the velocity vector of the particle, (v_x, v_y, v_z), so that $v^2 = v_x{}^2 + v_y{}^2 + v_z{}^2$.

Of course, there are now three components of the momentum. In vector notation we have

$$m = \frac{m_0}{\sqrt{1 - (v^2/c^2)}} \qquad (18\text{--}37)$$

$$p = m\mathbf{v} = \frac{m_0\mathbf{v}}{\sqrt{1 - (v^2/c^2)}} \qquad (18\text{--}38)$$

Each component of the total momentum of an isolated system is now conserved, along with its total mass.

The variation of mass with velocity is, of course, just what is predicted by the Lorentz theory, which regards it as a consequence of the "back emf" acting on the electron that is induced by the changing magnetic field produced by the electron as it is accelerated (see Chapter 6).

In Einstein's point of view we do not deny that a part, or perhaps even all, of the mass of the electron may thus be electromagnetic in origin. However, we do not regard the determination of the relationship of mass to velocity as dependent on particular models of the electron, such as that suggested by Lorentz. Rather, we see that *independent of the origin of the mass* it must have this particular dependence on the velocity, if the general features of the laws of physics described in this section are to be relativistically invariant, i.e., the same in all frames of reference related by a Lorentz transformation.

XIX

The Equivalence of Mass and Energy

We now come to a crucial further step made by Einstein, which greatly extended the revolutionary effect of his relativistic point of view, i.e., the demonstration of the equivalence of mass and energy through the by-now very well known formula $E = mc^2$.

To develop this notion, we begin with Eq. (18–37) for the mass of a moving object, $m = m_0/\sqrt{1 - (v^2/c^2)}$. For small v/c we can expand m as a series of powers of v/c, keeping only the terms up to v^2/c^2. The result is

$$m \cong m_0\left(1 + \frac{v^2}{2c^2} + \cdots\right) \qquad (19\text{–}1)$$

If we multiply this by c^2, we obtain

$$mc^2 = m_0c^2 + \frac{m_0v^2}{2} + \cdots \qquad (19\text{–}2)$$

But $m_0v^2/2$ is just the nonrelativistic expression for the *kinetic energy T* of a body moving with speed v, and m_0c^2 in just a constant. We then have, for such a body

$$mc^2 - m_0c^2 = T \tag{19-3}$$

The conservation of total mass of a system, obtained in the previous chapter, then becomes equivalent to the law of *conservation of total energy* of a collection of bodies, at least in the nonrelativistic limit. But the principle of relativity requires that if such a law holds in any one frame, it will hold in all frames. It follows then that Eq. (19–3) must represent the kinetic energy of a particle *in any frame*, even when the expansion in terms of v^2/c^2 is no longer a good approximation.

The significance of this result can be seen more clearly if one transfers m_0c^2 to the other side of the equation. We then write for the energy of the body

$$E = m_0c^2 + T = \frac{m_0c^2}{\sqrt{1 - (v^2/c^2)}} \tag{19-4}$$

We can always do this, because in nonrelativistic theory the energy is in any case undefined to within an arbitrary constant. Mathematically speaking, Einstein's procedure here is equivalent to defining this arbitrary constant, so that the energy of a particle at rest is taken to be

$$E_0 = m_0c^2 \tag{19-5}$$

Physically, this corresponds to assuming that even a particle that is not in motion has the *rest energy* given by (19–5).

What is the meaning of this rest energy? We can perhaps bring this out by noting that a typical object which is visibly at rest is constituted of parts (i.e., molecules, atoms, nuclei, etc.) which are actually in a state of violent movement, such that on the average the effects of the movement cancel out when observed on a macroscopic scale. Nevertheless, according to the arguments given in the previous chapter, all these movements are contributing to the masses of the constituent particles, according to the formula

$$m_i = \frac{m_{0i}}{\sqrt{1 - (v_i^2/c^2)}} \cong m_{0i} + \frac{m'_{0i}v_i^2}{2c^2} = m_{0i} + \frac{T_i}{c^2} \tag{19-6}$$

The total mass of the system is then

$$M = \sum_i \left(m_{0i} + \frac{T_i}{c^2} \right) = \sum_i m_{0i} + \frac{T}{c^2} \tag{19-7}$$

where T is the total kinetic energy of the various particles. On multiplying by c^2 we have

$$Mc^2 = \sum_i m_{0i}c^2 + T$$

Now, is there any way of checking experimentally whether the internal state of movement contributes to the mass? The answer is that there are several possible ways of doing this. The most obvious idea would be to raise the temperature of a body and to see if the weight increased by the amount Q/c^2, where Q is the heat energy absorbed by the body. The difficulty is that with temperature changes that are available (a few thousand degrees centigrade, at the most), Q/c_u^2 is too small a quantity to be detected by methods that are now available. (This is basically because c^2 is such a large number.) Similarly, if we allow two systems to combine chemically and to give off the energy ΔE, the sum of the masses should be less than its original value by $\Delta E/c^2$. But, once again, this is too small to be detected experimentally.

Some time after Einstein demonstrated the equivalence of mass and energy theoretically, experimental studies of nuclear transformations were carried out, in which great enough quantities of energy were given off, so that the difference between the sum of the masses of the products and that of the initial reactants was actually measurable with the equipment that was then available. Many such measurements were made; these all confirmed Einstein's prediction that the change in mass of the whole system is equal to Q/c^2.

The experiments cited above show that at least a *part* of the rest mass of an object can be ascribed to internal movements, in such a way that when these movements alter and give off an energy Q, the mass of the system decreases by Q/c^2. But can we verify Einstein's statement that *all* of the rest mass of an object can be related in a similar way to an energy?

Some years after the first nuclear transformations were investigated, new particles, called *positrons*, were discovered, having the same mass as an electron, but opposite charge. It was found that when an electron meets a positron, the two particles can *annihilate* each other, leaving no particles at all, but giving off gamma rays with total energy $Q = 2m_e c^2$ (which is ultimately transformed into heat as a result of collisions of the gamma rays with electrons and atoms). In this way it was shown that *all* of the rest energy of an electron is potentially transformable into other forms of energy, such as heat.

Since the discovery of the positron, particles called "antiprotons" (with negative charge and the same mass as that of the proton) have been found, which can similarly annihilate protons. Indeed, it is now known that to each kind of fundamental particle there exists an anti-particle, of the same mass and definitely related properties (such as charge and spin), which combines with the particle to give nothing but energy, in one form or another. Vice versa, it has been shown that a gamma ray colliding with a nucleus can be absorbed, and its energy transformed into the rest energy of, for example, an electron–positron pair, which is *created* in this process, under conditions in which no such particles existed before. So there has been conclusive experimental proof that either a part or the whole of the "rest energy" of a body can be transformed into other forms of energy, and that the inverse process of transforming other forms of energy into rest energy is also possible.

The only reason that the equivalence of mass and energy was not observed earlier is, as we have already suggested, that before the discovery of nuclear processes, the mass Q/c^2, associated with the energy Q, was too small to be detected. Conversely, this means of course that the enormous reserves are "locked" in the rest energy of matter. These reserves are what are being liberated, in part, by nuclear fission in atomic piles, as well as by "fusion" processes that go on spontaneously in the Sun and in the stars.

Einstein gave a simple physical way of seeing why mass and energy are related by the formula $E = mc^2$. To do this, he considered a box of mass M_B, at rest in the laboratory. Suppose that this box contained a distribution of radiant electromagnetic energy in thermodynamic equilibrium with the walls. Let the energy of this radiation be denoted by E_R.

Now, it is well known that electromagnetic energy exerts a radiation pressure in the walls of the box, similar to that produced by a gas. When the box is at rest or in uniform motion, the total force exerted on any one wall is cancelled by that exerted on the opposite wall. But if the box is given an acceleration a, then while the acceleration is taking place the radiation which reflects off the rear wall will gain more momentum than the radiation which reflects off the front wall will lose.

When one carries out a detailed calculation of the resulting changes of pressure on the moving walls, one discovers that the radiation exerts a net force on the box of $F_R = - E_R a/c^2$, which opposes the acceleration. The equation of motion of the system will then be

$$m_B a = - \frac{E_R a}{c^2} + F \qquad (19\text{--}8)$$

where F is the applied force. This reduces to

$$\left(M_B + \frac{E_R}{c^2} \right) a = F \qquad (19\text{--}9)$$

So the radiant energy E_R adds an "effective mass" E_R/c^2 in the sense that it contributes in the same way as such a mass would to the inertia, or resistance to acceleration, which is one of the characteristic manifestations of that physical property called by the name of "mass."

It can be seen that the case considered by Einstein is very similar to that discussed in the previous chapter, where we studied the effects on the total mass of the *internal movements* of its various particles. Einstein refers instead to the effects of the internal movements of electromagnetic radiation, thus helping to bring out the point that the contribution to the mass is independent of the nature of the energy.

XX

The Relativistic
Transformation Law
for Energy and Momentum

We have seen in earlier chapters that the momentum and energy of a given object (along with its mass, which is proportional to its energy) depends on the speed of that object, according to the formulas

$$E = \frac{m_0 c^2}{\sqrt{1 - (v^2/c^2)}} = \frac{E_0}{\sqrt{1 - (v^2/c^2)}} \qquad (20\text{--}1)$$

$$\mathbf{p} = \frac{m_0 \mathbf{v}}{\sqrt{1 - (\mathbf{v}^2/c^2)}} \qquad (20\text{--}2)$$

Suppose now that E and $\mathbf{p}$ are known in a given frame A. Can we find a transformation, analogous to the Lorentz transformation of $\mathbf{x}$ and t, which gives the values, E' and $\mathbf{p}'$ as measured in another frame B, moving at a velocity $\mathbf{V}$ relative to A?

To simplify the problem, we begin by restricting ourselves to the one-dimensional case (which we take to be in the direction of x). Suppose that we are given E and p in frame A. We wish then to calculate the corresponding E' and p' in frame B. Let v be the velocity of the body in frame A and v' in frame B.

In doing this we can begin with Eq. (18–22). Note, however, that in (18–15), (18–17), and (18–19) the symbol v' refers to the velocity of the object as measured in a frame moving at a speed $V' = -V$, relative to the frame A. Taking the reciprocal of both sides of the equation, and substituting $v' = -V$, we obtain

$$\frac{1}{\sqrt{1 - (v_2'^2/c^2)}} = \frac{(1 - v_1 V/c^2)}{\sqrt{1 - (v_1^2/c^2)}\sqrt{1 - (V^2/c^2)}} \qquad (20\text{–}3)$$

Since $E' = m_0 c^2/\sqrt{1 - (v'^2/c^2)}$, $E = m_0 c^2/\sqrt{1 - (v^2/c^2)}$, and $p = m_0 v/\sqrt{1 - (v^2/c^2)}$, this leads to

$$E' = \frac{E - Vp}{\sqrt{1 - (V^2/c^2)}} \qquad (20\text{–}4)$$

Moreover, by the relativistic law for the addition of velocities,

$$v' = \frac{v - V}{1 - (vV/c^2)}$$

so that

$$p' = \frac{m_0 v'}{\sqrt{1 - (v^2/c^2)}} = \frac{m_0(v - V)}{\sqrt{1 - (V^2/c^2)}\sqrt{1 - (v^2/c^2)}}$$

$$= \frac{p - VE/c^2}{\sqrt{1 - (V^2/c^2)}} \qquad (20\text{–}5)$$

Equations (20–4) and (20–5) are essentially the same relationship as the Lorentz transformation (14–3), with p taking the place of x and E/c^2 taking the place of t. Therefore, the energy and momentum of a body in one frame can be calculated from that in another frame by a transformation analogous to that of Lorentz.

This argument is easily extended into three dimensions. As happens with x and y we have

$$p_x' = p_x \qquad p_y' = p_y \qquad (20\text{–}6)$$

In vector notation this becomes

$$E' = \frac{E - (\mathbf{V} \cdot \mathbf{p})}{\sqrt{1 - (V^2/c^2)}} \tag{20-7}$$

$$\mathbf{p}' = \mathbf{p} - (\mathbf{p} \cdot \hat{V})(\hat{V}) + \frac{(\mathbf{p} \cdot \hat{V})\hat{V} - \mathbf{V}E/c^2}{\sqrt{1 - (V^2/c^2)}} \tag{20-8}$$

where $\hat{V}$ is a unit vector in the direction of $\mathbf{V}$.

It follows from the above that the same proof which shows that the expression (1-7) for the interval $s^2 = c^2 t^2 - x^2 - y^2 - z^2$ is invariant under a Lorentz transformation will suffice to demonstrate a similar invariance for the quantity, $E^2 - c^2 p^2$.

To see what this quantity means, let us evaluate it in a frame in which the body is at rest, so that $p = 0$. Then, $E_0^2 - c^2 p^2 = E_0^2 = M_0^2 c^4$. But $E^2 - c^2 p^2$ is an invariant, and so it must have the same value in every frame, which is

$$E^2 - c^2 p^2 = m_0^2 c^4 \tag{20-9}$$

A case of special interest arises when the rest mass is zero. Here we have

$$E^2 - c^2 p^2 = 0 \tag{20-10}$$

If we choose the direction of the z axis as that of $\mathbf{p}$, this becomes

$$E = \pm c p_z \tag{20-11}$$

The interesting point is that the theory of relativity implies that a particle of zero rest mass can have a nonzero energy and momentum. To see what this means, let us consider a particle of very small rest mass m_0, and then let m_0 approach zero. If its velocity is v, its energy and momentum are

$$E = \frac{m_0 c^2}{\sqrt{1 - (v^2/c^2)}} \qquad p = \frac{m_0 v}{\sqrt{1 - (v^2/c^2)}} \tag{20-12}$$

If v/c is fixed at a value less than unity, E and p approach zero as m_0 approaches zero. But if we let v/c approach unity, while m_0 approaches zero, in such a way that $m_0/\sqrt{1 - (v^2/c^2)}$ remains equal to a constant R, then we obtain

$$E \to RC^2 \qquad p \to RC \qquad E^2 - c^2 p^2 \to 0 \tag{20-13}$$

which is in accord with (10–10). Therefore, a body can have nonzero energy and momentum, even though its rest mass is zero, *if and only if it is moving at the speed of light.*

Another way of looking at this problem is to note that if $m_0 \neq 0$, then as a particle is accelerated toward the velocity of light, its energy, $E = m_0 c^2 / \sqrt{1 - (v^2/c^2)}$, and its momentum, $p = m_0 v / \sqrt{1 - (v^2/c^2)}$ approach infinity. Since, in reality, only finite sources of energy and momentum are available, such a particle can never actually reach the speed of light. But if $m_0 = 0$, then, as we have seen, it can be moving at the speed c with finite energy and momentum.

The conclusion that no object can ever be at the speed of light evidently applies, then, only to something with a nonzero rest mass. However, something having no rest mass can exist *only* in a state of movement at the speed of light. Thus, it may be said that while nothing can be *accelerated* to the speed of light, there can be things which move at the speed of light, not as a result of a previous acceleration, but rather, because that is the only state in which they can exist.

We shall discuss later the physical meaning of movement at the speed of light.

XXI

Charged Particles in an Electromagnetic Field

We have already seen that the relativistic expressions for momentum, mass, and energy are quite different from those applying in Newtonian theory, reducing to the latter only in the limit $v/c \to 0$. For an isolated system, the laws of movement then take the relativistic form

$$\frac{d\mathbf{p}}{dt} = 0 \qquad \mathbf{p} = m\mathbf{v} = \frac{m_0\mathbf{v}}{\sqrt{1 - (v^2/c^2)}} \qquad (21\text{--}1)$$

To these we must add the law of conservation of mass. In Newton's theory this was implicit in the assumption that m_i, the mass of the ith body is a constant, or that $dm_i/dt = 0$ [Eq. (18–3)]. In Einstein's theory, however, the mass of a given body can vary. However, mass and energy are equivalent, according to the relationship $E = mc^2$. Therefore, the conservation of the total mass $M = \Sigma_i m_i$, and the conservation of the total energy, $E = \Sigma_i E_i = \Sigma_i m_i c^2$, of an isolated system are essentially the same law, in the sense that one follows from the other.

The conservation law $dM/dt = 0$, or, alternatively, $dE/dt = 0$, now replaces the nonrelativistic law $dm_i/dt = 0$, as well as the nonrelativistic expression for the conservation of the total energy of the system.

We shall now generalize these laws to a nonisolated system, i.e., to a system on which a net force **F** is acting. To simplify the problem, let us consider a system consisting of a single body, with velocity **v**. Then, we tentatively propose as the proper relativistic laws

$$\frac{d\mathbf{p}}{dt} = \mathbf{F} \tag{21-2}$$

$$\frac{dE}{dt} = \mathbf{F} \cdot \mathbf{v} \tag{21-3}$$

These have the same *form* as do the corresponding expressions in the Newtonian theory. However, their physical meaning is different, because **p** and E are now defined by the relativistic expression $\mathbf{p} = m\mathbf{v}$, $E = mc^2$, with $m = m_0/\sqrt{1 - (v^2/c^2)}$, rather than by the Newtonian expression.

It is evident, however, that to obtain equations of motion which remain invariant in form (i.e., which constitute the same relationships) in every Lorentz frame, it is not enough to give **p** and E a proper relativistic definition. It is also necessary to define the force **F** in such a way that it will express the same kind of relationship, independent of the speed of the reference frame. Now, this cannot actually be done until we have some more specific expressions for the force, such as that due to an electromagnetic field, to gravitation, or to other forces (e.g., those arising in nuclear interactions). In this work we shall in fact discuss only the electromagnetic forces, showing in detail that they do lead to invariant relationships for the equations of motion. It may be stated, however, that all forces with properties that are known can be expressed in such a way as to lead to similarly invariant equations of motion, but the proof of the statement is beyond the scope of the present work.[1]

[1] There are further forces (notably the forces between atomic nuclei), which are so poorly understood as yet that little can be said about them in this regard. However, there is at present no reason to suppose that they lead to equations of motion that are *not* invariant under a Lorentz transformation.

The force on a body of charge q under an electric field $\mathscr{E}$ and a magnetic field $\mathscr{H}$ is

$$\mathbf{F} = q\left(\mathscr{E} + \frac{\mathbf{v}}{c} \times \mathscr{H}\right) \tag{21-4}$$

Noting that $\mathbf{v} \cdot (\mathbf{v} \times \mathscr{H}) \equiv 0$, we obtain the well-known Lorentz equations of motion for such a body:

$$\frac{d\mathbf{p}}{dt} = q\left(\mathscr{E} + \frac{v}{c} \times \mathscr{H}\right) \tag{21-5}$$

$$\frac{dE}{dt} = q(\mathscr{E} \cdot \mathbf{v}) \tag{21-6}$$

For our purposes these can more conveniently be expressed in differential form with $d\mathbf{x}/dt = \mathbf{v}$,

$$d\mathbf{p} = q\left(\mathscr{E}\, dt + \frac{d\mathbf{x}}{c} \times \mathscr{H}\right) \tag{21-7}$$

$$dE = q(\mathscr{E} \cdot d\mathbf{x}) \tag{21-8}$$

when $d\mathbf{x}$ is the vector for the distance moved by the body in the time interval dt.

The above laws were first observed to hold in frames of reference which are such that the velocity $\mathbf{v}$ of the electron is small compared with c. However, we are now investigating the conditions under which these laws will hold, independent of the speed of the frame of reference. In other words, if (21-7) and (21-8) hold in some frame A, we wish to find out how the quantities $\mathscr{E}'$ and $\mathscr{H}'$, as observed in another frame B, must be related to $\mathscr{E}$ and $\mathscr{H}$ in order that the equations in frame B will have the same form, when expressed in terms of the new variables.

$$d\mathbf{p}' = q\left(\mathscr{E}'\, dt' + \frac{d\mathbf{x}'}{c} \times \mathscr{H}'\right) \tag{21-9}$$

$$dE' = q(\mathscr{E}' \cdot d\mathbf{x}') \tag{21-10}$$

We now express $d\mathbf{p}'$ and dE' in terms of $d\mathbf{p}$ and dE by the Lorentz transformations (20-7) and (20-8) and express $d\mathbf{x}'$ and dt' in terms of $d\mathbf{x}$ and dt by the similar transformation (15-12). In doing this we take the differentials of the corresponding equations, noting that $\mathbf{V}$ and $\hat{V}$ are constants. We obtain [with $\gamma = 1/\sqrt{1 - (V^2/c^2)}$]

$$d\mathbf{p} + (\gamma - 1)(\hat{V}\cdot d\mathbf{p})\hat{V} - \frac{\gamma \mathbf{V}}{c^2}dE = q\gamma\mathscr{E}'\left(dt - \mathbf{V}\cdot\frac{d\mathbf{x}}{c^2}\right)$$

$$+ \frac{q}{c}(\gamma - 1)(\hat{V}\cdot d\mathbf{x})(\hat{V} \times \mathscr{H}') + \frac{q}{c}\gamma \, dt(\mathbf{V} \times \mathscr{H}') \quad (21\text{-}11)$$

$$\gamma(dE - \mathbf{V}\,d\mathbf{p}) = q\mathscr{E}'\cdot d\mathbf{x} + q(\gamma - 1)(\mathscr{E}'\cdot\hat{V})(\hat{V}\cdot d\mathbf{x}) - \gamma(\mathscr{E}'\cdot\mathbf{V})\,dt$$
$$(21\text{-}12)$$

Substitution of (21–7) and (21–8) for dE and $d\mathbf{p}$ yields

$$d\mathbf{p} + (\gamma - 1)(\hat{V}\cdot d\mathbf{p})\hat{V} - \frac{\gamma \mathbf{V}\,dE}{c^2} = q\left(\mathscr{E}\,dt + \frac{d\mathbf{x}}{c} \times \mathscr{H}\right)$$

$$+ q(\gamma - 1)\left[\hat{V}\cdot\mathscr{E}\,dt + \hat{V}\cdot\left(\frac{d\mathbf{x}}{c} \times \mathscr{H}\right)\right]\hat{V} - \frac{\gamma}{c^2}\mathbf{V}(\mathscr{E}\cdot d\mathbf{x})$$

$$(21\text{-}13)$$

$$\gamma(dE - \mathbf{V}\cdot d\mathbf{p}) = q\gamma\left[\mathscr{E}\cdot d\mathbf{x} - (\mathbf{V}\cdot\mathscr{E})\,dt - \frac{\mathbf{V}}{c}\cdot(d\mathbf{x} \times \mathscr{H})\right] \quad (21\text{-}14)$$

Equations (21–11) and (21–12) together yield [with $\mathbf{V}\cdot(d\mathbf{x} \times \mathscr{H})$ $= -(\mathbf{V} \times \mathscr{H})\cdot d\mathbf{x}$]

$$\left[\mathscr{E}' + (\gamma - 1)(\mathscr{E}'\cdot\hat{V})\hat{V} + \gamma\mathscr{E} + \gamma\left(\frac{\mathbf{V}}{c} \times \mathscr{H}\right)\right]\cdot d\mathbf{x}$$

$$+ \gamma(\mathscr{E}' - \mathscr{E})\cdot\mathbf{V}\,dt = 0 \quad (21\text{-}15)$$

Now, the above equation must be true for arbitrary particle velocity $\mathbf{v} = d\mathbf{x}/dt$. Hence it must hold independent of $d\mathbf{x}$ and dt. The reader will readily verify that this is possible only if the coefficients of $d\mathbf{x}$ and dt are separately zero, or if

$$(\mathscr{E}' - \mathscr{E})\cdot\mathbf{V} = 0$$

$$\mathscr{E}' - \gamma\mathscr{E} - (\mathscr{E}'\cdot\hat{V})(\hat{V}) + \gamma(\mathscr{E}'\cdot\hat{V})\hat{V} + \gamma\left(\frac{\mathbf{V}}{c} \times \mathscr{H}\right) = 0 \,(21\text{-}16)$$

It will now be convenient to express the field quantities $\mathscr{E}$, $\mathscr{H}$ and

$\mathscr{E}'$, $\mathscr{H}'$ in terms of components $\mathscr{E}_1$, $\mathscr{E}'_1$; $\mathscr{H}_1$, $\mathscr{H}'_1$ which are parallel to **V** and $\mathscr{E}_2$, $\mathscr{E}'_2$; $\mathscr{H}_2$, $\mathscr{H}'_2$, which are perpendicular to **V**. From $(\mathscr{E}' - \mathscr{E}) \cdot V = 0$ it follows that $\mathscr{E}'_1 = \mathscr{E}_1$. Since $\mathscr{E}'_1 - (\mathscr{E}'_1 \cdot \hat{V})(\hat{V}) = 0$ and $\mathscr{E}'_2 \cdot \hat{V} = 0$, it follows [using $\mathscr{E}'_1 \cdot \hat{V} = \mathscr{E}' \hat{V}$ and $\mathscr{E}_1 = (\mathscr{E}'_1 \cdot \hat{V}(\hat{V})]$ that

$$\mathscr{E}'_2 = \gamma\left(\mathscr{E}_2 + \frac{V}{c} \times \mathscr{H}_2\right) \tag{21-17}$$

By going through a similar procedure with Eqs. (21–11) and (21–13) the reader can verify that we obtain the corresponding equations:

$$\mathscr{H}'_1 = \mathscr{H}_1 \tag{21-18}$$

$$\mathscr{H}'_2 = \gamma\left(\mathscr{H}_2 + \frac{V}{c} + \mathscr{E}_2\right) \tag{21-19}$$

The equations for $\mathscr{E}'$ and $\mathscr{H}'$ can be combined into the set

$$\mathscr{E}' = (\mathscr{E} \cdot \hat{V})(\hat{V}) + \gamma\left[\mathscr{E} - (\hat{V} \cdot \mathscr{E})\hat{V} + \frac{V}{c} \times \mathscr{H}\right] \tag{21-20}$$

$$\mathscr{H}' = (\mathscr{H} \cdot \hat{V})(\hat{V}) + \gamma\left[\mathscr{H} - (\hat{V} \cdot \mathscr{H})\hat{V} - \frac{V}{c} \times \mathscr{E}\right] \tag{21-21}$$

The above equations define the transformation laws for $\mathscr{E}$ and $\mathscr{H}$ that will lead to the same equations of motion [(21–7) to (21–10)] for a charged particle, independent of the speed of the frame of reference.

It should be noted that the transformation relationships (21–20) and (21–21) can also be shown to lead to an invariant form for Maxwell's equations. (To do this is beyond the scope of the present work, but for a further discussion on this point see C. C. Moller, *The Theory of Relativity*, and W. Panofsky and M. Phillips, *Classical Electricity and Magnetism.*) Therefore, what has been achieved is the demonstration that the laws of electrodynamics (Maxwell's equations) and the laws of motion of a charged particle in an electromagnetic field can both be expressed in an invariant form (i.e., as the same set of relationships in all frames of reference connected by Lorentz transformations).

Finally, it should be noted that the transformation laws for $\mathscr{E}$ and $\mathscr{H}$ give the kind of results that would be expected from a consideration of the laws of electrodynamics. Thus Faraday's law of induction implies that a wire passing through a magnetic field $\mathscr{H}$ with velocity **V** will have emf induced in it proportional to **V** and the field $\mathscr{H}$ but perpendicular to both. Equations (21–20) and (21–21) express what is essentially the same conclusion. Thus, if in frame A we have $\mathscr{E} = 0$ and $\mathscr{H} \neq 0$, then on going to the frame B, moving at speed **V** in which the wire is at rest, we will have $\mathscr{E}' = \gamma[(\mathbf{V}/c) \times \mathscr{H})]$. The emf (as experienced in the frame on which the wire is at rest) will then be proportional to $\mathscr{E}'$.

Similarly, if in frame A we have $\mathscr{H} = 0$ and $\mathscr{E} \neq 0$, then (21–18) and (21–19) imply that in a frame moving at a velocity **V** relative to A, there will appear a magnetic field $\mathscr{H}' = -\gamma(\mathbf{V}/c) \times \mathscr{E}]$. This can be shown to lead to results equivalent to Maxwell's "displacement current," $\mathbf{j}_d = (c/4\pi)(\partial\mathscr{E}/\partial t)$, which implies that an object passing through a static electric field will, in the frame in which it is at rest, experience a corresponding magnetic field (which could be shown up, for example, if the object were a magnetic dipole tending to orient itself in relationship to this "induced" magnetic field).

XXII

Experimental Evidence for Special Relativity

We shall here give a brief review of the experimental evidence confirming the special theory of relativity. In doing this we must keep in mind that the special theory depends crucially on two points.

1. *The principle of relativity*, which asserts that the laws of physics are always the *same relationships* independent of the speed of the reference frame.

2. *The expression of the relationship* between two reference frames moving at different but uniform velocities as a Lorentz transformation.

The experimental evidence confirming the principle of relativity is actually overwhelming, in the sense that in no field has one ever discovered any dependence of the forms of the laws of physics on the velocity of the reference frame. We shall therefore confine ourselves here to a discussion of the evidence confirming the Lorentz transformation.

In our discussion of the ether theory (see Chapter 9) we saw that the Lorentz transformation is completely equivalent to a combination of three effects:

1. The Lorentz contraction of a moving object in the ratio $\sqrt{1 - (v^2/c^2)}$.

2. The lengthening of the period of a moving clock in the ratio $1/\sqrt{1 - (v^2/c^2)}$.

3. The change in reading of two equivalent moving clocks a distance **x** apart by $\Delta t = (\mathbf{v \cdot x}/c^2)/\sqrt{1 - (v^2/c^2)}$.

This means, of course, that two such moving clocks fail to register the same time after they are separated, even if they were in perfect synchronism while they were adjacent to each other.

As was shown in Chapter 6 the Michelson–Morley experiment may be regarded as an excellent confirmation of the Lorentz contraction. The more modern and very exact measurements of the velocity of light by the equivalent of the Fizeau method, as discussed in Chapter 7, depend on the combination of the Lorentz contraction and the change of periods of clocks. Since the Lorentz transformation itself is already checked by the Michelson–Morley experiment, we may regard the Fizeau method as confirming the variation of the rates of clocks, with their velocity, as predicted by the Lorentz transformation. However, there exists more direct verification of the variation of the rate of clocks. Thus in Chapter 16 we have discussed the observations on the mean time decay of rapidly moving mesons and the Doppler shift for light viewed perpendicular to the direction of motion of the source, both of which have provided very accurate confirmation of the predictions of the Lorentz transformation concerning the increase of period that should be observed for moving clocks.

The direct experimental confirmation of the remaining prediction concerning the nonsimultaneity of separated clocks is rather more difficult to obtain. At first sight it would seem that one could test this by considering the relativistic law for the addition of velocities (15–7) and (15–8), the derivation of which depended on the formula (15–6), expressing just the property of nonsimultaneity of such clocks that is under discussion. This law has been quite accurately confirmed, for example, by the measurement of the speed of light in flowing water, described in Chapter 17. Unfortunately, such a test is not unambiguous in its significance, because, as can be shown (see, for example, C. C. Moller, *The Theory of Relativity*) nonrelativistic theories of electromagnetic phenomena can be made to give the same results as relativistic theories to the order of the experiments that are available. As a result, the agreement of experiments measuring the speed of light in flowing water with the predictions of relativity does not prove *conclusively* that the formulas for nonsynchronization of moving clocks is correct, because other assumptions concerning electromagnetic processes might lead to essentially the same result.

Another line of approach, offering practically conclusive confirmation on this point, can be obtained by reconsidering the results of Chapter 8, when we showed in the development leading to Eq. (8–8) that once we accept the formula $T = T_0/\sqrt{1 - (v^2/c^2)}$ for the slowing down of clocks, it follows necessarily that when two initially synchronous moving clocks separate (slowly and without jarring movements) they will get out of synchronism by $[l_0 v/c^2]/[\sqrt{1 - (v^2/c^2)}]$. This conclusion is just a consequence of the fact that while the clocks are separating, they must run at different rates; and *it evidently follows quite independent of the hypotheses of an ether*. Since experiment has already confirmed the formula $T = T_0/\sqrt{1 - (v^2/c^2)}$, the prediction of the Lorentz transformation that equivalent clocks will get out of phase by $[l_0 v/c^2]/[\sqrt{1 - (v^2/c^2)}]$ may be regarded as essentially verified.

A more direct way of checking the above prediction has already been suggested at the end of Chapter 10, viz., to measure the speed of light on the basis of the time $t_A - t_B$ taken for light to pass between two points A and B, the times t_A and t_B being read from equivalent cesium clocks that were first synchronized and then separated. This experiment may perhaps soon be technically feasible. As indicated in Chapter 10, however, there seems to be little reason to suppose that the results would differ from those predicted with the aid of a Lorentz transformation.

The predictions of Einstein's theory with regard to the equivalence of mass and energy have been so thoroughly verified that further discussion of this point seems unnecessary. In this regard, even the detailed relationships (20–4), (20–5), and (20–6), expressing the Lorentz transformation of energy and momentum, have been verified in the study of collisions of particles of very high energy, such as those produced in accelerators in the laboratory and encountered naturally in cosmic rays.

Similarly, the invariance of the Lorentz equations (21–2) and (21–3) for a moving charged particle has been verified, even when v/c is close to unity, while the transformation laws, (21–20) and (21–21), for the electromagnetic field are also well verified experimentally.

The experimental evidence that we have cited as confirming the special theory of relativity seems very strong indeed. Besides, there is a great deal of additional evidence, which we have not discussed here. Moreover, it should be kept in mind that a large part of this evidence came, especially in the early days when the theory was new and not generally accepted, from experiments designed at least to probe and test the theory and, if possible, to refute it. In view of its ability to withstand such probes and criticisms, as well as to lead fruitfully to new results, many of them unexpected, it may be said that the theory of relativity is now as well confirmed as is any aspect of physics that is known today.

Nevertheless, as is true of any theory in science, it must not be supposed that relativity is an iron-clad certainty, which should not be questioned, and which could never be shown to be wrong in certain respects, an approximation to the facts, or of limited validity for other reasons. For example, there is even now an appreciable number of scientists who are inclined to suspect that the theory of relativity (both special and general) may be wrong when applied in the domain of very small distances (much less than the presumed size of the "elementary" particle). Besides, there seem to be reasons to suspect that relativity may not be adequate when applied to extremely large distances of the order of the presumed "size" of the universe (out to where the "red shift" becomes appreciable). In addition, the theory of relativity may break down in yet other ways. It is therefore necessary, especially when we enter into new domains of phenomena, to apply the theory of relativity in a tentative manner, being alert and ready to criticize it, and if necessary to replace it with a more nearly correct theory, which may be as radically different from relativity as relativity is from Newtonian mechanics.

XXIII

More About the Equivalence of Mass and Energy

The equivalence of mass and energy, which follows from the theory of relativity, is so much at variance with the older classical concepts that it seems worthwhile to discuss the general implications of this fact in some detail. Indeed, experience shows that students often have considerable difficulty in understanding the full implications of Einstein's notions of mass and energy. Typical questions that arise are: "Is mass the same thing as energy?" "Is the world constituted only of energy?" "What is mass, if it can be transformed into energy and vice versa?" And for that matter, "What is *energy?*"

Let us begin by considering where the common conception of a body with a well-defined and constant mass comes from. This idea is evidently based on the observation that the world contains a large number of objects and entities, which can be compared with regard to size, shape, weight, etc., and which can be regarded as constituted of definite quantities or masses of certain substances, such as rock, soil, water, metal, wood, etc. We find, of course, that these substances wear away, break down, melt, corrode, decay, evaporate, and burn up into nothing but gases. So it is evident that they are not in fact individually permanent or constant in mass, though they may undergo negligible visible changes in such properties, some for short periods of time and others over longer periods of time.

Our mode of thought is such, however, that somehow we seem to believe that somewhere there must be an absolutely permanent basis for everything.

Early scientists, for example, supposed that atoms were absolutely permanent entities, the basic "building blocks" of the universe, so that the ever-changing appearances of large-scale matter were regarded as nothing but consequences of the underlying movements of its permanent atomic constituents. But then the atoms were seen to be constituted of moving structures of "elementary particles" (electrons, protons, and neutrons) with the result that atoms could be altered, transformed into other atoms, built up and torn down, etc. It was then assumed, however, that there is something else that is absolutely permanent, i.e., the elementary particles. But as we have seen, nuclear and other processes have been discovered, in which even these particles are transformed into each other and annihilated and created, with the liberation and absorption of corresponding amounts of energy. So once again the search for absolutely permanent entities and substances has been foiled. Rather, it is clear that both in common experience and in scientific investigations, the objects, entities, substances, etc., that we actually experience, perceive, or observe have always (thus far) shown themselves to be only *relatively invariant* in their properties, this relative invariance having often been mistaken for absolute permanence.

If mankind has never yet encountered anything that is absolutely permanent, where then does this idea come from, an idea of great persistence which returns perennially in the face of new experiences and observations, which again and again show it to be contrary to the available facts? Some light can be thrown on this question by considering investigations of the development of the concept of the object in infants and young children. (These investigations have been carried out along with studies of the development of their concepts of space and time, and are discussed in more detail in the Appendix.) The existing evidence shows that very young infants do not seem actually to have the notion of a permanent object. Rather, their behavior in relation to objects is such as to suggest that they regard them as coming into existence when they are first seen and going out of existence when they vanish from the field of perception. Only gradually does the infant build up the notion of an object that exists even when he does not perceive it. The notion of a permanent *quantity* of matter is developed still later; and even children of three or four years of age are often quite confused on this question. But in time the concept is formed, and eventually it becomes habitual, so that in every field we automatically tend to seek bodies, entities, or substances of fixed characteristics, and even begin to feel that we cannot imagine a world that is not built out of some kinds of permanent entities or substances.

The notion that there must exist some absolutely permanent kinds of entities is not only based on habits of thought beginning in early childhood in the manner described above. As happens with the similar notions of absolute space and time, it also originates, at least in part, in the structure of our common language. Thus when we see something with *relatively invariant* properties we give it a name. But this name remains the same, even though the object changes. Because it has the same name, we tend to think of it as being the same thing. An extreme case is that of a human being. Each person has the same name that he had 10, 20 or 30 years ago. Yet he is evidently a very different person, both physically and mentally. In fact, he is different from what he was yesterday or even a minute ago. Similarly, a block of metal is always changing, its atoms are moving, it is oxidizing, becoming fatigued, etc. In certain limited contexts and for short periods of time, these changes can be neglected. So the constancy of the name of an object leads to an adequate conception of it only in a certain limited domain. Our difficulties arise because out of a habit that goes back to the very beginning of the use of language by the human race (as well as to its beginnings in the childhood of each individual), we *identify* things; i.e., we unconsciously assume that whatever has the same name is at least in essence the same thing.

Let us now return to the problem of mass and energy in physics. We have given the name "mass" to certain properties observed in common experience. These properties have since then been given more refined meanings in physics. Besides referring to the common notion of "quantity of the permanent substance of matter," mass refers in physics to two more precisely defined properties. One of these is inertia, or resistance to acceleration, and the other is gravitation.

We shall begin by discussing the *inertial aspect* of mass. In Newtonian mechanics, the equation $m\mathbf{a} = \mathbf{F}$ implies that the force needed to give an object a specified acceleration is proportional to its mass. But this mass would not have its usual significance if it were not a constant. In other words, Newton's equations (18-1) and (18-2) are not defined without (18-3), i.e., $(dm/dt) = 0$, or $m =$ constant. The importance of this latter equation is often missed, just because of our everyday habit of thinking of mass as a "permanent" property of substances. In reality, however, it is not from the common *idea* of mass that we know the constancy of the proportionality factor m between the force and acceleration of a given object. Rather, it is an observed fact that this proportionality factor is an *invariant* in all experiments referring to the domain of Newtonian mechanics.

The second important manifestation of the mass of an object in physics is that it occurs as a constant proportionality factor occurring in the law of gravitational force between it and another such object, $F = Gm_1m_2/r^2$, where r is the distance between the objects and G is the gravitational constant. An important further fact is that in all experiments available to date, the mass appearing in the above equation has always been proportional to the inertial mass appearing in the equations of motion. Because of this constancy of the ratio between gravitational and inertial masses, one tends to *identify* them; that is, one is led to give them the same name and, therefore, to regard them as the same thing. In doing this we are very likely also unconsciously to replace the precise physical meanings of gravitational and inertial masses by the common notion of mass as "quantity of the permanent substance of matter."

In the relativistic domain of large v/c we find (as we have seen in Chapter 20) that Newton's laws of motion must be replaced by Einstein's, which are

$$\frac{d\mathbf{p}}{dt} = \mathbf{F} \qquad \text{with} \qquad \mathbf{p} = \frac{m_0\mathbf{v}}{\sqrt{1 - (v^2/c^2)}} = m\mathbf{v}$$

The mass is therefore no longer an invariant in the broader domain. So it is clear that mass is in fact just a *relative invariant*, in the sense that its changes can be neglected only in the Newtonian domain.

The problem of the gravitational aspect of mass cannot be dealt with in the special theory of relativity; it requires the general theory. But it will suffice here to mention briefly that in the general theory Einstein regards the exact proportionality between gravitational and inertial masses, which has thus far been observed, as suggesting that these two kinds of mass represent different but related aspects of some single broader set of concepts and laws, which encompasses *both* the phenomena of inertia and those of gravitation. This notion he embodies in his "principle of equivalence" between the effects of acceleration of the coordinate frame and those of a gravitational field. Here the notion of equivalence has a meaning similar to that arising in the "equivalence" of mass and energy; i.e., it refers to an inherent relationship between two different quantities, implying that one is necessarily proportional to the other. On this basis Einstein succeeded in developing a coherent and unified theory, which, in effect, explains gravitational and inertial mass as different aspects of a single underlying process, treated by the laws of general relativity, of which restricted relativity is, of course, a special and approximate limiting case, more or less as Newtonian mechanics is a corresponding limiting and approximate case of special relativity.

It seems clear that we have been applying the same name "mass" to properties that become very different, as we go outside the Newtonian domain. Indeed, because the mass of a body is not invariant in the relativistic domain, it follows that the relativistic concept of mass contradicts the common notion of mass as "quantity of the permanent substance of matter." Since this common notion can be applied correctly only in the Newtonian domain, it follows that in the theory of relativity we are using the word "mass" in a sense that is not compatible with its common everyday meaning. Rather, in relativity mass refers merely to certain proportionality factors that enter into the laws of inertia and gravitation.

In this connection it is important to recall that, in any case, the common concept of mass is not an inevitable one, but has been built up in the development of the human race, and learned by each child, to such a degree that it becomes habitual and then seems to be a necessary idea, which could not be otherwise. As in the case of ordinary notions of space and time, these habits of thought appear to be adequate in a certain limited domain. It is important, however, not to continue with these habits beyond the domain in which they are appropriate.

Let us now consider what is the meaning of energy. In physics, energy was originally defined as "quantity of motion"; but this led to a great deal of argument in early days as to which was the "real" quantity of motion, energy or momentum. Since then, it has been seen that this argument was pointless, since there is no unique "quantity of motion." Rather, energy and momentum are both *invariant functions*, in the sense that the total of these quantities, summed over all component parts of an isolated system, does not change with time.

As different parts of a system interact there is a process of exchange of energy (and momentum) between them. In this process the total quantity is conserved, but the energy of each part will of course alter. For this reason alone the total energy of a system is only a *relatively invariant* function, being constant when the system in question is isolated, but not when it is brought into interaction with its environment.

Interactions may involve not only mechanical exchanges but also changes of energy into different forms. Thus, mechanical energy can be transformed into an equivalent amount of electrical energy and vice versa, while there is a similar possibility of a mutual transformation between both of these kinds of energy and equivalent quantities of heat (which is the energy of random molecular movement, a movement that cancels out as far as the large-scale level is concerned). This transformability between different forms in equivalent amounts is indeed what is most characteristic of energy in physics.

Because the total energy of an isolated system is conserved, there is a tendency for us to think of it as a *permanent substance*, like a fluid that flows from one part of the system to another. But no one has ever perceived, or otherwise observed, such a substance. Rather, the energy always appears as a *relatively invariant function* in a movement. Thus, for an isolated body, the function $mv^2/2$ is such an invariant, in the sense that it remains constant as long as the body is isolated, and that in a system of such bodies capable of interaction, the sum of the energies of the bodies remains constant (whereas, for example, the function $m_2v^5/2$ would not have these properties). Similarly, an electric current I flowing through a coil of inductance L has energy $LI^2/2$, which is conserved if there is no resistance, and which can be transformed into a corresponding quantity of mechanical energy with the aid of a motor, and into heat energy with the aid of a resistance. We emphasize then that energy is *always* an invariant, but transformable, *aspect and function* of some kind of movement and never appears as an independently existing substance. Even potential energy is defined just as the capacity for doing work, i.e., for creating a corresponding movement, measured in terms of mechanical, electrical, thermal, or other forms of energy.

In the earlier stages of the development of physics, it was in principle possible to think of all movement as a quality or property of some kind of particles. With the discovery that mass (and even the particles themselves) can be "annihilated," with the liberation of equivalent amounts of energy, this way of thinking ceased to be tenable. But if the energy does not belong to such particles, how then are we to conceive of it? If energy has meaning only as a relatively invariant function of movement, and if there are no basic and permanent constituents of the universe which possess this movement, what can we mean by the terms "energy" and "movement"?

To answer these questions it will be helpful to begin by introducing a distinction between two kinds of energy. On the one hand, there is the *energy of outward movement* which occurs on the large scale, for example, when a body changes its position or orientation as a whole. On the other hand, there is the *energy of inward movement*, for example, the thermal motions of the constituent molecules, which cancel out on the large scale. It is characteristic of inward movement that it tends to be to-and-fro, oscillating, reflecting back and forth, and so on. (In Einstein's example of the box containing radiation, discussed earlier, the light reflecting back and forth can be regarded as inward movement.)

It is evident that the terms "inward" and "outward" are inherently relational in their meanings. Thus, relative to the large-scale level, molecular movement is "inward," because its over-all outward effects cancel on the large scale. However, relative to the molecular level, it is "outward," because the molecules do undergo a displacement through space that is significant on *this level*. On the other hand, the electronic and nuclear motions are still "inward" relative to the molecular level, although they must be regarded as "outward" when we go to still deeper levels, where *their* movements result in significant space displacements.

With these notions in mind, let us now return to the question "What *is* mass?" We first point out that in Einstein's theory, mass and energy are not regarded as originating in *essentially different ways*. Rather, they are to be thought of as two different but related aspects of a single total process of movement. In such a movement there is a relatively invariant capacity to do work, to interact with other systems, and to set them in movement, at the expense of the movement in the original system. This is called *energy*. In addition, such a system has a certain inertia, or resistance to acceleration, as well as a certain gravitational attraction to other bodies. Both of these are proportional to a property called by the name of "mass." Now, we have already seen that if there is inward movement in a body (random molecular motion or the motion of light rays reflecting back and forth), then this movement contributes an amount, Δm, to the inertial mass, according to the formula $\Delta m = \Delta E/c^2$, where ΔE is the energy associated with this movement. Moreover, as we have also pointed out, in the general theory of relativity, Einstein shows that *such energy contributes to the gravitational mass in the same way*. Since relativity requires us, in any case, to set aside the notion of mass as "quantity of the permanent substance of matter," it follows from Einstein's theory that whenever a system possesses a certain kind of energy, contributing a part ΔE to its total energy E, it has *all* the properties (i.e., inertial and gravitational) that physics ascribes to a corresponding contribution $\Delta m = \Delta E/c^2$ to its mass, which is a part of the total mass $m = E/c^2$.

In this connection it must be noted that *every form of energy* (including kinetic as well as potential) contributes in the same way to the mass. However, the "rest energy" of a body has a special meaning, in the sense that even when a body has no visible motion as a whole, it is still undergoing inward movements (as radiant energy, molecular, electronic, nucleonic, and other movements). These inward movements have some "rest energy" E_0 and contribute a corresponding quantity, $m_0 = E_0/c^2$ to the "rest mass." As long as the energy is only "inward," the rest mass remains constant, of course. But as we have seen, internal transformations taking place on the molecular, atomic, and nuclear levels can change some of this to-and-fro, reflecting "inward" movement into other forms of energy whose effects are "outwardly" visible on the large scale. When this happens, the "rest energy" and with it, the "rest mass," undergo a corresponding decrease. But such a change of mass is seen to be not in the least bit mysterious, if we remember that inertial and gravitational masses are merely one aspect of the whole movement, another aspect of which is an equivalent energy, exhibited as a capacity to do work on the large scale. In other words, the transformation of "matter" into "energy" is just a change from one form of movement (inwardly, reflecting, to-and-fro) into another form (e.g., outward displacement through space).

It is particularly instructive to consider how, in this point of view, one understands the possibility for objects with zero rest mass to exist, provided that they are moving at the speed of light. For if rest mass is "inner" movement, taking place even when an object is visibly at rest on a certain level, it follows that something without "rest mass" has no such inner movement, and that *all* its movement is outward, in the sense that it is involved in displacement through space. So light (and everything else that travels at the same speed) may be regarded as something that does not have the possibility of being "at rest" on any given level, by virtue of the cancellation of inner "reflecting" movements, because it does not possess any such inner movements. As a result it can exist only in the form of "outward" movement at the speed c. And as we recall, the property of moving with the speed of light is invariant under a Lorentz transformation, so that the quality of the movement as purely "outward" does not depend on the frame of reference in which it is observed. (On the other hand, movements at speeds less than c can always be transformed into rest by a change to a reference frame with velocity equal to that of the object under consideration).

XXIV

Toward a New Theory of
Elementary Particles

The full development of the point of view outlined in the previous chapter, concerning the transformation between "rest energy" and other forms of energy, implies that we shall eventually have to understand the so-called "elementary" particles as structures arising in relatively invariant patterns of movement occurring at a still lower level than that of these particles. In such structures even the "rest energy" of an elementary particle would be treated as some kind of "inner," to-and-fro reflecting movement, on a level which is even below that on which nuclear transformations take place.

At present the study of the structure of the "elementary" particles is indeed one of the principal concerns of physical research. A great many clues have been accumulated, which suggest that there does actually exist a new level of the kind mentioned above, in terms of which such structure may perhaps eventually be understood. However, it seems likely that the laws of this level will be as new relative to those of the nucleonic and atomic levels as those of the latter are in relation to the large-scale level. The present situation in elementary particle physics may perhaps be compared with that existing in atomic physics before the time of Niels Bohr, in the sense that a great deal of systematic factual information has been collected, suggesting the need for a fundamentally new set of theoretical concepts, which is, however, yet to be developed. Nevertheless, it is already clear that the "creation" of a particle should correspond to setting up some characteristic relatively invariant kind of movement in a level below that of the elementary particles, with the aid of the necessary quantity of energy, and its "annihilation" to the ending of this pattern of movement, with the liberation of a corresponding quantity of energy. What seems essential here is to set aside the notion of "elementary" particles as the permanent substance of matter, and to regard them as only *relatively* fixed kinds of entities, which come into being when certain kinds of movement take place, and pass out of being when these kinds of movement cease.

At this point, questions naturally arise. · One is: "May we not find new kinds of entities below the level of elementary particles which do in fact constitute the real permanent substance of matter?" Of course, we have no way at present to know what will be discovered in future research on this problem. But it may perhaps be instructive to make a few observations here, which we can carry out on the basis of what we already know. Naturally, these observations will have to be somewhat speculative, but it is hoped that they will serve to help clarify the meaning of this question.

We begin by asking: "Does the assumption of the absolute permanence of entities or substances ever make a real contribution to the laws of physics, or is it not like the Ptolemaic epicycles and the ether theory, in the sense that it is factually not necessary and as far as the theory is concerned, a source of confusion?" To show that this question is well founded, we shall begin by considering everyday life, where as we have seen from our continually changing immediate perceptions, we have been able to abstract certain objects, entities, etc., having more or less constant characteristics, such as shape, size, hardness, and other qualities. Knowing that all these objects can be broken, corroded, melted, burned, or that they are subject to decay, is it not better to refer to them, in effect, as *relatively fixed and invariant*, rather than as entities with absolutely permanent properties? Indeed, if we do this, we can then think of their various movements and transformations, outward and inward, without contradicting the above-described facts, because we have not made the false assumption that since the objects have a fixed name they must always remain essentially the same sorts of things. Thus, it is evident that on the level of ordinary experience, clarity is gained and confusion is decreased if we admit, from the outset, that objects and entities need have only relatively invariant characteristics and that our descriptions of their actions are only approximations, in the sense that all the movements in the atomic, nuclear, and lower levels are (correctly for this level) being ignored. When these movements are taken into account, transformations in which "substances" such as liquids, solids, metals, and gases are created and destroyed can be understood quite simply, as the outcome of "inward" movements on lower levels.

But then when we come to the molecular, atomic, and "elementary" particle levels, we again note a similar process. Thus, an atom, which is a fixed entity on its own level (the very word "atom" means "indivisible" in Greek) is found to be just as capable of fundamental transformations which are the outcome of "inward" movements of its electrons, protons, and neutrons as are the entities on the large-scale level. And, indeed, nowhere have we ever encountered entities which do not have these characteristics.

Can we not then simply refrain from making assumptions concerning the absolute permanence of what is, in the nature of the case, unknown? As can be done in large-scale experience, we can instead regard entities and structures encountered on lower levels as *relatively invariant* or relatively fixed in their characteristics. In the domain in which these entities or structures are relatively invariant, we may refer to their movements and transformations in a way rather similar to that adopted with regard to the objects of everyday experience. Evidently nothing is lost when we thus replace the notion of absolute permanence by that of relative invariance.

The notion that something is absolutely permanent is moreover evidently one that can never be proved experimentally. For no one can be sure that even if certain things have not changed over a given domain of experience, they will *never* change, as our domain of experience is broadened (as has indeed actually happened with everything that was ever thought to be absolutely permanent).

It is evident then that by considering entities and structures as relatively invariant, with *an as yet unknown domain of invariance*, we avoid making unnecessary and unprovable assumptions concerning their absolute invariance. Such a procedure has enormous advantages in research, because one of the main sources of difficulty in the development of new concepts—not only in physics, but also in the whole of science—has been the tendency to hold onto old concepts beyond their domain of validity; this tendency is evidently enchanced by our habit of regarding the entities and structures that we know as absolutely permanent in their characteristics.

XXV

The Falsification of Theories

These concepts may perhaps be further clarified by the consideration of a point that has been very strongly emphasized by Professor Popper, i.e., that the *falsification* of a theory is, in many ways, even more significant than its *verification*. For example, the demonstration that the Galilean transformation is false led eventually to the revolutionary changes attending the development of the theory of relativity. Similarly, experiments showing the falsity of the predictions of classical physics for atomic spectra, the photoelectric effect, and the distribution of black-body radiation led to the even more revolutionary changes that the quantum theory brought in. And the more recent evidence suggesting that our ideas concerning the existence of "permanent" elementary particles are false seems to be laying the foundation for a transformation of our basic concepts that will make even the changes introduced by relativity and quantum theory seem comparatively small.

It is clear that the falsification of old theories has actually had a key role in the development of physics (and indeed of the whole of science). A little reflection on this problem shows, however, that such a process is a necessary part of the development of a science, and that in order to permit this development to take place properly, it is indeed essential that scientific theories be *falsifiable*.[1]

Consider, for example, the Ptolemaic theory, which allowed the addition of arbitrary sets of epicycles in such a way as to be able to accommodate any conceivable set of observations. Such a theory could not be disproved by any set of experiments whatsoever. *But theories which are inherently unfalsifiable in this way do not really say anything new about the world.* For their ability to accommodate themselves to any factual discoveries whatsoever means that they exclude no possibility at all, and therefore, have no well-defined implications concerning what is as yet unknown. At best, they constitute a useful way of summarizing existing facts. On the other hand, a theory such as that of Newton or Einstein cannot be adjusted to fit arbitrary experimental results, and is therefore capable of leading to *definite* predictions about phenomena that were not known when the theory was first formulated. If such a theory is wrong, it can therefore be checked and shown to be false. This possibility is inseparable from its ability to say something new about the world, and thus to constitute a genuinely scientific theory (i.e., genuine in the sense that it affords correct knowledge going beyond the experimental facts which helped lead to its proposal).

A theory that has a real predictive content must then, as it were, "stick its neck out." But if it does this it is likely in time to "have its neck chopped off." Indeed, this is what did happen eventually to a great many theories such as Newtonian mechanics, which were confirmed up to a point but then shown to be false. Moreover, it seems likely that eventually this will be the fate of *all* theories. Thus Einstein's special theory of relativity cannot be entirely true, if only because it is an approximation to the general theory. And Einstein implicitly recognized that even the general theory is not entirely true, when he engaged in his search for a still more general "unified field theory" that he hoped would contain general relativity, electrodynamics, and elementary particle theory, as approximations and limiting cases.[2] Moreover, as we have already remarked, classical mechanics has been

---

[1] For a more detailed discussion of Professor Popper's point of view on this question, see K. R. Popper, *Conjectures and Refutations*, Routledge and Kegan Paul, London, 1963.

[2] Recall also that, as pointed out in Chapter 22, there are yet other reasons why it is suspected that there may be limits to the validity of the theory of relativity.

shown to be false, in the sense that it is an approximation and limiting case of quantum mechanics, which is a very different kind of theory. And now it seems likely that current elementary particle theory, along with quantum mechanics, will be shown to be false, in the sense of being approximations to some as-yet-unknown theory of a new kind that is still more general.

If useful scientific theories are not only *falsifiable*, but also very probably *actually false*, what then can it mean to seek truth through scientific research? Does not Professor Popper's thesis thus disclose a deep kind of confusion in the whole purpose of science, its goals, aims, procedures, and achievements?

This problem has its roots in a certain attitude toward truth in science, which has, like the concepts of absolute space and time, and of permanent substance, become so habitual that it may seem inevitable. This attitude regards *basic* scientific laws as *absolute truths*, in the sense that such laws are assumed to hold exactly (i.e., without approximation) in unlimited domains, under all possible conditions, so that they will never be subject to modification, contradiction, and fundamental change. For example, before the advent of relativity and quantum theory, Newton's laws of motion, along with his concepts of space and time, were regarded as absolute truths of this kind. Later, many scientists probably began to regard relativity and quantum theory as "really absolute" truths, whereas they felt that Newtonian mechanics had been a false version of such "eternal verities."

Where did the notion of absolute truth come from? It is evident that at least as far back as the Middle Ages this notion was quite prevalent. For example, the doctrines of Aristotle were then commonly regarded as absolute truths. And if we go back further in time it seems clear that there is no society known in historical records which did not accept *some* kinds of doctrines, notions, or ideas as absolute truths. Thus, the search for an absolute truth seems to be based on the continuation of a tradition having very deep roots in the distant past.

But, as with the case of the permanent substance, mankind has never encountered any *general* statements that were not approximations, having limited domains and conditions of validity. Moreover, even if there did exist general statements which had not yet been shown to be thus limited in their validity, there would (as in the case of the hypothesis of absolutely permanent substances) be no way to be sure that they would continue to be verified, as the domain under consideration is extended indefinitely. Thus, the notion of absolute truth is not based on facts, and can indeed never be proved by any experiments.

It is clear, moreover, that the assumption that a given law is absolutely true is never necessary. For any laws that are thus asserted as absolute truths can, with greater faithfulness to the *facts of the case*, be asserted as relationships holding in *some domain*. The extent of such a domain can be indicated when the law is ultimately falsified in further research and investigation and replaced by a new law or set of laws containing the older ones as approximations or limiting cases. For example, Newtonian mechanics was found, as we have seen, to fail as the velocity becomes appreciable compared with that of light, where it has to be replaced by Einstein's theory, which showed that the domain of Newton's law is that of sufficiently low velocities.

It must not be supposed, however, that we can eventually come to know the domain of validity of a given law *completely* and *perfectly*, and thus obtain another kind of absolute truth, which would assert that at least in a specified and well-defined domain, a given law is *always* applicable. For our knowledge of this domain is itself incomplete. Thus, with regard to Newton's laws, it was found that even in the low-velocity domain delimited by the theory of relativity, these laws fail in the atomic level, where quantum theory is needed, and probably on the extra-galactic scale of space and time, as well as in the interiors of superdense stars, where general relativistic effects become important. As we cannot be sure that there are not further as-yet-unknown limitations on Newton's laws, which will be revealed in future research, we can only say that it is necessary always to be alert to the possibility of discovering additional limitations on the domain of applicability of any given law, even after some of the limitations of this kind have already been disclosed.

It seems clear, however, that as long as, generally speaking, laws can be discovered having domains of validity *going in any way at all beyond the facts in which they are based*, then the conditions will exist in which scientific research can be carried out by methods currently in use. For such research evidently does not require that any of these laws be absolute truths, provided that they can be confirmed objectively in certain domains and similarly falsified in broader domains.

In terms of the notion of law, described above, Professor Popper's thesis on the need for falsifiability of theories is seen to arise quite naturally. For now we need no longer suppose that a scientific theory is either completely true, and therefore an "eternal verity," or else completely false, and therefore of no significance whatsoever. Rather, a law of nature is, by our very way of conceiving it, seen to express the fact that in a certain set of changes taking place in nature, as well as in a corresponding set of changes of points of view, reference frames, modes of investigation, etc., certain general relationships can be discovered, which remain the same throughout all these changes. But this invariance is to be conceived of as *only relative*, in the sense that as the domain is broadened, we leave room in our minds to *entertain the notion* that the law may break down. That is to say, it may be falsified in some future set of experiments. We do not commit ourselves as to when, where, and how it will be falsified but leave this to be shown by future developments themselves. The essential point is only that our minds are not closed on this question. Instead, we are always ready for a falsification when it comes, without having at that time to face a "crisis" in which our notions of absolute truths and "eternal verities" are shattered and overthrown once again, as has happened perennially since the human race began its quest for this kind of truth.

As important as the falsifiability of a theory is, it is evident that we do not propose theories *merely* in order to show that they are wrong. Rather, as we have already indicated, an acceptable scientific theory must also be able to withstand a certain number of experimental tests and criticisms, which show that it leads to true inferences, going beyond the facts on which the theory was originally based. Of course, some statements may have such small domains of validity of their predictive inferences that they are either trivial or of a rather narrow significance (e.g., the pencil is on the table). A genuinely scientific law is one that has a fairly broad domain of validity. So one of the aims of scientific research is to find laws with the broadest possible domains of validity.

Indeed, without the development of such laws, science as we know it would be almost impossible. For a great deal of scientific research is, and must be, based on the effort to show that a theory already well-confirmed in a broad domain, can continue to be applied to ever greater accuracy and in ever new kinds of problems. A theory of this kind thus helps indicate the kinds of questions that are likely to be relevant in our investigations of nature. In the absence of such a theory, research tends to degenerate into a kind of random or disorderly collection of isolated facts, most of which are not, in general, very relevant to each other or to the disclosure of laws of nature.

Nevertheless, it will eventually happen, as we have seen, that further efforts to confirm a successful theory of the kind described above will eventually lead either to falsification or else to arbitrary *ad hoc* hypotheses, involving an intolerable degree of confusion and ambiguity, which is in essence more or less equivalent to a falsification. Such a result contributes to the delimitation of the domain of validity of the theory in question but, even more, it usually provides significant clues or indications, helping to lead to newer laws having broader domains of validity and yet incorporating those predictions of older laws that are known to be correct (in terms of suitable approximations as limiting cases). These clues do not, of course, directly show what forms the newer laws must take. Finding such laws actually depends on a creative step by some scientist, in which he sees a new way of looking at things (a new hypothesis, a new idea, etc.) that resolves the problems that were insoluble in the older point of view. Nevertheless, the possibility of such creative new steps depends on a background of scientific development in which the activities of confirmation and falsification of older theories work together in a complementary way, as equally necessary aspects of the development of scientific knowledge.

After a new theory has demonstrated that it has an additional predictive content going beyond the facts which helped to suggest it, it tends, in its turn, to take on the role of an accepted framework, the development and articulation of which will lead to the kinds of questions that are likely to be relevant in further investigation of nature. Eventually, however, the new theory suffers the fate of its predecessors.[1]

It is clear, then, that the discovery of truth in science is a process that is never finished, and is not the quest for some fixed and well-defined set of principles, the knowledge of which would constitute a final goal of scientific investigations. Moreover, the discovery of truth is not a process of *coming nearer* to some such set of principles step by step, as a limit which can never be reached, but which can be approached in some convergent way. Nor is truth to be compared to some substance

[1] For a further discussion of this kind of development of scientific theories see T. S. Kuhn, "The Structure of Scientific Revolutions," *International Encyclopedia of Unified Science*, Vol. 11, No. 2, University of Chicago Press, Chicago, 1962.

that can at least be gathered, bit by bit, to be accumulated into a continually growing pile or "treasure" of truths.

The idea of an absolute truth that *we do not know* and that we are nevertheless approaching continuously is evidently just as unprovable and unnecessary as is the idea that we already possess, or can come eventually to know completely, such an absolute truth. All that we actually know and all that we really need to say is that each set of scientific laws has some as-yet incompletely known domains of validity. It is not necessary to commit ourselves in any way at all about a supposititious absolute truth that we do not and cannot know but which we assume can be approached. Moreover, besides being unnecessary and unfounded, such a commitment tends to confuse us for it suggests that the march towards truth will be on some line, or set of lines, which continues previous trends in such a way that the difference between the predictions of our laws and the real state of affairs is always getting smaller. But the actual progress of science does not suggest such a process of steady convergence. Rather, as in the case of relativity and quantum theory, it shows that, generally speaking, older ideas are on a *completely wrong track* when extended beyond their proper domains, and that radically new ideas are needed, which contradict the old ones while at the same time containing them, in some sense, as limiting cases and approximations. So the notion of a steady and convergent approach toward some fixed kind of absolute truth is indeed very misleading.

In a similar way the idea of steadily accumulating pieces of an absolute truth is also contrary to the facts of the case. For this idea suggests that although we do not know the whole of the absolute truth, we do have parts of it, which are absolutely true, independent of other parts, which will be discovered later. But as we have seen, each such part (e.g., Newtonian mechanics) has only a certain domain of validity, the full and precise limits of which are never completely known, in the sense that later discoveries may always *contradict* earlier laws in some as yet unpredictable ways. Therefore, a given "partial truth" can in no sense be regarded even as a kind of "brick" that can be added to others, so that mankind can, for example, be regarded as building an ever-growing structure of truth, each part of which can *always* be relied on (at least in certain domains that have already been fully delimited).

Truth is thus seen to be apprehended in an essentially dynamic way, in the sense that our knowledge of it can undergo fundamentally new developments at any point, developments that contradict the older structure of ideas in unexpected ways and contain unexpected basically new features. At each stage this knowledge has the form of a body of theories which have thus far demonstrated the ability not only to explain the facts known when they were first proposed, but which have also correctly predicted broad ranges of further phenomena, going beyond these facts. It may be expected that most of these theories will continue to be valid in *some* range of further experiments, which are designed to apply them, articulate them, question them, and test them in broader domains. But from time to time, parts of the whole body of theory, either large or small, will be falsified, with the result that new theories will have to be developed. In this process there is no permanent accumulation of theories, nor is there an approach to any particular form as a convergent limit. What has been achieved at any given stage is, of course, eventually recorded in journals and textbooks, which make it available for technical application, for study, and for further development and criticism by investigators. But it is in the confrontation of new problems to which older theories are always giving rise that scientific truth has its essential life in a kind of "growing region" where man is always meeting what has hitherto been unknown to him.

We shall go into this question further in Section A-4 of the Appendix.

XXVI

The Minkowski Diagram and the K Calculus

Thus far we have discussed Einstein's relativistic notions of space and time from a physical and mathematical point of view—the mathematical treatment being based largely on the formulas (14–3) and (14–4) for a Lorentz transformation. We shall now give a *geometrical* way developed by Minkowski for considering the meaning of the theory of relativity, which helps to bring out the significance of the theory in a different light.

We begin with the so-called "Minkowski diagram" for space and time (see Figure 26–1). In discussing this diagram we first consider an observer Ω_1, at rest in the laboratory. We represent the time coordinate as measured by this observer by the line OA and one of the space coordinates (z) by the line OB. In principle we should include the other two space coordinates, x and y, so that the diagram ought to be four-dimensional. However, for many purposes it will be sufficient to deal with z and t, so that a two-dimensional diagram will suffice.

Each point on this diagram refers to an *event* (such as the flashing of a light signal). Every real event must, of course, take place during some interval of time and occupy some region of space. However,

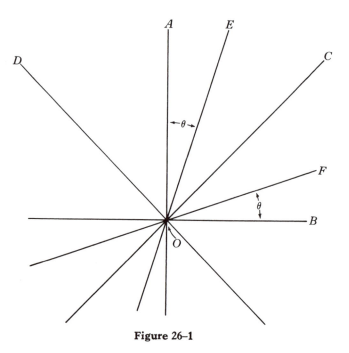

Figure 26–1

if the time interval is very short and the region of space is correspondingly small, we may replace the actual *extended event* by the simplifying abstraction of a *point event*.

Let the point O represent such an event, happening at the time $t = 0$ to an observer, located at $z = 0$. If the observer is at rest relative to the laboratory, then the events which describe what happens to him over a period of time will be located on the line OA, which is the t axis of our diagram. Such a line is called a *world line*. The line OB then represents all the events which are simultaneous to O, as measured by such an observer.

It will be convenient to adopt time units such that the velocity of light c is unity. We can do this by writing $\tau = ct$. Then, if we suppose that the axis OA represents the time in terms of units of τ, we see that the paths of light rays, $z = \pm \tau$, are represented by the two lines OC and OD, at 45° relative to the z and τ axes.

Of course in three dimensions there are many possible directions for a light ray, so that the whole set of light rays through O is represented by a cone. The lines OC and OD then correspond to the intersection of this "light cone" with the z-τ plane.

Let us now consider a second observer, Ω_2, moving in a rocket ship at a speed v relative to the laboratory. His trajectory, $z = (v/c)\tau$, then defines a corresponding world line OE with an inclination relative to the τ axis, given by $\tan \theta = v/c$. In accordance with the results of Chapter 13, such an observer will ascribe simultaneity to a different set of events than that regarded as simultaneous by the observer Ω_1, fixed in the laboratory. Indeed, if τ' and z' are the coordinates as measured by Ω_2, then the expression $\tau' = 0$ determines which events are taken by him to be simultaneous. But from Eq. (14–3) we see that $\tau' = ct' = 0$ implies $t = (v/c^2)z$, or $\tau = (v/c)z$. This locus is indicated by the line OF, inclined at the angle $\theta = \tan^{-1}(v/c)$ relative to the z axis.

According to the principle of relativity, as described in Chapters 16 and 17, there is no "favored" system of coordinates, so that *all* the basic laws of physics constitute the same relationships in every reference frame. It should therefore be just as correct to use a Minkowski diagram, in which the rocket-ship observer is taken to be at rest while the laboratory is moving at a speed $-v$ relative to the ship. We illustrate this possibility in Figure 26–2, where $O'A'$ represents the world line of the rocket ship and $O'B'$ represents the set of events regarded as simultaneous by the observer in the rocket ship. The world line of the laboratory observer is then given by $O'E'$, while the events that are simultaneous to O' for the laboratory observer are on the line $O'F'$ (corresponding to the velocity $-v$ of the laboratory relative to the ship).

One of the simplest and most elegant ways of further developing the meaning of the principle of relativity in terms of the Minkowski diagram is with the aid of what has been called the "K calculus." This calculus[1] begins by considering a set of observers, each of whom is equipped with an equivalently constructed clock, and with a radar set capable of sending out pulses that are timed by this clock, so that they are spaced at regular intervals. Besides having a radar transmitter, each observer is supposed to be equipped with a receiver, which can

[1] This calculus was exposed by H. Bondi in a public lecture.

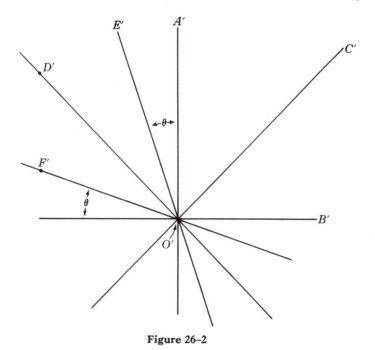

Figure 26-2

register the times of arrival (as measured on his clock), both of his own
signals as they come reflected back from objects in his environment
and of the signals emitted by other observers.

Let us begin by considering ourselves to be at rest in the laboratory,
which is sending out signals at the regularly spaced intervals N_1, N_2, N_3,
etc., as indicated in Figure (26-3). These travel at the speed of light,
and are received by the rocket observer (with world line OE) at intervals
indicated by N_1, N_2, N_3, etc. Let T_0 be the time between pulses, as
measured by the laboratory clock. Now the rocket observer will measure
some other time, T, as the interval between *reception* of successive
pulses. In general, T and T_0 must evidently differ. Indeed, even in
Newtonian theory, T will not be the same as T_0, because of the Doppler
shift. In relativity theory, however, we shall see that the ratio

$$k = \frac{T}{T_0} \tag{26-1}$$

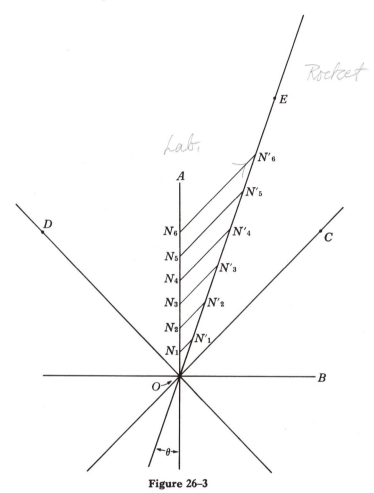

Figure 26–3

is a different function of the velocity of the rocket ship than it is in Newtonian theory.

Now, according to the principle of relativity there should exist a corresponding possibility of a similar experiment, in which the rocket observer sends out regular pulses at M_1, M_2, M_3, etc., as shown in Figure 26–4, the interval between these pulses being T_0, as measured by *his* clock. The pulses are received by the laboratory observer at

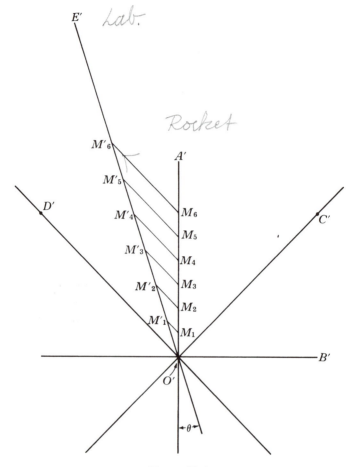

Figure 26–4

M'_1, M'_2, M'_3, etc., with an interval between them which we denote by
T'.. We then define the ratio

$$k' = \frac{T'}{T_0} \tag{26-2}$$

which we shall presently evaluate with the aid of further arguments.

Note that in Figures 26–3 and 26–4 we have drawn the lines M_1M_1', M_2M_2', etc. (and also N_1N_1', N_2N_2', etc.), which indicate the paths of radio signals, with a slope of 45°, indicating that in both frames the speed of light has the same value, c. This is how we embody in the Minkowski diagram the observed fact that the speed of light is invariant, the same for all observers.

Evidently the experiments carried out in the two frames are equivalent, and are to be symmetrically described, when each is referred to the frame of the corresponding observer. Thus in each experiment regular signals are being sent out at intervals of T_0, as measured by the clock that controls the emission of the signals in question. In each experiment the signals move at the speed c, and are received by an observer receding from the source at a speed, v. According to the principle of relativity, whenever two different observers thus carry out equivalent procedures, the laws applying in these procedures should be the same. We conclude then that the ratio $k' = T'/T_0$ must be the same as the ratio $k = T/T_0$, or that

$$k = k' \qquad (26\text{–}3)$$

It must be remembered, however, that the above is true only in a relativistic theory, in which light has the same speed in every frame of reference. Thus in Newtonian mechanics the light rays would be represented as lines at 45° to the axes only in a frame at rest in the ether, so that the reasoning by which we showed the equality of k and k' would not have gone through.

We can now go on to derive the value of k as a function of the relative velocity v of the two observers. To do this we consider an experiment in which the laboratory observer (indicated by the world line OA in Figure 26–5) exchanges signals with the moving observer (with world line OE). Let us suppose that at the beginning of the experiment the two observers pass very close to each other, at the place and time corresponding to the origin O. Then, because a signal takes a negligible time to pass between the observers at this moment, they will be able to synchronize their clocks. For the sake of convenience we suppose that both observers set their clocks so that the moment O corresponds to

$$t = 0, \quad t' = 0$$

The laboratory observer then sends a signal at the point corresponding to N and the time T_0, as measured by *his* clock. This is received on the

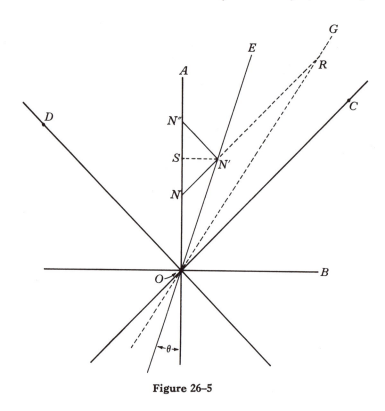

Figure 26–5

rocket ship at the point corresponding to N'. The rocket observer attributes to the time

$$T = kT_0 \tag{26-4}$$

But now let us suppose that on receiving the signal at N' the rocket observer immediately sends out a signal of his own. This will be received in the laboratory at the point corresponding to N'', at the time T_1. However, as we have seen, the principle of relativity implies that from which it follows that

$$T_1 = kT = k^2T_0 \tag{26-5}$$

We shall now do a bit of elementary geometry. Because (NN') and

$(N'N'')$ both correspond to light rays at 45° to the axis, we have

$$(SN') = (NS) = (SN'') = \frac{(NN'')}{2}$$

$$(SN') = (NS) = (OS)\tan\theta = (OS)\frac{v}{c} = \frac{(NN'')}{2}$$

$$(OS) = (ON) + (NS) = (ON) + \frac{(NN'')}{2}$$

$$(ON) = T_0$$

$$(NN'') = T_1 - T_0 = \frac{k^2 - 1}{2}T_0$$

$$(OS)\frac{v}{c} = \frac{k^2 + 1}{2}\frac{v}{c}T_0 = \frac{k^2 - 1}{2}T_0 \tag{26-6}$$

$$\frac{v}{c} = \frac{k^2 - 1}{k^2 + 1} \tag{26-7}$$

$$k = \sqrt{\frac{1 + v/c}{1 - v/c}} \tag{26-8}$$

We have thus obtained the factor K, which is the essential quantity in the K calculus. Note that it is unity for $v = 0$, as it must be. For positive v it is greater than unity, and for negative v it is less than unity.

The K factor is, in fact, just the relativistic Doppler shift (for a zero angle of viewing), which we have previously obtained in a much more roundabout way in Eq. (17–12) with the aid of the Lorentz transformation. However, this time we have derived the formula very directly from the principle of relativity, using the invariance of the velocity of light as measured by observers moving at different speeds.

The K calculus can, in fact, be used to obtain the basic formulas that we have previously derived from the Lorentz transformation. To illustrate this possibility, let us begin by deducing the formula comparing the rates of equivalent clocks moving at different speeds. Now, referring to Figure 26–5, we know that in the interval corresponding to (ON') the rocket observer will register a time of

$$T = kT_0 \tag{26-9}$$

On the other hand, because the line $(N'S)$ is perpendicular to the axis OA, the laboratory observer will regard the event N' as simultaneous with S. Therefore, the laboratory observer will attribute to N' the time coordinate

$$t = (OS) = (ON) + (NS) = (ON) + \frac{(NN'')}{2} = \frac{1 + k^2}{2}T_0 \quad (26\text{--}10)$$

It follows then that the ratio t/T of times measured for the same event (N') by the laboratory observer and the rocket observer, respectively, is

$$\frac{t}{T} = \frac{k + k^{-1}}{2} = \frac{1 + k^2}{2k} = \left[1 + \frac{1 + (v/c)}{1 - (v/c)}\right]\frac{1}{2k}$$

$$= \frac{1}{\sqrt{1 - (v/c)}}\frac{1}{\sqrt{1 + (v/c)}} = \frac{1}{\sqrt{1 - (v^2/c^2)}} \quad (26\text{--}11)$$

We have thus directly deduced the "slowing down" of moving clocks, without the aid of the Lorentz transformation. We can now deduce the relativistic formula for addition of velocities with equal directness. To do this consider a third observer, as indicated in Figure 26–5, with world line OG, one having a velocity w relative to the laboratory. It is possible to obtain the K factor corresponding to this observer in two different ways. First, we begin in the laboratory frame, emitting a signal at the point N corresponding to the time T_0. This is received by the observer OG at the point R, at the time corresponding to

$$T_2 = k(w)T_0 \quad (26\text{--}12)$$

where $k(w) = \sqrt{[1 + (w/c)]/[1 - (w/c)]}$. But we can also obtain the formula for T_2 in two stages. First, we consider the signal from N arriving at N' at the time (measured by the rocket-observer's clock)

$$T_1 = k(v)T_0 \quad (26\text{--}13)$$

where $k(v) = \sqrt{[1 - (v/c)]/[1 + (v/c)]}$. Then, the rocket observer immediately sends out a signal (which coincides with $N'R$). If the observer OG has a velocity of u, as measured in the frame of the rocket ship, then according to the principle of relativity we have

$$T_2 = k(u)T_1 = \sqrt{\frac{1 + (u/c)}{1 - (u/c)}}\sqrt{\frac{1 + (v/c)}{1 - (v/c)}}T_0 \quad (26\text{--}14)$$

From this it follows that

$$\frac{(1 + u/c)\,(1 + v/c)}{(1 - u/c)\,(1 - v/c)} = \frac{1 + w/c}{1 - w/c} \tag{26-15}$$

$$k(w) = k(u)k(v) \tag{26-16}$$

Thus, the K factor for a pair of transformations in sequence is just the product of the individual K factors for each of the transformations. With the aid of a little algebra we obtain

$$w = \frac{u + v}{1 + (uv/c^2)} \tag{26-17}$$

which is just the relativistic formula for addition of velocities, given in Eq. (15-8).

Finally, the K calculus can be used to obtain the Lorentz transformation itself. Before doing this, it is useful to note that because the speed of light is the same for all observers, we do not need separate standards of time and distance. Rather, once one has a clock, the standard of distance is already implied. For if one sends out a radar signal to an object at a distance d, then if δt is the time needed for the signal to go from the source to the object and be reflected back, the distance d of the object is

$$d = \frac{c\,\delta t}{2} = \frac{\delta \tau}{2} \tag{26-18}$$

For this reason it is sufficient if all observers have equivalently constructed clocks. It is not necessary to assume in addition that they have standard meter sticks. This makes the logical foundations of the procedure of measurement very simple, because one can use the periods of vibrations of atoms or molecules as standard clocks, which can be depended on to function in equivalent ways for all observers.

To deduce the Lorentz transformation we refer to Figure 26–6. Let us suppose that the laboratory observer OA and the rocket observer OE pass each other at O, corresponding to the zero of time for both of them. The laboratory observer sends a pulse at M, corresponding to a time T_1 as measured by his clock. At N this pulse passes the rocket observer, who simultaneously sends out his own pulse, at the time T_1, as measured by his clock. The two pulses travel together until they reach an object with world line ST, striking it at P. The reflected pulses return, striking the rocket ship at Q, at the time T_2' indicated by the clock of the rocket observer. The pulses continue to strike the laboratory at R, at the time T_2 indicated on the laboratory clock.

Figure 26–6

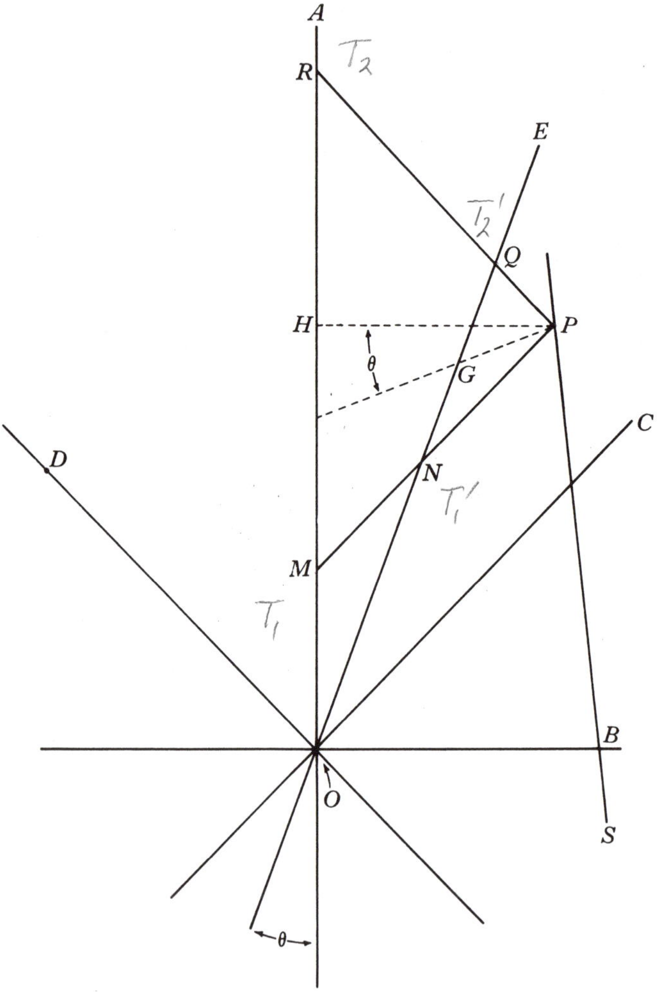

Now, the laboratory observer attributes to the event P the time and space coordinates

$$\tau = ct = cT_1 + c\frac{T_2 - T_1}{2} = c\frac{T_2 + T_1}{2} \qquad (26\text{–}19)$$

$$x = c\frac{T_2 - T_1}{2} \qquad (26\text{–}20)$$

$$\tau + x = cT_2 \qquad \tau - x = cT_1 \qquad (26\text{–}21)$$

By the principle of relativity, the rocket observer will have an equivalent set of formulas.

$$\tau' = ct' = \frac{c}{2}(T_1' + T_2') \qquad x' = \frac{c}{2}(T_2' - T_1')$$

$$\tau' + x' = cT_2' \qquad \tau' - x' = cT_1' \qquad (26\text{–}22)$$

But according to the K calculus,

$$T_1' = kT_1 \qquad T_2 = kT_2'$$

$$T_1'T_2' = T_1T_2 \qquad (26\text{–}23)$$

From the above, we have (with $\tau = ct$),

$$\left(t' + \frac{x'}{c}\right)\left(t' - \frac{x'}{c}\right) = (t')^2 - \frac{(x')^2}{c^2} = T_1'T_2' = T_1T_2 = t^2 - \frac{x^2}{c^2}$$

$$(26\text{–}24)$$

This gives (for the one-dimensional case) the invariance of the formula for the interval obtained in Eqs. (9–7) and (9–8) from the Lorentz transformation.

From (26–20) we obtain

$$t = \frac{kT_2' + T_1'/k}{2}$$

$$x = \frac{kT_2' - T_1'/k}{2} \qquad (26\text{–}25)$$

And after a bit of algebra, this reduces to

$$t = \frac{t' - (vx'/c^2)}{\sqrt{1 - (v^2/c^2)}} \qquad x = \frac{x' - vt'}{\sqrt{1 - (v^2/c^2)}} \qquad (26\text{–}26)$$

which is, of course, just the Lorentz transformation.

In terms of the K calculus, it can fairly directly be seen why two different observers attribute simultaneity to a different set of events. Indeed, Eqs. (26–20) to (26–22) merely assert that when any observer sends out a radar pulse, then that observer *defines* the time of the event P to be simultaneous with an event in his world line that is halfway between the point of emission of the radar pulse and the point of reception of its reflection. Thus, in Figure 26–6 the laboratory observer defines P to be simultaneous with H, which is the midpoint between M and R, while the rocket observer defines P to be simultaneous to G, which is halfway between N and Q. We have already called attention to the conventional aspect of simultaneity in the theory of relativity in Chapter 12, where we discussed it qualitatively in terms of the example of observers on a railway train and on the embankment. Here we see in more precise terms just how the equality of the velocity of light for both observers, plus the fact that they use equivalent conventions for defining simultaneity, implies that they cannot agree on which events occur at the same time; and thus we exhibit the source of the different loci of simultaneous events for different observers, as shown in Figures 26–1 and 26–2.

It is evident that the K calculus provides us with a very direct way of obtaining many of the relationships that were historically derived first on the basis of the Lorentz transformation. The advantage of the K calculus is that it makes the connection between these relationships and the basic principles and facts underlying the theory very evident. Indeed, starting with the principle of relativity and the invariance of the velocity of light, we have seen that the Lorentz transformation itself follows simply from certain geometrical and structural features of the patterns of certain sets of physical events. Nevertheless, as elegant and direct as it is, the K calculus has not yet been developed far enough to replace the Lorentz transformation in *all* the different relationships that are significant in the theory of relativity. Thus, the situation at present is that the Lorentz transformation approach and the K-calculus approach complement one another, in the sense that each provides insights that are not readily obtained in the other. In addition, the K calculus is fairly new, so that most of the existing literature is expressed in terms of the Lorentz transformation approach. Although it is possible that the K calculus may eventually be developed far enough to replace the Lorentz transformation as a foundation of the mathematical theory, it seems that for some time, at least, the Lorentz transformation will continue to be the main mode of expressing the theory, while the K calculus will serve to provide additional insights into the meaning of the theory.

XXVII

The Geometry of Events and the Space–Time Continuum

In the previous chapter we saw in terms of the Minkowski diagram how physical phenomena are described in terms of *events* (such as the emission and absorption of signals) and *processes* (such as the transmission of a radar signal from emitter to receiver). Even a continuously existing object (such as an observer) is described by his *world line*, which is really, in effect, the locus of a continuous series of events, representing the successive places and times at which he exists. Actually, of course, all real objects (including observers) are extended in space as well, so that they are described by means of "world tubes" (one of which is indicated in Figure 27–1 by its boundaries as *MM'* and *NN'*). Inside such a tube, a very complex set of events and processes is generally taking place (e.g., movements of the various constituent parts of the object, going all the way down to its molecules, atoms, electrons and protons, etc.).

Implicit in the Minkowski diagram is a very radical change in our concepts concerning the general nature of things. To see how this comes about we begin by recalling that in Newtonian theory there is a unique meaning to simultaneity. It therefore makes sense to suppose that at each moment the world is constituted by various objects

146

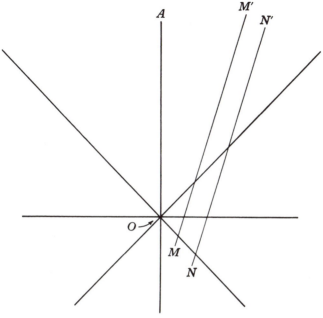

Figure 27–1

(whether they be on the large-scale or on the atomic or electronic level). In the next moment these objects will still be in existence, but each of them will have moved from one place to another. The task of physics is then regarded as the analysis of the world into the permanent basic objects which constitute it, including following the movements of these objects with the passage of time.

In Chapter 24 we indicated that because all known objects (including the so-called "elementary particles") can be created, destroyed, and transformed in various ways, the notion described in the previous paragraph has already demonstrated itself to be inadequate, with regard to the *experimental facts* that are now known concerning physical phenomena. But relativity provides further *theoretical reasons* against the notion that at each moment the world is constituted of some arrangement of uniquely defined objects. For as we have seen, the notion of "the same time" now has meaning only in relationship to the frame of the observer. Different observers do not agree on which events constitute "the same time," and therefore they do not agree on what are the basic properties of the "objects" (such as length, mass, etc.).

By introducing the Minkowski diagram we have dealt with the problem described above. For the "object" is now replaced by a structure and pattern of events and processes (e.g., the world line or the world tube representing an observer). The usual type of relatively permanent object now corresponds to a pattern of events and processes that tends to remain similar to itself over an indefinitely long period of time. An object that is not permanent corresponds, of course, to a pattern that alters and transforms, beginning in some region (where the object is "created") and ending in another region (where the object is "destroyed").

In the procedure described above, *the analysis of the world into constituent objects has been replaced by its analysis in terms of events and processes*, organized, ordered, and structured so as to correspond to the characteristics of the material system that is being studied. It follows that *space and time* taken jointly constitute the means by which the characteristics of physical phenomena are to be treated. In this sense, space and time together are playing a role similar to that played by space alone in Newtonian mechanics. That is to say, the nature of things is being described in terms of a kind of "geometrical" pattern in space and time, as exhibited in the Minkowski diagram.

In the geometry of space, there is a thoroughgoing unification of its three dimensions, based on the fact that each of the dimensions can be related to the others by means of a rotation. Algebraically, a rotation through an angle about the z axis is represented by the transformation

$$x = x' \cos \alpha + y' \sin \alpha$$
$$y = y' \cos \alpha - x' \sin \alpha \qquad (27\text{--}1)$$

Without such a transformation we would hardly even be justified in regarding the three dimensions as united into a single space as "continuum" (e.g., in an arbitrary graph, in which one physical quantity such as temperature is plotted against another, such as pressure, there is no such unification). The question then naturally arises as to whether, in the "geometry" of space and time taken together, there is not a similar unification of space and time dimensions, so that they also form a single continuum. (Recall that in Newtonian mechanics, time is independent of space, so that no such unification occurs there.)

To see that there is in fact *some kind* of unification of space and time in the theory of relativity it is necessary only to refer to the Lorentz transformation, in which the coordinates z, τ are expressed in terms of z', τ'. This transformation evidently at least *resembles* a rotation. To bring out this resemblance in more detail we can introduce a *hyperbolic angle* β, defined by

$$\sinh \beta = \frac{e^\beta - e^{-\beta}}{2} = \frac{v}{c} \frac{1}{\sqrt{1 - (v^2/c^2)}} \qquad (27\text{--}2)$$

$$\cosh \beta = \frac{e^\beta + e^{-\beta}}{2} = \frac{1}{\sqrt{1 - (v^2/c^2)}} \qquad (27\text{--}3)$$

The Lorentz transformation can then be written

$$\tau = \tau' \cosh \beta - z' \sinh \beta$$
$$z = z' \cosh \beta - \tau' \sinh \beta \qquad (27\text{--}4)$$

We see that (27–4) differs from the rotary transformation (27–1), first, in that the hyperbolic functions $\cosh \beta$ and $\sinh \beta$ replace the trigonometric functions $\cos \alpha$ and $\sin \alpha$, and, second, in that the coefficients of $\sinh \beta$ *both* have a minus sign, whereas in (27–1) one of the coefficients of $\sin \alpha$ has a plus sign, while the other has a minus sign. Nevertheless, the analogy to a rotation is still quite strong, and for this reason the transformation (27–4) is called a *hyperbolic rotation*.

The essential difference between trigonometric rotations and hyperbolic rotations is in the functions that are invariant under these respective transformations. Thus in a trigonometric rotation, in the XY plane, what is invariant is the distance function, $x^2 + y^2$. In a hyperbolic rotation in the $z\tau$ plane, what is invariant is $\tau^2 - z^2$, which differs from distance function in that τ^2 and z^2 enter with *opposite* signs, whereas in the latter, x^2 and y^2 enter with the *same* sign.

If we now consider the three dimensions of space as well as the dimension, we see from Eq. (9–7) that the function

$$s^2 = \tau^2 - x^2 - y^2 - z^2 = \tau'^2 - x'^2 - y'^2 - z'^2 \qquad (27\text{--}5)$$

is an invariant both under arbitrary Lorentz transformations in space and time and under arbitrary rotations in space (as well as under reflections of x, y, z, τ). And more generally, if one considers two events with coordinates x_1, y_1, z_1, τ_1 and x_2, y_2, z_2, τ_2, then the corresponding invariant, which is called the *interval* between the two events, is

$$s^2 = (\tau_1 - \tau_2)^2 - (x_1 - x_2)^2 - (y_1 - y_2)^2 - (z_1 - z_2)^2$$

$$(27\text{--}6)$$

It is easily seen that the function (27–6) is a generalization of the distance functions (11–3) that apply in ordinary three-dimensional space. However, (27–6) applies in space and time together, provided that τ undergoes a Lorentz transformation, which is a hyperbolic rotation, rather than an ordinary rotation.

It seems clear then that in relativistic physics, space and time are united into a four-dimensional continuum, in which they can be transformed into each other in such a way that the function s^2 given in (27–6) is invariant. This continuum is called *space-time* rather than "space and time," the hyphen emphasizing the new kind of unification.

It should be noted that in spite of the above-described unification of space and time brought about in the theory of relativity, there remains a rather important and peculiar distinction between them, resulting from the fact that $(\tau_1 - \tau_2)^2$ and $(x_1 - x_2)^2 + (y_1 - y_2)^2 + (z_1 - z_2)^2$ appear with *opposite* signs in the formula for the invariant interval s^2. Because of this, it is possible for s^2 to be positive, negative, or zero, for distinct pairs of events. Indeed, since $s^2 = 0$ represents the light cone, it is clear that this cone constitutes the boundary between events with positive and negative values of s^2. If in Figure 27–2 we choose one of the events, O, as the origin of coordinates (so that $x_2 = y_2 = z_2 = \tau_2 = 0$), then we see that for another event, P, *inside* the light cone, s^2 is positive, while for events such as E, which are outside the light cone, s^2 is negative. But because s^2 is an invariant, it follows that *the property that one event is inside, outside, or on the light cone of another is the same in every frame of reference.* So although space and time can, to some extent, be transformed into each other in a change of reference frame, there are certain limits on this transformation, in the sense that an interval inside the light cone cannot be transformed into one outside the light cone, or on the light cone.

Now, the simplest case of an interval inside the light cone is one in which $x = y = z = 0$. Such an interval represents only a time difference. Under a Lorentz transformation, this interval goes over to one with new coordinates, x', y', z', τ', such that x', y', and z' are in general not zero. Nevertheless, the square of the interval, being invariant, will remain positive. For this reason, intervals with positive values of s^2 are called "time-like," because in some reference frames they correspond to a simple time difference of events happening at the same place.

On the other hand, the simplest case of an interval outside the light cone is one in which $\tau = 0$. Such an interval, which corresponds to a separation of events in space, is represented by a negative value of s^2. If one transforms to a new frame of reference, then in general τ' will cease to be zero, but s^2 remains invariant, and therefore negative.

Figure 27–2

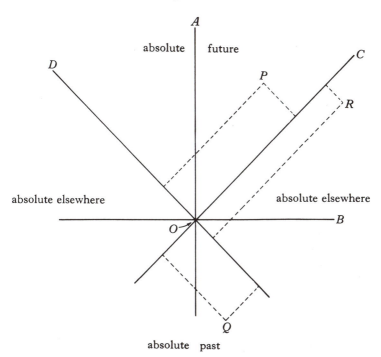

Such intervals are called "space-like," because in some reference frames they correspond to a spatial separation of simultaneous events.

To sum up, then, it is clear that while space and time coordinates can be transformed into each other as a result of a change of velocity of the reference frame, the distinction between space-like and time-like events is an invariant, the same for all observers. Likewise, the character of being on the light cone, and therefore neither a space-like nor a time-like interval, is also an invariant one. So a certain subtle kind of difference between space and time is preserved (in the sense of a lack of *complete* interchangeability under transformation), in spite of the fact that space–time is unified into four-dimensional continuum (whereas if z and τ had been subject to an ordinary trigonometric rotation, a *complete* equivalence of space and time would have resulted, so that an interchange of z and τ would have been possible, as one can interchange x and y by a $90°$ rotation).

One can obtain further insight into the invariant distinction between space-like, time-like, and "null" intervals (i.e., intervals on the light cone, for which $s^2 = 0$) by measuring the coordinates u, v of an event P in the Minkowski diagram along the direction of the light rays. Such a procedure corresponds to a $45°$ rotation of the $z\tau$ axes. We obtain

$$u = \frac{\tau - z}{\sqrt{2}} \qquad v = \frac{\tau + z}{\sqrt{2}}$$

$$uv = \frac{\tau^2 - z^2}{2} = \frac{s^2}{2} \qquad\qquad (27\text{--}7)$$

So in terms of our new set of axes, the invariant s^2 is the *product* of u and v. A light ray corresponds to $s^2 = 0$, and therefore either to $u = 0$ or $v = 0$. The locus $u = 0$ signifies the line OC, while $v = 0$ signifies OD.

A point such as P, which is (see Figure 27–2) inside the light cone and later than O, has positive values for both u and v. On the other hand, a point such as Q, which is inside the light cone but earlier than O, has *negative* values of u and v. Points outside the light cone (such as F) must have either positive u and negative v or positive v and negative u.

Let us see how u and v change under the Lorentz transformations (27–4). We have

$$u = \frac{\tau - z}{\sqrt{2}} = \frac{(\cosh \beta)\tau' - (\sinh \beta)z' - (\cosh \beta)z' - (\sinh \beta)\tau'}{\sqrt{2}}$$

$$= \frac{e^{\beta}}{\sqrt{2}}(\tau' - z') = e^{\beta}u' \quad (27\text{–}8)$$

$$v = \frac{\tau + z}{\sqrt{2}} = \frac{(\cosh \beta)\tau' - (\sinh \beta)z' + (\cosh \beta)z' - (\sinh \beta)\tau'}{\sqrt{2}}$$

$$= \frac{e^{-\beta}}{\sqrt{2}}(\tau' + z') = e^{-\beta}v' \quad (27\text{–}9)$$

We see then that under a Lorentz transformation, u and v undergo an especially simple transformation, in that each is respectively multiplied by a factor (e^{β} and $e^{-\beta}$) which is the reciprocal of that by which the other is multiplied (so that uv remains invariant). As a special case we consider a light ray ($u = 0$, or $v = 0$), which now immediately leads to $u' = 0$ or $v' = 0$, thus showing the invariance of the speed of light in a very direct way.

The Lorentz transformation is evidently a stretching along the direction of one of the light rays by a factor e^{β} and a contraction along the direction of the other one by the reciprocal factor, $e^{-\beta}$. If we consider any element of "area" in space-time, it is clear that under such a transformation this element is subject to a kind of "shearing," with the "axes" of the shear on the lines corresponding to the two light rays. So instead of a real (or trigonometric) rotation, the space–time transformation is a hyperbolic rotation, which is, as we have seen, actually a shearing in the pattern of events.

Now in the shearing transformation described above, u and v are multiplied by factors e^{β} and $e^{-\beta}$, which are always *positive*. From this it follows that the distinction of events inside the light cone of O as earlier or later than O is an invariant one. Thus, we have not only the invariant characteristic of events as being inside, outside, or on the light cone of O, but also the invariance of the property that events inside the light cone are in the future of O (later than O) or in the past of O (earlier than O).

In a similar way one easily sees that for events *on* the light cone there is also an invariant distinction between those that are earlier and those that are later. For on the light cone, either $u = 0$ or $v = 0$, and whichever is not zero must be positive for an event later than O, negative for one earlier than O.

On the other hand, the characteristic of being earlier or later than O is not invariant, for an event *outside the light cone*. Referring to Figure 26–1 let us consider, for example, the event B, which is simultaneous with O in the laboratory frame. In the frame of the observer Ω_2, moving at a speed v relative to the laboratory (with world line OE), an event measured by him to be simultaneous to O will correspond to a point, such as B', which is on the line OF, and which is therefore *not* simultaneous to O in the laboratory frame. If we consider *all possible* values for the velocity v, we see that *any* point outside the light cone through O will be regarded as simultaneous to O by *some* observer and either in the past of O or in the future of O by different observers with suitable velocities. So while events inside each other's light cones do have a unique time order (in the sense that all observers will agree on which is earlier and which is later), events outside each other's light cones do not.

XXVIII

The Question of Causality and the Maximum Speed of Propagation of Signals in Relativity Theory

We have seen in the previous chapter that for a pair of events outside each other's light cones, different observers will not in general agree on which is earlier and which is later. At first sight one might think that this ambiguity could mix up the question of causality. Thus it is a truism that if A is a cause of B, it must occur either earlier than B or at the same time as B. An event that is expected tomorrow cannot be taken as a cause of what is already happening today. For, by the cause of an event B, one means one of the conditions A that, being present and active, leads to the arising of B. Thus a fire acting today may set off some explosives now, but tomorrow's fire will not set off these explosives today.

It seems clear that if we were allowed to interchange the order of past, present, and future in a completely arbitrary way, the result would be confused, both in physics and in everyday life. Suppose, for example, that one observer sees that the burning of some fuel is *followed* by the heating of water, and that for another observer, the water was heated first, while the fuel was seen to be burned later. Or suppose that one observer first became hungry and then ate food which satisfied his hunger, while another observer who was satisfied ate food and then became hungry. One could go on to multiply such instances without limit, showing clearly that we could not make sense of the world if we could make *arbitrary* changes in the time order of events. The question is then to see whether or not the relativistic ambiguity in time order of events outside the light cone of an observer will confuse the problem of cause and effect.

In answering this question we first recall that, as pointed out in Chapter 14, no object, influence, or force, etc., can move or otherwise be transmitted faster than the speed of light *c*. It is then easy to see that as long as this condition is satisfied, the relativistic ambiguity in time order will not mix up the question of causality. For if one event *A* is to be a cause of another event *B*, there must be some kind of physical action of contact between them. (If there is no physical contact at all, then one cannot be a cause of the other.) But if such physical action is not transmitted faster than light, then any two events which are causally connected will, as we have seen in the previous chapter, have a unique and unambiguous time order. In other words, if a cause *A* is earlier than its effect *B* for one observer, this relationship will hold for all observers. Therefore, the order of cause and effect will be invariant, so that no confusion will result in this order when different observers consider the same set of events, each in his own frame of reference.

On the other hand, if any influence could go faster than light, then the notion of the order of cause and effect would become completely mixed up. To see this, consider an extreme case, in which one assumes that physical influences could be transmitted with infinite velocities, so that two distant observers could be in *simultaneous* contact. Let one of these observers, Ω_1, be represented in Figure 28–1 by the world line *OA*, while the other, Ω_3, with the same speed, is taken to have the world line *MN*. By our hypothesis, the observer Ω_1 at the time represented by *O* could be in immediate physical contact with the other observer Ω_3 at the time represented by *M*, so that each could, for example, use this contact to signal to the other.

Now, if there were no principle of relativity with the invariance of the speed of light, this assumption would entail no logical self-contradictions. Indeed, it corresponds only to the "common-sense" notion that what we see at a given moment is in immediate contact with us and is all happening at the same time, which we call "now."

Let us go on, however, to consider the further implications of the principle of relativity, as developed by Einstein, i.e., that the laws of physics have the same form for *all* observers, and that all observers ascribe the same speed to light. As we have seen earlier, it follows from this that two relatively moving observers do not agree with each other as to which set of events is simultaneous. Thus the observer Ω_2 with world line OE will regard the events on the line OF as simultaneous with O, while Ω_1 (with world line OA) regards events on OB as simultaneous. But according to the principle of relativity all the general laws holding in the frame of Ω_1 also hold in the frame of Ω_2. Therefore, if it is assumed that Ω_1 can be in contact with an event M

Figure 28–1

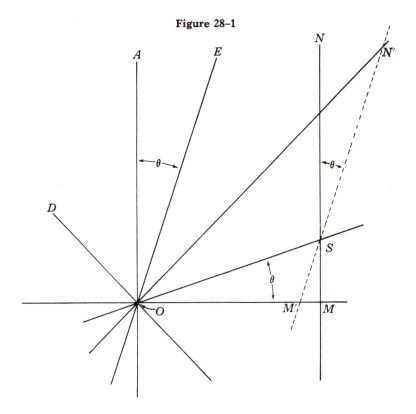

that is simultaneous to O in *his* frame, the relatively moving observer, Ω_2, can be in contact with an event S that is simultaneous to O in *his* frame of reference.

Let us now consider the observer Ω_3 with world line MN. At the time corresponding to S his world line would intersect that of an observer Ω_4, with world line $M'N'$, moving at the same speed as Ω_2. Two observers at the same point S, but with different speeds, can evidently be in essentially immediate contact, so that there need be no time lapse (or a negligible one) for a signal to pass from one to the other. Then, according to the principle of relativity, Ω_4 should have the same ability to signal immediately to Ω_2 at O (which is simultaneous with S in *his* frame) that Ω_1 has to signal to Ω_3 at M. The observer Ω_2 could then signal to Ω_1 at O, and Ω_1 could signal to Ω_3 at M (which is simultaneous to O in the frame of reference of Ω_1 and Ω_3). By this cycle of signals S could communicate with M and vice versa. But M is in the *past* of S. So, in effect, S could communicate with his own past at M, and tell his past self what his future is going to be. But on learning this M could decide to change his actions, so that his future at S would be different from what his later "self" said it was going to be. For example, the past self could do something that would make it impossible for the future one to send the signal. Thus, there would arise a logical self-contradiction.

By a generalization of the above line of argument, it can easily be shown that a similar contradiction would arise if one assumed that physical contact were transmitted with any speed greater than that of light.

We see then that as long as we accept Einstein's theory of relativity it leads to an absurdity to suppose that there is any action through physical contact capable of constituting the basis of a signal that is transmitted faster than light. In other words, either we have to assume that no physical action faster than light is possible, or else we have to give up Einstein's form of the principle of relativity. But thus far this form of the principle of relativity has been factually confirmed. Besides, as we have already seen, no physical actions have ever been discovered which are actually transmitted faster than light (e.g., material objects cannot be accelerated to the speed of light, because this would require infinite energy, while no fields are known which propagate influences faster than light). Of course, Einstein's theory is, like all other theories, in principle capable of being falsified as experiments are extended into broader domains. But as long as we remain in the domain where this theory is valid (and thus far, known experiments are and have been in such a domain), it will not be possible to have physical actions that are transmitted faster than light.

Given an event O, any other event P must, as we have seen, fall into one of a certain set of regions of space-time, which are subject to an invariant distinction (see Figure 27–2). If it is inside or on the light cone, then this event is either in the future of O or in the past of O. Because this distinction is independent of the frame of reference, it can be said to be in a certain sense "absolute" (at least in the domain in which Einstein's theory holds). The "forward" light cone through O, plus all that is in it, is then called the "absolute future" of O, while the corresponding "backward" light cone, and all that is in it, is called the "absolute past" of O. The region outside the light cone has very aptly been called the "absolute elsewhere" of O. For this region has no direct contact with O at all, and therefore it is essentially "elsewhere." Thus, if we consider a distant star, we have contact only with what that star *was* a long time ago. That this star exists "now" is only a likely inference, based on our general knowledge of the properties of stars. But actually we do not *know* that it exists "now." For example, it may already have exploded. *Later* we (or other observers) may see this explosion. But whatever happens to this star in what is "now" our absolute elsewhere can have no contact with us "now." (Later we shall have to be represented by another point on our world line, which is different from the one that represents us now.)

When two events are in each other's absolute elsewhere, so that they can have no physical contact, it makes no difference whether we say they are before or after each other. Their relative time order has a purely conventional character, in the sense that one can ascribe any such order that is convenient, as long as one applies his conventions in a consistent manner. And as we have seen, observers, moving at different speeds, and correcting for the time Δt, taken by light to reach them from a point at a distance r by the formula $\Delta t = r/c$, will arrive at different conventions for assigning such events as before, after, and simultaneous with some event taking place in the immediate neighborhood of the observer. But as long as there is no physical contact, which is the basis of the relationship of causal connection of events, it does not matter what we say about which is before and which is after. On the other hand, as we have seen, where such casual contact is possible, the order of events is unambiguous, so that the Lorentz transformation will never lead to confusion as to what is a cause and what is an effect.

XXIX

Proper Time

Until now we have been discussing the implication of the special theory of relativity, which is valid for observers moving with a constant velocity. As we remarked earlier (Chapter 16) the principle of relativity cannot correctly be applied in the reference frame of an accelerated observer, if we stay within the domain of the special theory. In other words, to obtain laws which constitute the same relationships (i.e., have the same form), even for accelerated frames of reference, it is necessary to broaden our conceptual basis and to go onto the general theory of relativity. Nevertheless, this does not mean that the special theory can make no predictions at all as to what will happen to accelerated observers. It only means that if we wish to make such predictions we shall have to adopt the standpoint of an unaccelerated observer, when we formulate the basic laws of physics. Starting from this standpoint it is then possible, at *each moment*, to transform their implications, so as to see what they would entail, when viewed from the accelerated frame. (A similar procedure is in fact developed in Newtonian mechanics, whose laws are based on an inertial frame, and can yet be transformed into an accelerated frame leading to additional terms in the equations of motion, such as centrifugal and Coriolis forces.)

To study this question we first note that in the reference frame of an observer moving with constant velocity, an accelerated observer

161

is represented by a curved world line (see Figure 29–1) which stays somewhere inside the light cone of any point O, through which it passes. Now consider a particular point P on this world line, and a nearby point Q. If Q is sufficiently close to P we can approximate the curve by differentials of the coordinates $t_Q - t_P = dt$ and $z_Q - z_P = dz$. At the point P let the velocity of the accelerated observer be v and at Q let it be $v + dv$.

The basic notion which makes possible the deduction of the implications of the special theory of relativity in an accelerated frame of reference is that of the *locally co-moving unaccelerated frame*. To see what this notion implies, let us begin at the point P, moving at velocity v. The actual observer is, as we have assumed, accelerated. But we can imagine an unaccelerated observer at P moving with (constant) velocity v. The important point with regard to such an observer is that over a sufficiently short period of time, dt, the *velocity of the accelerated observer relative to the co-moving observer will be of the order of dv, which is very small.* We have already seen that for low velocities

Figure 29–1

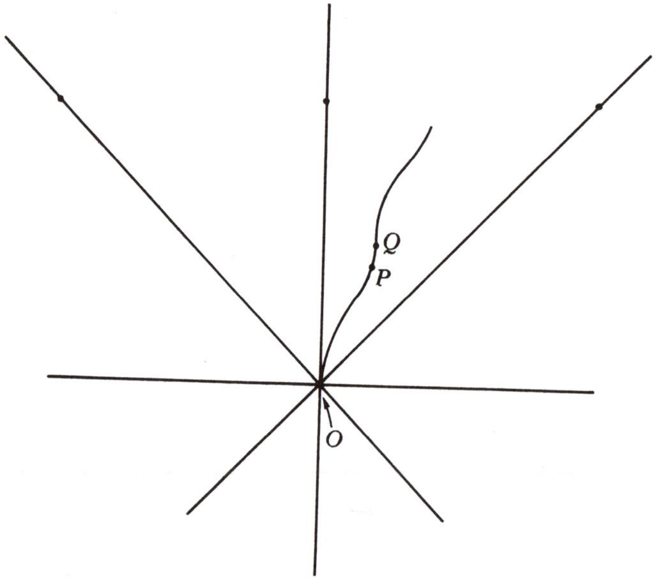

Einstein's theory approaches Newton's laws as a limiting case. There-fore, at least over some period of time dt, one can discuss the movements of the system in terms of Newton's laws applying in the reference frame having the constant velocity v. One can then see the implications of these laws in the laboratory frame by means of a Lorentz transforma-tion. When dv becomes appreciable we simply go to another frame with constant speed $v + dv$, etc. Thus by considering a series of such co-moving frames, we can calculate what will be seen by an observer with a fixed velocity (e.g., in the laboratory frame) with the aid of a corresponding series of Lorentz transformations. Or, vice versa, we can use a similar procedure to start with what is observed in the laboratory frame, to calculate what would be seen by a co-moving observer at any given moment.

An important example of the procedure described above is the calculation of the so-called "proper time" that is registered by a clock accelerated along a given world line, such as OPQ. In doing this we make use of the principle described above, i.e., that during a sufficiently short interval of time, dt (in which dv is very small), the clock as seen in the co-moving reference frame will behave essentially as it would according to Newtonian mechanics, which asserts that the rate of properly constructed clocks do not depend on how they are accelerated. Therefore, over the interval dt, the clocks will register an interval dt_0 that is related to dt by a Lorentz transformation from the frame of the co-moving observer to that of the laboratory. This relationship is most easily obtained by considering the invariant function

$$ds^2 = c^2 (dt)^2 - (dz)^2 \qquad (29\text{--}1)$$

In the co-moving frame we have $dt' = dt_0$ and $dz' = 0$ (because in this frame the clock is at rest). Therefore $ds^2 = c^2 dt_0^2$ and

$$\frac{ds^2}{c^2} = dt_0^2 = (dt)^2 - (dz)^2/c^2$$

$$\frac{dt_0}{dt} = \sqrt{1 - (dz/dt)^2/c^2} = \sqrt{1 - (v^2/c^2)} \qquad (29\text{--}2)$$

The interval Δt_0 of "proper time" registered by the accelerated clock in its movement between t_1 and t_2 can then be calculated by integrating (29–2). The result is

$$\Delta t_0 = \int\limits_{t_1}^{t_2} \sqrt{1 - \frac{v^2(t)}{c^2}}\, dt \qquad (29\text{–}3)$$

This formula is easily extended to the three dimensions of space, for which it continues to hold if we replace v^2 by the square of the total velocity $v_x^2 + v_y^2 + v_z^2$.

It is clear from (29–3) that because $\sqrt{1 - (v^2/c^2)} \leqslant 1$, the proper time registered by a clock moving in relation to a given frame of reference is generally less than the time difference, as measured by clocks which are fixed in that frame of reference.

XXX

The "Paradox" of the Twins

On the basis of the results of the previous chapter we can now describe a well-known apparent paradox to which the theory of relativity leads.

Consider a pair of "identical" twins. Let one of them take a voyage in a rocket ship, which we suppose to be capable of attaining a speed close to that of light, while the other remains on the Earth. When the twin who has made the voyage returns to the Earth, the clocks in his rocket ship will show the elapse of a time interval,

$$\Delta t_0 = \int_{t_1}^{t_2} \sqrt{1 - \frac{v^2(t)}{c^2}}\, dt$$

while similarly constructed clocks of the twin who remained on the Earth will show the elapse of a time interval $t_2 - t_1 > \Delta t_0$. But as we have seen earlier, all physical, chemical, nervous, psychological, etc., processes will be subject to the same Lorentz transformation that applies to clocks. Therefore, the twin who took the journey will in every way have experienced less time than did the one who remained on the Earth. And if the speed of the rocket ship was close to that of light, this time difference could be quite appreciable. For example,

165

if 20 years passed for a man who remained on the Earth, only one or two years might have passed for the man who was in the rocket ship.

Before proceeding to discuss the significance of this conclusion, let us first note that it does not violate the principle of relativity, which asserts that the laws of physics must constitute the same relationships, independent of how the frame of reference moves. For as we pointed out in the previous chapter we have thus far restricted ourselves to the special theory of relativity, in which the laws of physics are invariant only for observers moving at a constant speed. The conclusions of this theory evidently cannot be applied symmetrically in the frames of both observers, since one of them is accelerated and the other is not. For this reason it is not legitimate to interchange observers, and to say, for example, that the observer in the rocket ship should equally well see his twin in the laboratory as having aged less than he has. Rather, as long as we remain within the special theory of relativity, we must give the unaccelerated reference frame a unique role in the expression of the laws of physics; and in this way we explain how observers who have suffered different kinds of movements can, on meeting again, find that they have experienced different amounts of time.

To obtain laws that are the same for accelerated as for unaccelerated observers, we must go on to the general theory of relativity. But to do this we must bring in the *gravitational field*. As Einstein has shown, in an accelerated frame of reference, new effects must occur, which are equivalent to those that would be produced by a gravitational field. Indeed, from the point of view of the accelerated observer, one could say that there is an additional effective gravitational field, which acts on the general environment (stars, planets, Earth, etc.) and explains its acceleration relative to the rocket ship.

According to the general theory of relativity, two clocks running at places of different gravitational potential will have different rates. If the observer on the rocket ship uses the same laws of general relativity that are used by the observer on the Earth, but considers the different gravitational potentials that are appropriate in his frame of reference, he will then predict a difference of the rates of the two kinds of clocks. And, as a further calculation shows, he will come to the same conclusions about this time difference as are obtained by the observer on the Earth (for whom the laws of general relativity reduce to those of special relativity because he is not accelerated). So the different degree of "agings" of the two twins is fully compatible with the principle of relativity, when the theory is generalized sufficiently to apply to accelerated frames of reference.

Why does the different aging of the two twins seem paradoxical to most people, when they first hear of it? The answer is basically in the habitual mode of thought, whereby we automatically regard all that is co-present in our sense perceptions as happening at the same time, which we call "now." Thus, on looking out at the stars in the night sky we cannot avoid seeing the whole firmament as existing "now," simultaneous with our act of perception. As a result we are led, almost without further conscious thought, to the supposition that if a rocket ship went out in space, we could keep on watching it, or otherwise remain in immediate contact with it, comparing each event that happened to it (e.g., the ticking of a clock) with corresponding events that are happening to us at the same time. When it returned, it would then be seen to have experienced the same amount of time, as indeed does happen with all systems with which we are familiar (which latter of course move at speeds that are very low in relation to that of light).

It is of course by now very well known to us that what we see in the night sky is not actually happening at the same moment at which we perceive it, but rather that all that we see is past and gone (the distant nebulae, for example, are seen as they were a hundred million years ago or more). Moreover, our judgement as to *when* what we see actually did exist is based on the correction, $\Delta t = r/c$, for the time light takes to reach us. And, as we have brought out in earlier chapters, this correction is not the same for all observers, but depends on their speeds. As a result, our habitual procedure of assigning a unique time to each event no longer has much meaning. And if distant events do not have a unique time of occurrence, the same for all valid methods of measuring it, then there is no longer any good reason to suppose that two observers who separate and then meet will necessarily have experienced the same amount of time.

To bring out more sharply the kind of problem to which our intuitive notions of simultaneity tend to give rise, let us consider what would actually happen if each observer were to send out to the other a regular light or radio signal (say one per second) as measured by his own clocks. Each observer could then "see" how time was passing for the other one, so that he could presumably check up on just how it was possible for the two of them to experience different amounts of time.

Let us begin with a discussion of what would be seen by the observer who remained in the laboratory. To simplify the problem, we suppose that the rocket ship is initially accelerated to a velocity v in so short a time interval that we can regard the acceleration as effectively instantaneous. We suppose the the rocket ship moves away from the laboratory at constant velocity v in the z direction over a time interval $T/2$, as measured in the laboratory frame. Then another burst is fired, and the velocity is reversed ($t_0 - v$). The ship continues for another time interval of $T/2$ until it returns to the Earth, after which it is very suddenly decelerated to the speed of the Earth. (This assumption of sudden bursts of acceleration does not change any essential feature of the problem.) The world line of the rocket ship is shown in the Minkowski diagram (Figure 30–1) as OEA. The regular light signals given off by the moving observer are indicated by lines such as M_1M_1', N_1N_1', etc.

At first the observer OA will receive signals at M_1', M_2', M_3', etc., whose frequency is reduced by the effects of the Doppler shift, according to the *relativistic* formula (17–12).[1] If τ_0 is the period of the clock in the rocket ship, which determines these pulses, then the time τ_1 between pulses as seen in the laboratory will be (since $\theta = 0$)

$$\frac{\tau_1}{\tau_0} = \frac{\nu_0}{\nu} = \left[1 + \frac{v}{c}\right]\frac{1}{\sqrt{1 - (v^2/c^2)}} \qquad (30\text{–}1)$$

On the other hand, after the rocket ship is accelerated at E it will be approaching the laboratory, so that after E the laboratory observer will see pulses with a decreased period.

$$\frac{\tau_2}{\tau_0} = \frac{\nu_0}{\nu_2} = \left[1 - \frac{v}{c}\right]\frac{1}{\sqrt{1 - (v^2/c^2)}} \qquad (30\text{–}2)$$

Because of the equality of the velocity of recession of the rocket and its velocity of approach, it is clear that the rocket ship will put out the same number, $N/2$, of pulses on its way out and on its way back (N being the total number of pulses emitted over the whole journey).

---

[1] Alternatively, one could use the K calculus, as developed in Chapter 26.

The total time over which these pulses are received by a laboratory observer will be

$$\frac{N}{2} \frac{\tau_0}{\sqrt{1-(v^2/c^2)}}\left(1 + \frac{v}{c} + 1 - \frac{v}{c}\right) = \frac{N\tau_0}{\sqrt{1-(v^2/c^2)}}$$

(30–3)

which shows, of course, that these pulses will be received in the laboratory over a period of time longer than $N\tau_0$, which would be regarded as being taken by an observer on the rocket ship.

The important point to note here is that the laboratory observer cannot *directly* know how time is passing for the rocket observer,

Figure 30–1

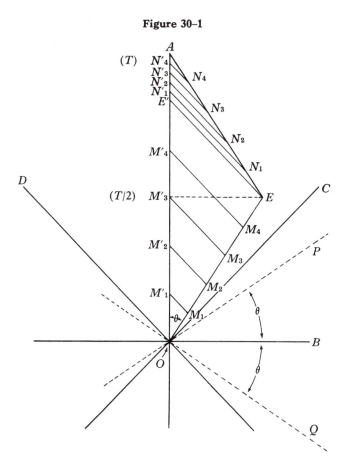

because signals between the two are altered by the Doppler shift. In other words, what is directly observable in the laboratory frame is, first of all, a set of slower pulses and later, another set of faster ones (e.g., if he were to watch the moving observer, he would first see the latter's life slowed down, and then speeded up). It is only by means of a *calculation* that the laboratory observer can "correct" for the effects of the recession or approach of the rocket ship. In this calculation he takes the speed of light to be c. But, as we have seen, if all observers take the speed of light to be c, then those with different speeds are in fact making a different correction. As a result, the twin in the laboratory attributes simultaneity to events on lines parallel to OB, while the twin on the rocket attributes simultaneity to events in lines parallel to OP, until he reaches the point of acceleration E, after which he attributes simultaneity to events in lines parallel to OQ. Thus, as the twin on the rocket goes, say, from M_3 to M_4 he does not attribute the same lapse of time to the process as the observer in the laboratory does, because he takes his zero of time to correspond to the sloping line OP and not the horizontal line OB. After acceleration at E, he takes the line OQ to be corresponding to his zero of time. In this way we see that there is room for a difference in how much time is actually registered by the clocks of observers who separate and then meet again.

One can obtain further insight into this problem by considering what the rocket-ship observer would find as he looked at a set of light signals sent out uniformly by the laboratory observer (see Figure 30–2). Because of the Doppler shift, the pulses sent out between O and E' would be received between O and E with a reduced frequency, while those sent out between E' and A would be received with an increased frequency.

Just before the acceleration at E, the observer on the rocket ship regards events on the line EG (parallel to OP) simultaneous with E, but just after acceleration he takes events on the line EH (parallel to OQ) as simultaneous with E. So we see that there is a sudden jump in the time coordinate ascribed to a given event, and that after the acceleration at E an event such as N_4' is ascribed a smaller time coordinate than it had before (the difference corresponding to the line GH). It is this jump in the ascription of time coordinates that implies that there is room for more signals to come from the laboratory observer to the

moving observer than the other way round, even though both are
using similarly constructed clocks. And since this jump occurs only
in the rocket frame and not in the laboratory frame, it is clear that the
situation is not symmetrical between both observers.

If the rocket observer were watching the fixed observer, he would
then see the life of the latter slowed down at first and later speeded up,
but he would find over the whole course of the journey that the effect
of the speeding up more than balanced that of the slowing down.
He would not therefore be surprised to discover on meeting with his
twin that the latter had experienced more of life than he had.

Figure 30–2

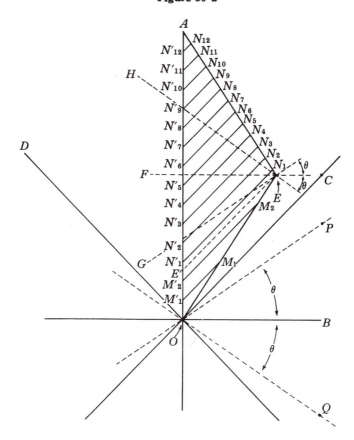

We see then that there is actually nothing paradoxical in the relativistic conclusion that an accelerated clock will register less time in passing between two points than would an unaccelerated clock passing between the same points. This is possible because in relativity theory time is not an absolute, with a universal moment "now," the same for all coexistent observers. Rather it is a much more subtle sort of notion, which can be different in relation to different frames of reference. There is room for many different kinds of time, as registered by clocks and physical processes that are subject to different kinds of movement. In many ways physical time thus begins to show some of the properties of our own experience with time in immediate perception. Thus, it is well known that a given interval as measured physically by a clock may seem long or short, an eternity or a mere moment, depending on how much is happening during the interval. (In Section A-3 of the Appendix we shall go into this problem of perception of time in more detail.) Until the development of the theory of relativity, it seemed that physical or chronological time did not share such a relativity and dependence on conditions. But now we see that this is because it had been studied only in the limited domain of low velocities. As the domain is broadened to include velocities appreciable in comparison with c, we have begun to find in chronological time a dependence on conditions that is not entirely dissimilar to what we experience in immediate perception. In other words, all forms of time, including the chronological and the perceptual, are means of ordering actual events and measuring their relative duration. The notion that there is one unique universal order and measure of time is only a habit of thought built up in the limited domain of Newtonian mechanics. It is valid in that domain, but becomes inadequate as the domain is extended. And perhaps as the domain is broadened still further we may well have to modify our conceptions of time (and space) yet more to enrich them, and perhaps to change them radically, in such a way that even current relativistic notions are treated as approximations and special limiting cases.

XXXI

The Significance of the Minkowski Diagram as a Reconstruction of the Past

Because of the relativistic unification of space and time into a single four-dimensional space-time continuum, there is a tendency to interpret the Minkowski diagram as representing a kind of arena or field of action, the whole of which an observer can actually see at any given moment. That is to say, almost unconsciously, one is led to adopt the point of view of an observer who is, as it were, standing outside of space and time, surveying the whole cosmos from beginning to end, as a man in an aeroplane surveys the landscape beneath him. The world lines of other observers then tend to be thought of as tracks which are being traversed by these observers, much as a railway train observed from an aeroplane would be seen to progress along its own track.

A little reflection shows, however, that this view of the Minkowski diagram must be very far from the truth indeed. Consider, for example, an observer at rest in the laboratory, whose world line is given by OA in Figure 31–1. At each moment such an observer is to be represented by some point in the diagram such as P. Such an observer cannot survey the whole Minkowski diagram. On the contrary, he can only know of events that are inside his past light cone, PM, and PN. Therefore, both his absolute future and his absolute elsewhere are unknown to him.

The real situation, as experienced by an observer at some moment P, is indeed strikingly different from what is shown in the Minkowski diagram. Not only is an observer's knowledge restricted to the part of the Minkowski diagram that is in his absolute past, but, even more, he never sees his own past actually happening, *as it is represented in this diagram.* For at any given moment we are experiencing only what is actually present at that moment. What we see at a given moment as past no longer actually exists at that moment. What is

Figure 31–1

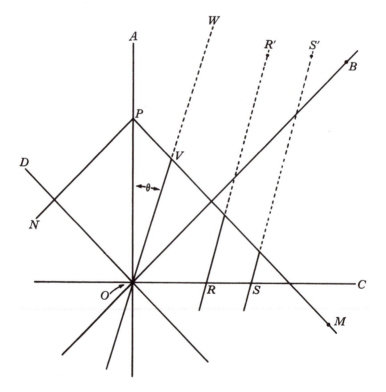

left of the past is only a trace, existing in the present. This trace may be in our memories, or in a photographic plate, or it may be left in the structure of things (e.g., the rings of trees, the skeletons of prehistoric animals, the layers of rock and earth studied in geology, etc.). From these traces we *reconstruct* the past in our thoughts, as well as with the aid of pictures and models. Thus it is evident that the reconstructed dinosaur is not the real dinosaur, just as the photograph of a past event is not that event itself. Because memories are so full of life, movement, color, and feeling, we often tend to become confused about them, and in effect to treat them as if what we remember still existed. But in fact all that appears in memory is also only a trace of the past that is gone. This trace is in our brain cells and, as it were, "replayed" in the present, much as one can replay a phonograph record, or re-project a film.

On the basis of our knowledge, not only of immediate events and facts from the past, but also of general regularities, trends, and laws that have been abstracted, either consciously or intuitively from this experience, both individual and collective, we are able to project a probable future. But while we are projecting it, this future also does not exist. It is in fact nothing more than an image, an expectation, a thought. If our projections are well founded, then the actual future, when it comes, may be close to what was expected. But, generally speaking, our projections are very often wrong, either because our knowledge of the laws and regularities of nature is inadequate, or because our knowledge of the relevant facts is inadequate. Moreover, it is clear from our general experience that all such predictive projections are subject to contingencies, i.e., to factors originating outside the domains that are accessible to our investigations at a given moment, factors which are thus unknown to us and which may yet play a crucial role in determining what will actually happen.

An important example of the significance of contingencies is provided by the theory of relativity. Thus, as we have seen, an observer at a given moment P can have information only about what is in his absolute past. Even if he is in communication with other observers, he can only hear what they have seen in *their* absolute pasts, at times which are also in *his* absolute past. So whether knowledge originates in the experience of the individual or in the collective experience of a group of people or of a society, it must always be based on what is past and gone, at the moment when it is under consideration. However, a great many features of nature are so regular and ordered that they do not change significantly with the passage of time. For such features knowledge based on the past in this way will provide a good approximation. Nevertheless, as we have seen in earlier chapters, we can never know *a priori* what is the proper domain of laws found to hold in past investigations, so that we must always be ready for the possibility that in later experiments in new domains, past regularities will cease to hold.

Even if we have some fairly reliable knowledge about the general laws of nature, as abstracted from past experience, observation, and experiment, it seems clear that we cannot avoid contingencies, just because we cannot know completely and with certainty what is in the absolute elsewhere. For example, if in Figure 26–4 an observer P has seen a particle moving on a world line OV in his absolute past, he can reasonably assume that the particle continues to exist on the line VW, which is the extension of OV into the region outside the light cone of P. If he had a great deal of information about what happened inside his past light cone, he might then be able to develop a fairly extensive projected notion of what is going on outside his light cone. But this projected picture is always subject to contingencies, because something unknown to P may always be taking place in his absolute elsewhere (e.g., a meteor. might enter the laboratory unexpectedly from outer space, thus altering the instruments, and deflecting the particle away from the projected continuation of its world line along VW). And evidently what happens in the absolute future of P is dependent on what is in his absolute elsewhere, so that his future is also subject to contingencies.

At first sight, one might be inclined to ask whether or not a *complete and certain* knowledge of the absolute past of P would not make possible a correspondingly complete and certain projection of what is happening in the absolute elsewhere of P, and thus in principle permit the removal of contingency. But this question is not very relevant, because such a complete and certain knowledge of the past is evidently impossible. Indeed, such a knowledge would entail going infinitely far back, and making observations and measurements of correspondingly great sensitivity and precision, since in many cases what happens in our future may be critically dependent on small things that took place long ago. But the traces of the distant past tend to be wiped out and confused to our observations. The further back one goes, the more sensitive and accurate must be the measurements and the better must be our knowledge and understanding of the laws of nature, in order to interpret the traces that we observe at present so as to reconstruct the past correctly. Evidently, it is impossible to have the perfect sensitivity and accuracy of instruments and the perfect knowledge and understanding of the totality of the laws of nature that would be needed to obtain *complete and certain* information about our own absolute past, even at a given moment of our existence. This means that projections from our absolute past to our absolute elsewhere are necessarily incomplete. There is therefore always much that is unknown in our absolute elsewhere; and, for this reason alone, predictions concerning the future will be subject to contingencies, arising from what is unknown at the moment when the prediction is made. Of course, we may come to know about these later (when they will have become a part of our absolute pasts), but then there will be a new absolute elsewhere, not known at the moment in question. So there will always be that which is unknown.

It can be seen that all these considerations arise out of the need to take into account the important fact that *the observer is part of the universe*. He does not stand outside of space and time, and the laws of physics, but rather he has at each moment a definite place in the total process of the universe, and must be related to this process by the same laws that he is trying to study. As a result, because of the very form of these laws of physics, which imply that no physical action can be transmitted faster than light, there are certain limitations on what can be known by such an observer at a given moment.

In the quantum theory the consequences of the fact that the observer is part of the universe are even more striking. For when one takes into account the indivisible quanta of action which connect the observer with what he observes, one sees that every act of observation brings about an irreducible *participation* of the observer in what he observes, a participation which entails a *disturbance* of the observed system. As a result, there is, as Heisenberg showed in his discussion of the indeterminacy principle, a minimum uncertainty in the accuracy of every kind of measurement. But it is perhaps not so generally realized that the relativity theory by itself leads to the necessity of a sort of inherent uncertainty in our predictions, different from that which follows from quantum theory, and yet not entirely dissimilar in its implications.

Let us now return to the fact that the past of a given moment, such as P, does not actually exist, as shown in the Minkowski diagram, but that is in reality only a *reconstruction* (from which we can, of course, project a probable future). We have seen an example of this in the previous chapter, where one person in the laboratory observes his twin in the rocket ship and vice versa. What each of these people *actually observes* is at first a slowing down of the processes seen to be happening in the other, because the rocket ship is going away from the laboratory, and later a speeding up of these processes, because it is approaching. At a given moment an observer has a memory or some other record of what has been seen up to that moment. He does not take this memory or record as representing directly what actually happened. Rather, he must interpret or "correct" it for the effects of the time needed by light to reach him, this correction being based on his *knowledge* of the general laws of physics, at least in so far as they relate to the propagation of light and other kinds of signals. Such a procedure evidently amounts to a *reconstruction* of what is supposed actually to have happened to the other observer. The correctness of this reconstruction depends on the correctness of his knowledge of the laws of propagation of signals. Thus he may know only the nonrelativistic laws, in which case his reconstruction would contain certain kinds of errors (significant at high velocities) which could be avoided by the use of relativistic laws.

A similar reconstruction is needed to arrive at the length of an object. Thus consider a ruler, moving with velocity v, relative to the laboratory, with end points indicated in Figure 27–1 by the world lines RR' and SS'. What is its length at the time corresponding to the moment O in the world line of the laboratory observer? Evidently this observer could not be in contact with the events R and S at the time corresponding to the event O. Rather, he could learn about these (e.g., with light signals) *only later*; and from this knowledge he could make a kind of mental reconstruction of the ruler as it had been at the time corresponding to C.

By definition the length of the ruler must be, of course, the distance between its end points, *taken at the same time*, as calculated by the observer in question, taking into account the time needed for light to reach him from various parts of the ruler. To obtain the necessary data for such a calculation, he could, for example, take a series of photographs of the ruler, and knowing the distance of the camera from the ruler and the direction in which the camera was sighting, he could use well-known geometrical methods to calculate the length of the ruler. In studying how he must do this, we can see very clearly how certain relativistic properties such as the Lorentz contraction of moving objects are very much a matter of conventional definition of the properties in question. Thus, if the ruler had been moving along the direction of its length and photographed from a long distance away at some angle, θ, to its direction of motion, then this photograph would *not* by itself show the distance between the end points of the ruler at the same time (Figure 31–2). Rather, the camera merely selects all the light rays that happen to pass through the shutter in the (negligibly short) interval during which the latter is open. Using the approximations following from the assumption that the ruler subtends a very small angle, $\Delta\theta$, at the camera C, we readily calculate that the light rays thus selected from the rear, B, of the ruler have started later than those from the front, A, by a time interval $\Delta t = (l - v\,\Delta t/c)\cos\theta$, where l is the length of the ruler. Thus $\Delta t = (l/c)[\cos\theta/1 + (v/c)\cos\theta]$. Because of the movement of the ruler the length that it shows *on the photograph* will be $l' = l/[1 + (v/c)\cos\theta]$. Therefore, the observer will have to "correct" for this effect, if he wishes to obtain the "length" of the ruler at a given value of his time coordinate. To make this correction he must know the velocity of the ruler. This he can find, for example from a series of photographs taken over a sequence of

Figure 31–2

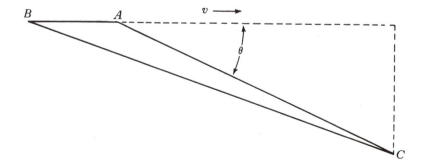

times, as measured by his clocks, if he observes the changes in position of the ruler.

In the above examples we have illustrated how abstract are properties, such as length and frequency, in the relativistic domain. They are seldom, if ever, directly perceived as such. Rather, they come out only after a process of reconstruction, based on a great deal of knowledge of the past, both general and specific.

Basically, however, all our knowledge has the character described above. Thus it is evident that what we know about prehistoric times comes entirely from reconstructions of traces of these times that still exist. But our knowledge of historic times is also only a reconstruction, based in addition on records of what people have said and done (records that are often false, misleading, incomplete, etc.). And even our knowledge of our own immediate past is also a similar reconstruction, based on what we can remember of it. So the whole of the past is a kind of reconstruction. To be sure, much of it is carried out by habitual expectation of certain kinds of regularities, requiring little or no conscious thought. Yet it cannot be denied that the past is gone, and that all that is left of it are traces, which we interpret, organize, and structure into some approximate and generally incomplete knowledge of what actually happened. This knowledge has a certain limited and partial degree of truth, which makes it a useful general guide for future actions, provided that one is alert to recognize its errors as they show themselves.

With all this in mind, let us now come to the question of what the Minkowski diagram can actually mean. The answer is that this diagram is a kind of map of the *events* in the world, which can correctly give us the order, pattern, and structure of real events, but which is not in itself the world as it actually is. Thus, everyone is familiar with the fact that a map of the world is made of paper, ink, etc., and that *the map is not the world*. Nevertheless, a good map has a *structure* that is in certain ways similar to the structure of the world. Thus, on such a map, if a certain city C is shown to be between two other cities A and B, we shall actually find as we go from A to B that C is encountered between them. (A bad map would, of course, be one whose structure was not similar to the structure of that of which it was supposed to be the map).

It may be said then that physics has developed a kind of map of the events taking place in the world such that for example, if event B is seen on the map as lying between events A and C, we should find that C is actually observed to happen after A and before C. In Newtonian mechanics the associated map implied a complete unrelatedness of space and time, so that if any observers found that a given event A was before another B, it was implied that all observers would actually encounter the same order. On the basis of Einstein's theory, however, physicists have now developed a more subtle map, in which space and time are inherently related, in the manner specified in the Minkowski diagram. On this map, if two events are in each other's absolute elsewhere, it is implied that observers moving at different speeds may attribute a different time order to the events, some saying that A is before B and others that B is before A. However, if the events are inside each other's light cones, the map implies that all observers will agree on which is earlier and which is later (so that there can be no ambiguity in the order of causally connected sets of events).

It is clear that even in the case of the geography of the Earth, a map is an elaborate reconstruction, based on a tremendous number of observations, organized, ordered, and structured in accord with certain geometrical principles that have been abstracted from a wide range of past experiences. Very often there are errors in the map that are corrected on the basis of further observation; and at times there have been fundamental changes in the *structure* of the map, resulting from the extension of experience into broader domains (e.g., when the notion of a flat Earth was replaced by that of a spherical Earth). Moreover, no one expects the map to be *complete*. Rather, it is only a general guide, so that to see what a given country is actually like you must go there.

In a similar way the physicist's notions of space and time are based on a reconstruction, in accord with appropriate geometrical, dynamical, and structural principles that have been abstracted from a wide range of past experiences. These too have errors that have to be corrected on the basis of further observations, and can be subjected to fundamental structural alterations, as experience is extended into new domains. And, likewise, the map is never complete. Indeed, it is based only on what is past and gone. But when all of this is put into the structure of a good conceptual map, it can serve as a general guide for what to expect in the future. However, to see what the future is really like, we must, of course, wait until it actually takes place. And from time to time, there will be surprises, not corresponding at all to what is on our map.

The difference between a map and the region of which it is the map is so self-evident that no one is likely to confuse the map with what it is supposed to represent (any more than someone is likely to confuse a picture of a meal with a real meal that can nourish him). But our ideas of space and time (whether gained in common experience or in physical research) seem to be comparatively easily confused with what actually happens. Thus, when Newton proposed the idea of absolute space and time physicists did not say that this is only a kind of conceptual map, which may have a structure that is partly true to that of real physical processes and partly false. Rather, they felt that *what is* is absolute space and time. Now that this notion has been seen to have only a limited degree of validity, the tendency is probably to feel that *what is* is relativistic space-time, as shown in the Minkowski diagram.

Much confusion can be avoided on this point if we say that both Newtonian and Einsteinian space-time are conceptual maps, each having a structure that is, in its domain, similar to that of real sets of events and processes that can actually be observed. Room is then left in our minds to entertain the notion that as physics enters new domains, still other kinds of conceptual maps may be needed.

Any map of this kind *is* what the world *is not*. That is, the map is an idea, a picture, a description, or a representation, while the world is not any of these things. But as happens with all thought, adequate ideas imply a structure similar to the structure of *what is*. And the test for the adequacy of an idea is to see whether the structure disclosed in actual experience is similar to that implied by our ideas. If it is not, then we need new concepts, implying another structure, which is adequate to that disclosed in the facts that are actually observed.

In all maps (conceptual or otherwise) there arises the need for the user to locate and orient himself by seeing which point on the map represents *his* position and which line represents the direction in which *he is* looking. In doing this, one recognizes, in effect, that every point and direction of observation yields a unique perspective on the world. But with the aid of a good map having a proper structure, one can relate what is seen from one perspective to what is seen from another, in this way abstracting out what is invariant under change of perspective, and leading to an ever-improving knowledge and understanding of the actual character of the territory under investigation. Thus, when two observers with different points of view communicate what they see, they need not argue, offering opinions as to which view is "right" and which view is "wrong." Rather, they consult their maps, and try to come to a common understanding of why each man looking at the same territory has a different perspective and comes therefore to his own view, related in a certain way to that of the other. (Of course, if after reasonable efforts they cannot do this they may begin to suspect that they may need maps with different structures.)

In Newtonian mechanics the importance of the location and perspective of the observer was very much underemphasized. Of course, physicists have probably always realized that each observer does actually have a perspective. However, they may have felt that such a perspective need play no part in the fundamental laws of physics. Rather, they assumed that a physical process takes place in an "absolute" space and time that is independent of the way in which it is measured and observerd, so that the perspective of the observer (or of his instruments) does not appear at all in these laws. On the other hand, in Einstein's point of view, it is clear that any particular example of a Minkowski diagram is a map corresponding to what will be observed in a system moving in a certain way and oriented in a certain direction. Therefore, this map already has some of the observer's perspective implicit in it. Moreover, as we have seen, even an observer with a given velocity has, at each moment, a different perspective on the universe, because he has information only about his absolute past, which corresponds to a different region of space-time in each moment of such an observer's existence. Thus, whether we consider what is seen by different observers or by the same observer at different times, it is necessary continually to relate the results of all these observations, by referring them to a space-time map with a correct structure, and in this way to develop an ever-growing knowledge and understanding of what is invariant and therefore not dependent on the special perspective of each observer.

It is seen then that while relativity does emphasize the special role of each observer in a way that is different from what is done in earlier theories, it does not thereby fall into a kind of "subjectivism" that would make physics refer only to what such an observer finds convenient or chooses to think. Rather, its emphasis is on the hitherto almost ignored *fact* that each observer does have an inherent perspective, making his point of view in some way unique. But the recognition of this unique perspective serves, as it were, to clear the ground for a more realistic approach to finding out what is actually invariant and not dependent on the perspective of the observer.

APPENDIX

Physics and Perception

A-1. INTRODUCTION

Throughout this book we have seen that in Einstein's theory of relativity, the notions of space, time, mass, etc., are no longer regarded as representing absolutes, existing in themselves as permanent substances or entities. Rather, the whole of physics is conceived as dealing with the discovery of what is *relatively invariant* in the ever-changing movements that are to be observed in the world, as well as in the changes of points of view, frames of reference, different perspectives, etc., that can be adopted in such observations. Of course, the laws of Newton and Galileo had already incorporated a number of relativistic notions of this kind (e.g., relativity of the centre of coordinates, of the orientation, and speed of the frame of reference). But in them the basic concepts of space, time, mass, etc., were still treated as absolutes. Einstein's contribution was to extend these relativistic notions to encompass the laws, not only of mechanics, but also those of electrodynamics and optics, in the special theory, and of gravitation in the general theory. In doing this he was led to make the revolutionary step to which we have referred, i.e., of ceasing to regard the properties of space, time, mass, etc., as absolutes, instead treating these as invariant features of the relationships of observed sets of objects and events to frames of reference. In different frames of reference the space coordinates, time, mass, energy, etc., to be associated to specified objects and events will be different. Yet there are various sets of transformations (e.g., rotations, space displacements, Lorentz transformations) relating the many aspects of the world, as observed in any one frame to those as observed in another. And in these transformations, certain functions (such as the interval and the rest mass) represent invariant properties, the same for all frames of reference, within the set in question. Of course, such invariance will in general hold only in some domain, so that as the domain under investigation is broadened, we may expect to come to new invariant relationships, containing the older ones as approximations and limiting cases. The lawfulness of nature is thus seen to correspond just to the possibility of finding what is invariant. But because each kind of invariance is only relative to a suitable domain, science may be expected to go on to the discovery of ever new kinds of invariant relationships, each of which contributes to the understanding of some new domain of phenomena.

At first sight the point of view described above may seem to be very different to that of "common sense" (as well as of the older Newtonian physics). For are we not in the habit of regarding the world as constituted of more or less permanent objects, satisfying certain permanent laws? That is to say, in everyday life we never talk about "invariant relationships," but rather we refer to tables, chairs, trees, buildings, people, etc., each of which is more or less unconsciously conceived as being a certain kind of object or entity, which, added to others, makes up the world as we know it. We do not regard these objects or entities as *relative invariants* which along with their properties, and the laws that they satisfy, have been abstracted from the total flux of change and movement. There appears then to be a striking difference between the way we conceive the world as observed in immediate experience (as well as in the domain of classical nonrelativistic physics) and the way it is conceived in relativity theory.

In this Appendix we shall show that the difference between the notions of common experience and those of relativity theory arise mainly because of certain habitual *ideas* concerning this experience, and that there is now a great deal of new, but fairly well confirmed, scientific evidence suggesting that our actual mode of *perception* of the world (seeing it, hearing it, touching it, etc.) is much closer in character and general structure to what is suggested by relativistic physics than it is to what is suggested by prerelativistic physics. In the light of this evidence it would seem that nonrelativistic notions appear more natural to us than relativistic notions, mainly because of our limited and inadequate understanding of the *domain of common experience*, rather than because of any inherent inevitability of our habitual mode of apprehending this domain.

A–2. THE DEVELOPMENT OF OUR COMMON NOTIONS IN INFANTS AND YOUNG CHILDREN

The evidence in favor of the suggestion at the end of Chapter 1 comes from many different fields. We shall begin with the fascinating studies of the development of intelligence in infants and young children carried out by Piaget.[1] On the basis of long and careful observations of children of all ages from birth up to 10 or more years, he was actually able to see the development of our customary ideas of space, time, the permanent objects, the permanent substance with the conserved total quantity, etc., and thus to trace the process in which such notions are built up until they seem natural and inevitable.

The very young infant does not behave as if he had the adult's concept of a world separate from himself, containing various more or less permanent objects in it. Rather, Piaget gives good evidence suggesting that the infant begins by experiencing an almost undifferentiated totality. That is to say he has not yet learned to distinguish between what arises inside of him and outside of him, nor to distinguish between the various aspects of either the "outer" or the "inner" worlds. Instead there is experienced only one world, in a state of continual flux of sensations, perceptions, feelings, etc., with nothing recognizable as permanent in it. However, the infant is endowed with certain inborn reflexes, connected with food, movements, etc. These reflexes can develop so as to selectively accommodate different aspects of the environment; and in this way the environment begins effectively to be differentiated to the extent of taking on certain "recognizable" features. But at this stage recognition is largely *functional* (e.g., some objects are "for eating," some "for drinking," some "for pulling" etc.), and there seems to be little or no development of the adult's ability to

[1] J. Paiget, *The Origin of Intelligence in the Child*, Routledge and Kegan Paul, London, (1953). J. Piaget and B. Inhelder, *The Child's Conception of Space*, Routledge and Kegan Paul, London, (1956).

recognize an object by the shape, form, structure, or other perceived characteristics.

At first these reflexes and functions are carried out largely in the satisfaction of primary needs, indicated by sensations, such as hunger, etc. In the next stage, however, there develops the so-called "circular reflex," which is crucial to the development of intelligence. In such a reflex there is an outgoing impulse (e.g., leading to the movement of the hand) followed, not mainly by the satisfaction of need, but rather by some incoming sensory impulse (e.g., in the eye, ear, etc.). This may be said to be a beginning of real perception. For the most elementary way of coming into contact with something that is not just the immediate satisfaction of a bodily need is by incorporating it into a process in which a certain impulse toward action is accompanied by a certain sensation.

This principle of the circular reflex is carried along in all further developments. Thus, at a certain stage, the infant begins to take pleasure in operating such reflexes, in order, as Piaget puts it, "to produce interesting spectacles." He finds, for example, that pulling a certain cord will produce an interesting sensation of movement in front of him (e.g., if the cord is attached to a colored object). It must not be supposed that he understands the causal connection between the cord and the movement, or even that he foresees the sensation of movement in his imagination and then tries to realize it by some operation. Rather, he *discovers* that by doing such an operation he gets a pleasant sensation that is *recognizable*. In other words, recognition that a past event has been repeated comes first; the ability to call up this event in the memory comes only much later. Thus, at this stage, he only knows that a certain operation will lead to some recognizable experience that is pleasurable.

The ability to recognize something as similar to what was experienced before is certainly a necessary prerequisite for beginning to see something relatively permanent in the flux of process that is very probably the major element in the infant's early experiences. Another important prerequisite for this is the coordination of many different kinds of reflexes that are associated to a given object. Thus, at first the infant seems to have little or no realization that the object he sees is the same as the object he hears. Rather, there seem to be fairly separate reflexes, such as listening, looking with the eyes, etc. Later, however, these reflexes begin to be coordinated, so that he is finally able to understand that he sees what he hears, grasps what he sees, etc. This is an important step in the growth of intelligence, for in it is already implicit the notion that will finally develop—of a single object that is responsible for all of our different kinds of experience with it.

The infant is, however, as yet far from the notion of a permanent object, or of permanent causal relationships between such objects. Rather, his behavior at this stage suggests that when presented with something familiar he now abstracts certain vaguely recognizable totalities of sensation and response, involving the coordination of hand, eye, ear, etc. Thus there is a kind of a germ of the notion of the invariant here; for in the total flux of experience he can now recognize certain invariant combinations of features of the pattern. *These combinations are themselves experienced as totalities*, so that the object is not recognized outside of its customary context.

Later the infant begins to follow a moving object with his eyes, being able to recognize the invariance of its form, etc., despite its movement. He is thus beginning to build up the reflexes needed for perceiving the continuity of existence of certain objects, apart from their customary contexts. However, he still has no notion of anything permanent. Rather, he behaves as if he believed that an object comes into existence where he first sees it and passes out of existence where he last sees it. Thus, if an object passes in front of him and disappears later from his field of view, he looks for it, not in the direction where he has *last* seen it, but rather toward the place where he *first* saw it, as if this were regarded as the natural source of such objects. Thus, if an object goes behind an obstacle, he does not seem to have any notion of looking for it there. The realization that this can be done comes only later, after the child has begun to work with what Piaget calls "groups of operations." The most elementary of these is the "group of two." That is, there are operations such as turning something round and round, hiding it behind an obstacle and bringing it back to view, shaking something back and forth, etc., which have in common that there is an operation, the result of which can be "undone" by a second operation, so that the two operations following each other lead back to the original state of affairs. It is only after he understands this possibility that the infant begins to look for an object behind the obstacle where it vanished from view. But his behavior suggests that he still does not have the idea of a permanent object, existing even when he doesn't see it. Rather, he probably feels that he can "undo" the vanishing of an object, by means of the "operation" of putting his hand behind the obstacle and bringing forth the object in question.

In this connection we must recall that the infant still sees no clear and permanent demarcation between himself and the world, or between the various objects in it. However, he is building up the reflexes and operations needed to conceive this demarcation later. Thus, he is beginning to develop the notion of causality, and the distinction of cause and effect. At first he seems to regard causality as if it were a kind of "sympathetic" magic. He may discover that certain movements applied to a string or other object near him will produce corresponding movements elsewhere. He does not immediately realize the need for a connection, but often acts as if he expected the results to follow directly as a kind of magical response to his movements. This is, of course, not really unexpected, if one considers that the child does not yet clearly distinguish what is inside him from what is outside. Thus, in many cases, movements will in fact produce perceptible *internal* effects without a visible intermediary connection. Therefore, as long as the child views all aspects of his experience as a single totality, with no clear distinction of "within" and "without," there is nothing in his experience to deny the expectation of such sympathetic magical causality. Later, however, he begins to see the need for intermediate connections in causal relationships, and still later he is able to recognize other people, animals, and even objects as the causes of things that are happening in his field of experiencing.

Meanwhile, the notions of space and time are being built up. Thus as the child handles objects and moves his body he learns to coordinate his changing visual experiences with the tactile perceptions and bodily movements. At this stage, his notion of groups of movements is being extended from the "group of two" to more general groups. Thus, he is learning that he can go from one place A to another B by many different paths, and that all these paths lead him to the same place (or alternatively that if he goes from A to B by any one path, he can "undo" this and return to A by a large number of alternative paths). This may seem to be self-evident to us, but for an infant living on a flux of process it is probably a gigantic *discovery* to find out that in all of this movement there are certain things that he can always *return* to in a wide variety of ways. The notion of the *reversible* group of movements or operations thus provides a foundation on which he will later erect that of *permanent places* to which one can return, and *permanent objects*, which can always be brought back to something familiar and recognizable by means of suitable operations (e.g., rotations, displacements, etc.).

Meanwhile the child is gradually learning to call up images of the past, in some approximation to the sequence in which it occurred, and not merely to *recognize* something as familiar only after he sees it. Thus begins true *memory*, and with it the basis for the notion of the distinction of past time and present time (and later future time, when the child begins to form mental images of what he expects).

A really crucial step occurs when the child is able to form an image of an absent object, as existing even when he is not actually perceiving it. Just before he can do this he seems to deal with this problem as if he regarded the absent object as something that he (or other people) can *produce* or *create* with the aid of certain operations. But now he begins to form a mental image of the world, containing both perceived and unperceived things, each in its place. These objects, along with their places, are now conceived as permanently existing, and in a set of relationships corresponding perfectly to the groups of movements and operations already known to him (e.g., the picture of a space in which each point is connected to every other by many paths faithfully represents the invariant feature of his experience with groups of operations, in which he was able to go from one point to another by many routes).

At this stage it seems that the child begins to see clearly the distinction between himself and the rest of the world. Until now he could not make such a distinction, because there was only one field of experiencing what was actually present to his total set of perceptions. However, with his ability to create a mental image of the world, i.e., to *imagine* it, he now conceives a set of places which are permanent, these places being occupied by various permanent objects. But one of these objects is *himself*. In his new mental "map" of the world he can maintain a permanent distinction between himself and other objects. Everything on this map falls into two categories—what is "inside his skin" and what is not. He learns to associate various feelings, pleasures, pains, desires, etc., with what is "inside his skin," and thus he forms the concept of a "self," distinct from the rest of the world, and yet having its place in this world. He similarly attributes "selves" to the insides of other people's skins, as well as to animals. Each "self" is conceived as both initiating causal actions in the world and suffering the effects of causal actions originating outside of it. Eventually he learns to attribute to inanimate objects a lower and more mechanical kind of "selfhood" without feelings, aims, and desires, but still having a certain ability to initiate causal actions, and to suffer the effects of causes originating outside of it. In this way the general picture of a world in space (and time), constituted of separate and permanent entities which can act on each other causally, is formed.

The notions of an objective world and of a subject corresponding to one of the objects in the world are, as we have seen, thus formed together, in the same step. And this is evidently necessary, since the mental image of the world that serves as a kind of conceptual "map" requires the singling out of one of the objects on this "map" to represent the place of the observer, in order that his special perspective on the world at each moment can be taken into account. That is to say, just as the relativistic "map," in the form of the Minkowski diagram (as discussed at the end of Chapter 29), must contain something in it to represent the place, time, orientation, velocity, etc., of the observer, so the mental map that is created by each person must have a corresponding representation of that person's relationship to the environment.

It must not be supposed, of course, that the child knows that he is making a mental image or map of the world. Rather, as Piaget brings out very well, young children often find it difficult to distinguish between what is imagined or remembered in thought and what is actually perceived through their senses (e.g., they may think that other people are able to see the objects that they are thinking about). Thus the child will take this mental map as equivalent to reality. And this habit is intensified with each new experience, because once the map is formed it *enters into and shapes all immediate perceptions*, thus interpenetrating the whole of experience and becoming inseparable from it. Indeed, it is well known that how we see something depends on what we know about it. (E.g., an extreme case is that of an ambiguous picture, subject to two interpretations, one obvious and the other less so. Once a person is told about the second interpretation, in many cases, he can no longer see the picture in the original way.) Thus, over a period of years we learn to see the world through a certain structure of ideas, with which we react immediately to each new experience before we even have time to think. In this way we come to believe that certain ways of conceiving and perceiving the world cannot be otherwise, although in fact they were discovered and built up by us when we were children, and have since then become habits that may well be appropriate only in certain domains of experience.

It is very hard to do full justice to the scope and range of Piaget's work in a summary of this kind. Besides covering a great many points concerning the period of infancy that have not been mentioned here, he goes on to discuss the development of intelligence after the child learns to talk and to engage in thought more or less as it is known by adults. Here, the child has to solve a new set of problems. For he must translate into the structure of thought and language that immediate perceptual structure of the world which is represented on the mental "map" to which we have referred. This process is inevitably attended by a great deal of confusion, in which the child's ideas and words frequently contradict what he must be perceiving. Yet, step by step, the child learns to know which figures are closed, which curves are smooth, which things are inside or outside others, etc. These are the so-called "topological" relationships. He then discovers the facts of perspective (which are behind projective geometry) and learns how to recognize the sizes and shapes of objects, thus becoming familiar with that set of relationships the essence of which is summed up in Euclidean geometry. In this process, he also learns the need for logical thought, when he wishes to reflect on the structure of the world, and to communicate with other people, as well as when he wishes to apply his ideas to a practical problem. (Piaget makes it clear that at first logic plays only a very small role in the thinking of children.) Thus in a continuing process of development the child builds up his knowledge and understanding of the world, with the aid of related sets of mental images, ideas, descriptions in words, etc., implying a structure similar to that of various aspects of the world as he directly perceives it.

It will be relevant for our purposes here to discuss briefly the development of the child's concept of the constancy of the number of objects, and of the total quantity of matter in them, because these concepts have evidently played a fundamental role in physics. As Piaget demonstrates, a child who has recently begun to talk does not at first have the notion that a set of objects has a fixed number, independent of how they are moved and rearranged. Rather, he forms at each instant a general perceptual estimate of whether a given collection seems to be more, or less, or equal to another, and does not hesitate to say that two initially equal collections are unequal, after they have been subject to some rearrangements in space (even though the numbers of objects have actually remained constant).

The results described above will be seen to be not surprising, if one keeps in mind the fact that the child does not yet have the idea of the conservation of the number of objects as they move and change their relationships to each other and to the observer. Indeed, this notion is developed only in a series of stages. First, the child learns to establish a one-to-one *correspondence* between objects that are in simple relationship, such as parallel rows. When he loses sight of this correspondence (e.g., when the objects are rearranged and are no longer in rows) he cannot yet think of them as having the same number. Later, as he learns to put them into correspondence again, he forms an idea similar to that of the "reversible group," i.e., that certain sets of objects can be brought back by suitable operations into their original state of one-to-one correspondence. From here he forms a new concept or "mental map" of the objects as having at all times a fixed number, which faithfully portrays the structure of his operations with such sets as capable of being put back into correspondence. Then, gradually, he forgets the operations that establish correspondence and thinks of the number of objects as a fixed property belonging to a given total set, even when these move and rearrange.

The procedure of thinking of numbers as an inherent and permanent property of a set becomes so habitual that the problem "What is number?" is considered as being too obvious to require much discussion. Yet when modern mathematicians came to study this question, what they had to do was in effect to uncover the operational basis on which each child originally develops his concept of number (thus reaching the definition of equality of cardinal numbers of two sets in terms of one-to-one correspondences between numbers of a set). We see then that the deepest problems are often found in the study of what seems obvious, because the "obvious" is frequently merely a notion that summarizes the invariant features of a certain domain of experience which has become habitual and the basis of which has dropped out of consciousness. So to understand the obvious it is necessary very often to go to a broader point of view, in which one brings to light the basic operations, movements, and changes, within which certain characteristics have been found to be invariant.

A very similar problem arises with regard to conservation of the quantity of matter or substance. Thus, when a given quantity of liquid is distributed into many containers of various shapes, the young child does not hesitate to say that the total quantity of water has increased or decreased, according to the impressions that the new distribution produces in his immediate perceptions. Later, when he sees the possibility of bringing the water back into the original container, where it has the same volume as it had originally, he is led to the idea of a constant quantity of liquid. The necessity for this step in the development of the child's conceptions is evident. For *a priori* there is no reason to suppose that the quantity of a given substance is conserved. This idea comes forth only as a result of the need to understand certain kinds of experience. Then later, one forgets that such an idea had to be developed. It becomes habitual, and eventually it seems inevitable to suppose that the world is made of certain basic substances that are absolutely permanent in their total quantities. Then, when we do not find this absolute permanence in the level of common experience, we postulate it in the atomic level or somewhere else.

As in the case of numbers, some very deep problems arise here in the effort to understand what seems obvious. Nothing seems more obvious than the notion of a permanent quantity of substance. Yet, to understand this idea more deeply, we must go on to a broader context, in which such a notion need not apply. We can then see that such conceptions arise when the child discovers a kind of *relative invariance* under certain operations, e.g., of pouring the liquid back into the original container. So we find that in the *understanding* of immediate perception, one must do essentially what is done in the theory of relativity, i.e., to give up the concept of something that is absolutely permanent and constant, to see the constancy of certain relationships or properties in a broad domain of operations involved in observation, measurement, etc., in which the conditions, context, and perspective are altered.

To sum up the work of Piaget, then, we recall that the infant begins with some kind of totality of sensation, perception, feeling, etc., in a state of flux, in which there is little or no recognizable structure with permanent characteristics. The development of intelligence then arises in a series of operations, movements, etc., by which the child *learns* about the world. In particular, what he learns is always based on his ability to see invariant relationships in these operations and movements, e.g., an invariant kind of correspondence between what he sees and what he hears, etc., an invariant relationship between cause and effect, an invariant form to an object as he follows it with his eye, an invariant possibility of "undoing" certain changes by means of suitable operations, etc., etc. The perception of each kind of invariance is then followed by the development of a corresponding mental image (and later a structure of organized ideas and language) which functions as a kind of "map" representing the invariance relationships correctly, in the sense that it implies invariant features similar to those disclosed in the operations (e.g., the mental image of a space with permanent positions connected by an infinity of possible paths corresponds to the operational experience of being able to reach the same place by many different routes). Very soon immediate perception takes on the structure of these "maps," and, after this, one is no longer aware that the map only *represents* what has been found to be invariant. Rather, the map begins to interpenetrate what is perceived in such a way that it seems to be an inevitable and necessary feature of the whole of experience, so obvious that it is very difficult to question its basic features.

The work of Piaget indicates that in order to understand the process of perception it is necessary to go beyond the habitual standpoint, in which one more or less confuses the general structural features of our mental "maps" with features of the world that cannot be otherwise, under any conceivable circumstances. Rather, one is led to consider the broader totality of our perceptive process as a kind of flux, in which certain *relatively invariant* features have emerged, to be represented by such "maps," in the sense that these faithfully portray the structure of such features. But as we have seen in this book, a similar step is involved in going from a nonrelativistic point of view in physics to a relativistic point of view. For in doing this we cease to regard our concepts of space, time, mass, etc., as representing absolutely permanent and necessary features of the world, and, instead, we regard them as expressing the invariant relationships that actually exist in certain domains of investigation.

A-3. THE ROLE OF THE INVARIANT IN PERCEPTION

The work of Piaget, discussed in the previous section, shows that the development of intelligence seems to be based on the ability to realize what is invariant in a given domain of operations, changes, movements, etc., and to grasp these relationships by means of suitable mental images, ideas, verbal expressions, mathematical symbolism, etc., implying a structure similar to that which is actually encountered. We shall now cite some evidence coming from the direct study of the process of perception, which strongly confirms the implications of this point of view, and considerably extends their domain of applicability.

There is a common notion of perception as a sort of *passive* process, in which we simply allow sense impressions to come into us, there to be assembled into whole structures, recorded in memory, etc. Actually, however, the new studies make it clear that perception is, on the contrary, an *active* process, in which a person must do a great many things in the course of which actions he helps to supply a certain *general structure* to what he perceives. To be sure, this structure is objectively correct, in the sense that it is similar to the structure of the kind of things that are encountered in common experience. Yet the fact that a great deal of what we see is ordered and organized in a form determined by the functioning of our own bodies and nervous systems has very far reaching implications for the study of new domains of experience, whether in the field of immediate perception itself or in science (which generally depends on instrumentally aided perception, in order to reach new domains).

One can see the active role of the observer most clearly by first considering tactile perception. Thus, if one tries to find the shape of an unseen object simply by feeling it, one must *handle* the object, turn it round, touch it in various ways, etc. (This problem has been studied in detail by Gibson and his co-workers.[1])

In such operations one seldom notices the *individual sensations* on the fingers, wrist joints, etc. Rather, one directly perceives the general structure of the object, which emerges, somehow, out of a very complex change in all the sensations. This perception of the structure depends

[1] See J. G. Gibson, *Psychological Review,* **69,** 477 (1962).

on two nervous currents of energy—not only the inward current of sensations to which we have referred above, but also an outward current determining movements of the hand. For knowledge of this structure is implicit in the *relationship* between the outward and the inward currents (e.g., in the response to certain movements of turning, pressing, etc.).

It is evident, then, that tactile perception is evidently inherently the result of a set of active operations, performed by the percipient. Nevertheless, the outgoing impulses leading to the movement of the hand and the influx of sensations are either not noticed or else they are only on the fringe of awareness. What is perceived most strongly is actually the structure of the object itself. It seems clear that out of a remarkably complex and variable flux of movement with their related sensual responses, the brain is able to abstract a *relatively invariant* structure of the object that is handled. This invariant structure is evidently not in the individual operations and sensations but can be abstracted only out of their totality over some period of time.

At first one might think that in *vision* the situation is basically different, and that one just passively "takes in" the picture of the world. But more careful studies show that vision involves a similar active role of the percipient, and that the structure of what one sees is abstracted out of similar invariant relations between certain movements and the changing sensations which are the eye's response to these movements.

One of the most elementary movements that is necessary for vision has been demonstrated by Ditchburn,[1] who has discovered that the eyeball is continually undergoing small and very rapid vibrations, which shift the image by a distance equal roughly to that between adjacent cells on the retina of the eye. In addition, it has a slower regular drift, followed by a "flick" which brings the image more or less back to its original center. Experiments in which a person looked at the whole field of vision through mirrors arranged to cancel the effects of this movement led at first to a distorted vision and soon to a complete breakdown of vision, in the sense that the viewer could see nothing at all, even though a clear image of the world was being focussed on his retina.

[1] R. W. Ditchburn, *Research*, **9**, 466 (1951), *Optica Acta*, **1**, 171 and **2**, 128 (1955).

Ditchburn has explained this phenomenon by appealing to the fact that when a constant stimulus is maintained on nerve cells for some time, they *accommodate*; i.e., the strength of their response tends to decrease, eventually falling below the threshold of what is perceptible. Under conditions in which the pattern of intensity of light on the whole retina is kept fixed by mirrors that compensate for the movements of the eyeball, it is then to be expected that such a process of accommodation will take place. In this way one can explain the distortion and eventual fading away of what is in the field of view, as observed in the experiments of Ditchburn. In normal vision, however, accommodation will be only partial, because the vibration and other movements of the eyeball will always be producing corresponding changes in the pattern of light on the retina. The response of the nerves connected to a given retinal cell will therefore depend less on the light intensity at the point in question than on the way in which this light intensity *changes* with position. This means that the excitation of the optic nerve does not correspond to the pattern of light on the retina, but rather to a modified pattern in which contrasts are heightened, and in which a strong impression is produced at the boundaries of objects, where the light intensity varies sharply with position. In this way one obtains an emphasis on the outlines and forms of objects which helps to lead to their being perceived as separate and distinct, a perception that would not be nearly so clear and noticeable if the eye were sensitive to the light intensity itself, rather than to its changes.

Platt[1] has made the interesting suggestion that our ability to discern the straightness of lines with great accuracy depends on the drift and "flick" motions which we have mentioned, or on motions that are similar to them. Now, Hubel and Wiesel[2] have shown by following the connections from the optic nerve through the retinal ganglion cells into the brain that certain kinds of regions on the retina resembling segments of short linear bars are mapped into corresponding cells of the cortex. This mapping could explain our ability to make relatively crude discriminations as to which segments of the visual field are lines (with an accuracy corresponding to the width of the bars, which is

---

[1] J. R. Platt, *Principles of Self Organising Systems*, Zopf and von Fuerster (eds)., Pergamon, 1961; *Information Theory in Biology*, Yockey, Quastler, and Platzman, (eds.), Pergamon, 1958; and *Scientific American*, **202**, 121, June 1960.
[2] D. H. Hubel, *Scientific American*, **209**, 54, November 1963.

generally of the order of several times the space between retinal cells). On the other hand, as Platt has pointed out, one can observe breaks in perfect linearity corresponding on the retinal image to about a thirtieth of the space between cells. The problem that interested Platt is that of explaining how this remarkable accuracy is made possible.

Platt's proposal is based on noting that the movements of the eyeball are rotations. In a small rotation of the eyeball around an axis in a plane parallel to the foveal part of the retina (i.e., the small region of central vision that is involved whenever precise discrimination of shape, size, etc., is to be made), the effect is to give the image in this region a corresponding linear movement. For a general figure, such a movement will produce *some* change in the pattern of stimulus, which will, of course, be perceptible. But for the special case of a segment of a straight line that is parallel to the direction of displacement of its image, the line will displace into itself. Therefore, the image will be *invariant* under this movement. Platt then postulates that the brain has a way of being sensitive to such invariance, thus permitting it to recognize the property of straightness.[1]

It is evident that the accuracy of discrimination in the process need not be limited by the distance between cells of the retina. For if a line is not straight it will produce a variation in the pattern of excitation of the nerves. This variation can be detected even if the failure of perfect linearity is in a region smaller than the size of a retinal cell, provided that there is sufficient *sensitivity* to small changes in the pattern of light intensity following on such cells.[2]

It is characteristic of perception, however, that usually there are *many* alternative mechanisms for obtaining the same kind of information, which can reinforce or aid each other. Thus, the mapping of bar-like regions on the retina into cells of the cortex of the brain disclosed by Hubel and Wiesel can give us a rough perception of straight lines, which may be supplemented by the process suggested by Platt, when

---

[1] The fact that straight lines do not disappear altogether from the field of vision as a result of accommodation could be accounted for by many possible mechanisms, e.g., by supposing that when their observed intensity starts to fade significantly the eyeball undergoes a "flick" that moves the line over to a fresh section of the foveal region.

[2] Rotations of the eyeball around an axis perpendicular to the plane of the fovea would permit a correspondingly accurate process of recognizing uniform curvature (i.e., that there are no changes of curvature in a small region of arc.)

finer discriminations are to be made. Moreover, from a consideration of Piaget's work discussed in Section 2A, it seems likely that, starting from childhood, each person builds up certain ways of *knowing* which lines are straight, by comparison with a sort of memory of grids of lines, learned by experience over a long period of time. In addition, yet other mechanisms are implicit in the work of Held, Gibson, and others, which we shall discuss presently.

The essential point that we wish to emphasize in the work concerning the eye is that nothing is perceived without movements or variations in the image on the retina of the eye, and that the characteristics of these variations play a large part in determining the structure that is actually seen. It is important that such variations shall not only be a result of changes that take place naturally in the environment, but that (as in the case of tactile perception) they also can be produced actively by movements in the sense organs of the observer himself. These variations are not themselves perceived to any appreciable extent. What is perceived is something relatively invariant, e.g., the outline and form of an object, the straightness of lines, the sizes and shapes of things, etc., etc. Yet the invariant could not be perceived unless the image were actively varied.

Experiments by Held and his co-workers and by Gibson[1] make it clear that movements of the body also play an essential role in optical perception, particularly the coordination between such movements and the resulting changes that are seen in the optical image of the world. For example, when people are furnished with distorting spectacles (which cause straight lines to appear to be curved) and allowed to enter a room patterned in a way that is not previously known to them, they eventually learn to "correct" the effects of this distortion by the spectacles, and *cease to see the curvature that must actually be present in the image of a straight line on the retinas of their eyes.* Later, when they take off the spectacles, they see straight lines as curved, at least for a while. (A more extreme case of such an experiment is to allow a person to see the world through spectacles that invert the image. After some time he sees it right side up, but when he takes off the spectacles he sees it upside down again, for a while.)

---

[1] For a discussion of these experiments see R. Held and S. J. Freedman, *Science*, **142**, 455 (1963); *Psychology, A Study of Science*, S. Koch (ed.), McGraw-Hill, New York, 1959, p. 456; R. Held and J. Rekosh, *Science*, **141**, 722 (1963).

The interesting point of these experiments is that the "relearning" of what corresponds to a straight line depends very strongly on the ability to move the body actively. Thus people who are free to walk around are able to adjust their vision to their spectacles fairly rapidly, whereas people who passively undergo equivalent movements in chairs either never learn to do so or else are very much less effective in such learning. So it is clear that what is essential is not only that there shall be appropriate *variations* of the image on the eye, resulting from movement, but also that some of these variations shall be produced *actively* by the percipient. In other words, as in the case of tactile perception, what one actually sees is determined somehow by the abstraction of what is invariant from a set of variations in what is seen, this variation having been produced, at least in part, as an essential aspect of the process of observation itself.

In the above experiment one may conjecture plausibly that through experiences with movement starting with early childhood (as discussed in the work of Piaget), each person already has some sort of Euclidean structure built into his bodily movements. As far as one can verify by trying to walk to the edge of a room with his eyes closed, he seems to have in his nervous system some kind of ability or skill which makes it possible for him to abstract from all the changing movements and sensations in his body some information concerning the straightness of his path, the amount of turning, etc. In normal vision (without distorting spectacles), when one walks along such a mechanically sensed straight line, the image on the retina of the eyes undergoes a *projective transformation* (at least approximately) in which the apparent shapes of figures change, but in which straight lines are transformed into straight lines. Therefore, as one walks in a straight line, the mechanically derived information on the invariance of direction of movement will agree with what is implied by the corresponding optical information, abstracted from the projective transformation of lines in the field of vision. However, when one is wearing distorting spectacles, what is mechanically sensed as walking a straight line will be optically sensed as walking a curved line. Thus, there is a contradiction between what one sees and what one perceives through feeling, movement, kinesthetic sensations, etc. It seems then, that below the level of consciousness, the brain and nervous system are trying to resolve this contradiction by testing various hypotheses as to what actually constitutes a straight line.[1] When a hypothesis is found that removes the contradiction between what is seen and what is felt mechanically, then this hypothesis is, as it were, embodied directly in the structure that we perceive. Therefore, a person who is wearing distorting lenses eventually ceases to perceive an optically curved line under conditions in which he mechanically senses a straight line, but rather he comes to *see* and *feel* the same straight line (as in the work of Piaget discussed in the previous section, where the child learns to perceive an invariant correspondence between what he sees, what he hears, what he grasps, etc.).

In the discussion of the work of Ditchburn, Hubel and Wiesel, and Platt we have already seen that the optic nerve does not transmit a simple "copy" of the image on the retina of the eye, but rather that it tends to emphasize certain structural features by heightening contrasts and being sensitive to the presence or absence of lines and other such figures. From the work of Held and Gibson, however, it is clearly seen that the picture that we perceive actually contains structural features which are *not even on the retina of the eye at a given moment*, but which are detected with the aid of relationships observed over some period of time.

The perceived picture is therefore not just an image or reflection of our momentary sense impressions, but rather it is the outcome of a complex process leading to an ever-changing (three-dimensional) *construction* which is present to our awareness in a kind of "inner show." This construction is based on the abstraction of what is invariant in the relationship between a set of movements produced actively by the percipient himself and the resulting changes in the totality of his sensual "inputs." Such a construction functions, in effect, as a kind of "hypothesis" compatible with the observed invariant features of the person's over-all experience with the environment in question. (For example, the perception of a straight line corresponds to a hypothesis on what is invariant in the optical, mechanical, and other changes that have been experienced in relationships with this line, as a result of the movements that have been made in a person's perceptual contacts with it.)

---

[1] Platt, for example, has suggested that the brain may find some new combination of rotations of the eyeball, about an axis parallel to the retina and perpendicular to it, which can consistently be coordinated with the mechanically sensed straight line.

Not only is the process of construction dependent on the abstraction of invariant relationships between movement and sense perceptions, as described above; it also depends on all that is *known* by the percipient. For example, if a person looks at a letter at a distance too great for clear distinct vision, he will see something very vague and indistinct in form. But if he is *told* what the letter is, its image will suddenly appear with comparatively great clarity. Or alternatively, he can drop a small coin on a highly patterned carpet, where he will generally find that it is lost to his sight. Then, if he catches a glint of reflected light, the coin that he *knows* that he has lost will suddenly stand out in his perception. Its image must have been on the retina of the eye all the time, but it did not enter the "inner show" of perception until the reflected glint contradicted the perception of a carpet with nothing on it, and also suggested the lost coin that he knows about.

Gibson[1] describes a great many experiments which further bring out the general properties of perception described above. He shows that in the perception of depth, or the three-dimensional character of the world, binocular vision is only *one* of the relevant factors. Another important factor is just the changing optical appearance of things as we move. Thus, as we walk, the image of an object that we are approaching gets larger. The closer the object is, the more rapidly does its apparent size change. In this way (as well as in many other ways, such as the placing of shadows, the relative haziness of distant objects, etc.), the brain is able to abstract information concerning the distance of objects in the dimension along the line of sight. On the basis of such information, it is continually "constructing" the field of what is perceived in the manner that has already been described, i.e., by introducing various "hypotheses" as to what is invariant. For example, if one misjudges the distance of something, one will also misjudge its size. As one walks, one may sense that the object is not varying its apparent size in the way implied by our judgement of its distance. Suddenly, there will appear in the field of perception a different way of seeing the object, which is consistent with the new information.

We see then that what actually appears in the field of perception, at least when one is viewing something relatively static, is a structure, order, and arrangement of things regarded as invariant in their sizes,

[1] J. G. Gibson and E. J. Gibson, *Journal of Experimental Psychology*, **54,** 129 (1957).

shapes, and spatial relationships. This construction in the "inner show" is such that the assumption that it is invariant explains not only its present optical appearance but also the alterations in its appearance that have been experienced as a result of past movements, as well as all that we know or think we know about it. At each moment such a construction has a tentative character, in the sense that it may be subject to changes, if what it implies leads to contradictions in later experiences attending subsequent movements, probings, tests, etc. Here we see an essential role of the *active* movements of the percipient, for it is through these that the current "hypotheses" in the "inner show" of perception are always being tested, corrected, modified, etc.

Thus far we have been considering only the case in which a percipient moves in a relatively static environment. If movements are taking place in his environment as well, then there is the additional problem of knowing which of the observed changes are due to the movements of the observer and which are due to movements of what is in the environment. This problem is dealt with, in effect, by the capacity to abstract a higher order type of invariant, i.e., *a relatively invariant state of movement*.

Generally speaking, as a person moves in his environment his brain begins (largely unconsciously) to note those features which do not change significantly as a result of these movements. These are treated as a distant and relatively fixed background, against which other movements can be perceived. The closer objects do, of course, change their apparent sizes, shapes, etc., appreciably in a systematic way as a person walks, moves his head, etc. It seems that the brain has developed the ability to be sensitive to such apparent movements and changes in the nearby environment, especially when they are coordinated with movements produced by the percipient himself. This permits the elimination of the self-produced movements in the field of what is perceived, so that the construction of the "inner show" corresponds to a generally static world, in which the percipient himself is seen to be moving. Therefore, as a person walks around a room, he does not feel the room to be moving, whirling around, and changing its shape, etc. Rather, he perceives the room as fixed and himself as moving, in such a way as to explain all the variations in what he has perceived. But if, for example, he has suffered damage to the delicate balancing mechanism in the inner ear, he can no longer coordinate his mechanical perceptions with his optical perceptions. He may then suffer vertigo, and feel that the world is moving around him. The difference between these two modes of perception is very striking to anyone who has ever experienced it.

On the basis of the elimination of the movement of the percipient, the brain is then able to go to the next level of abstraction, in which it senses the movement of some part of the field of vision against a background that is perceived as fixed. The simplest case arises when a given object merely suffers a dislocation in space and perhaps also a rotation. In this case one is able to perceive the object as actually having a constant size and shape, despite the fact that its image on the retina is changing all the time. This perception is inextricably bound up with the ability to see such an object as possessing a *certain state of motion*, rather than as a series of "still" pictures of the object in question, each in a slightly different position. It is almost as if the brain were able to establish a co-moving reference frame, in which a moving object could be seen to have a constant shape. In this way, the brain seems to include in its construction process the ability to abstract a certain state of movement, which under the assumption of an object of a given shape is compatible with the changes that have been perceived in the appearance of the object over some period of time.

Of course, there will then be further kinds of changes which cannot be explained in this way (e.g., an object may actually grow in size, change its form, etc.). These will have to be perceived in terms of more subtle internal changes in the object in question.

The problem of how movement is perceived is far from being fully solved. Yet it is already clear that such perception cannot be based merely on "sense impressions" at a given moment. Rather, the "inner show" that we perceive embodies certain structural features, based not only on abstractions from immediate sensations, but also on a series of abstractions over a more or less extended set of earlier perceptions. Indeed, without such a series of abstractions we could not be able to see a world having some well-defined order, organization, structure, etc. Even a static environment is effectively presented in the "inner show" as a tentative and hypothetical structure, which when assumed to be invariant, will be compatible with the changing experiences that the percipient has had with this environment, in movements that he himself has produced. And an environment which is itself changing is presented in the "inner show" as a structure expressed in terms of invariant states of movement of parts of the environment which account for earlier changing experiences that are not explained by the movements of the percipient.

There may also arise an ambiguity in the attribution of movements to the observer or to various parts of the environment. Thus, if a person is sitting in a train that is not moving, and watches another moving train through the window, he may find that he perceives himself as moving, and that he even gets some of the physical (kinesthetic) sensations of movement. But when he fails to feel the expected shaking and vibration of the train, he begins to look more carefully, and can soon see in the environment certain further clues, suggesting that the other train is moving and that he is at rest. Suddenly his mode of perception of the world changes. This is a striking demonstration of how our perceptions of the world are a construction in the "inner show," based on the search for a hypothesis that is compatible with all that we have experienced in connection with a certain situation. So we do not perceive *just* what is before our eyes. We perceive it organized and structured through abstractions of what kind of invariant state of affairs (which may include invariant *states of movement*) will explain immediate experience and a wide range of earlier experiences that led up to it.

Results of the kind described above led Gibson[1] to suggest a new concept of what constitutes perception. He emphasizes the need to drop the idea that perception consists of passively gathering sense impressions, which are organized and structured through principles supplied only by the observer. Indeed, the isolated sense impression is seen to be an extremely high level abstraction, which does not play any significant part in the actual process of perception. Instead, we are sensitive directly to structure of our environment itself. In the last analysis the observer therefore does not *supply* the structure of his perceptions, so much as he *abstracts it*. Or as Gibson himself puts this point, the structure of our environment is the *stimulus* that gives rise to what we perceive (i.e., to the construction in the "inner show" that is presented in our awareness). With regard to optical perception, for example, Gibson points out that through each region of space there passes an infinity of rays of light, going in all directions. These rays of light *implicitly* contain all the information about the structure of the

[1] J. G. Gibson, *American Psychologist*, **15**, 694 (1960).

world that we can obtain from vision.[1] But an eye fixed in a certain position cannot abstract this information. It must move in many ways, and at least some part of these movements must be produced by the observer himself, because (as was first brought out by Held and his co-workers) structural information is abstracted mainly from invariant relationships between the outgoing nervous excitations that give rise to these movements and the corresponding ingoing nervous excitations that result from them.

Gibson raises a related set of questions regarding the role of time in perception. A typical question is, for example; "When does a particular stimulus come to an end?" The older way of looking at this problem is to refer to what is called the "specious present." That is, it is found that there is an interval of time, of the order of a tenth of a second, which is "speciously" experienced as a single moment, in the sense that people do not seem to be able clearly to discriminate changes that take place in times less than this. From this notion it would follow that all our perceptions can in principle be uniquely ordered in time, within an accuracy of a tenth of a second or so. Nevertheless, Gibson raises questions which suggest that it is a source of confusion to try to understand the essential features of the process of perception by referring it in this way to such a time order.

To see why Gibson questions the simple time order of perceptions described above, let us recall that we do not perceive momentary sensations, to any appreciable extent. Rather, we perceive an over-all structure that is abstracted from these, a structure evidently built up over some period of time. We have already seen in connection with optical perception, for example, that clues obtained over some time may come together at a given moment and give rise to a new structure of what is perceived. It evidently makes no sense to say that this new structure is based only on the very last clue to be received. Rather, it is based on the whole set of clues. This means that a given stimulus to our perceptions is not restricted to the smallest time interval that can be discriminated. Rather, it may be said that some stimuli take place over much longer intervals.

In music the property of stimuli is much more clearly seen. As one is

---

[1] The same principle applies to the radio telescope, which is in contact (as it were) with the structure of the whole universe, through a similar set of radio waves.

listening to a tune, the notes heard earlier continue to reverberate in the mind, while each new note comes in. One may suddenly understand (i.e., perceive the over-all structure) of a piece of music at a certain moment in this process. But evidently the very last note to be received is not the sole basis of such an understanding. Rather, it is the whole *structure of* tones reverberating in the mind. These tones have manifold relationships, which are not restricted to their time order. To grasp these relationships is essential to the understanding of the music. The effort to regard the essential content of the music in terms of its time order could then lead to too narrow a way of looking at the problem, which would tend to produce confusion.

In a similar way one can consider the problem of how one perceives rhythm. At any moment there is only one beat to be heard. But one beat is not a rhythm. Evidently it is the reverberation of a whole set of beats in the mind, all in a certain relationship that constitutes the perception of rhythm. The stimulus that constitutes a rhythm cannot then refer only to a single moment of time. So it seems important to realize that the essential features of perception will not always be understood by stringing out what is perceived in a time order.

Indeed, in many cases it is not possible to assign a unique moment of time to a given feature of what is perceived. While listening to a piece of music one may be appreciating a rhythm that is based on many seconds, a theme that may require a minute or more to be apprehended, and we may be looking at a stop-watch, seeing the movements of the hand that perhaps indicates some fraction of a second. When one says "now," what does one mean by this? Does it refer to the perception of a certain position of the indicator on the watch, the perception of a certain part of the rhythm, the perception of some part of the theme, or perhaps to something else?

It would seem then that the effort to order the *totality* of one's perceptions in terms of a single, unique time order must lead to confusion and absurdity. Certain perceptions *can* thus be ordered (e.g., those that are similar to seeing the indicator on the watch dial). But to understand the process of perception in a broader context, we must see that the structures that are perceived are not as rigidly related to such a time order as our customary notions might lead us to think. There is a loose time order, in the sense, for example, that today's perceptions are not strongly related to yesterday's events (although these do in fact still "reverberate" in us and help to shape present perceptions). Yet the hard and fast notion that each perception is uniquely ordered as earlier, later, or simultaneous with another (within the period of the "specious present") seems to lead to a kind of confusion, indicating that it probably has little relevance to the actual facts of perception.

It may perhaps be instructive to consider a simple example of a physical problem in which the attempt to regard the time order of events as basic to the understanding of a process leads to a type of confusion similar to that in which it results when applied to perception. Suppose, for the sake of our discussion, that there were beings on Mars, and that they had become interested in studying the radio signals coming from the Earth. When they came to observe television signals they would not be able to make a great deal of sense of them, if they supposed that the essential principle of these signals were some kind of formula or set of relationships determining their *time order*. The signals can in fact be understood properly only when it is realized that they originate in a series of *whole pictures*, which are then translated systematically into a time series of pulses. The principles governing the actual order of pulses are therefore to be grasped in terms of a spatial structure very different from that of the time order that is received in the radio signals. Or, to put it differently, *the order of the signals is not essentially related to the order of time.* In a similar way, the structure of our perceptual process may also not be essentially related to some hypothetical series of instants, but may be based on entirely different kinds of principles involving (like the television signal) the integration of what is received over suitable intervals of time, extending far beyond the period of the "specious present."

If a given perception integrates what comes in over such extended periods of time, does this mean that *memory* is the main factor that determines the general structure of what we perceive? (Memory being the ability, for example, to recall approximately the sensations, events, objects, etc., that were experienced in the past.) Gibson does not accept the notion that the structure in our perceptions comes *mainly* from memory, although of course memories do evidently have *some* influence in shaping such perceptions. He suggests that the main process is what he calls "attunement" to what one perceives. Thus, as one sees something new and unfamiliar he first vaguely perceives only a few *general* structural features. Then as he moves in relation to what he is looking at and perhaps probes as well, he starts to abstract more of the details of the structure, and his perceptions sharpen. Perhaps one could compare this process to a kind of skill, which is also not based simply on memory of all the steps by which the skill was acquired.

Both in the case of perception and in that of building a skill, a person must actively meet his environment in such a way that he coordinates his outgoing nervous impulses with those that are coming in. As a result the structure of his environment is, as it were, gradually incorporated into his outgoing impulses, so that he learns how to meet his environment with the right kind of response. With regard to learning a skill it is evident how this happens. But in a sense the perception of each kind of thing is also a skill, because it requires a person actively to meet the environment with the movements that are appropriate for the disclosure of the structure of that environment. (This fact would also be evident if it were not for our habitual notion that perception is a purely passive affair.)

If we learn the structure of things by "attunement" it seems clear that the very general features of our ability to apprehend the structure of the world will, in many cases, go back to what was learned in early childhood. It is here that the studies of the process of perception can link up with the work of Piaget, discussed in the previous section. For there we saw how the infant begins with a limited set of inborn reflexes. When these are developed into the "circular reflex" he has the most basic feature of perception, i.e., the ability to be sensitive to a relationship between outgoing and incoming nervous impulses, a relationship that is characteristic of what is to be perceived. From here on he is able to "attune" himself step by step with his environment, by abstracting from such relationships what is invariant in its general structure. In doing this he builds up his notions of space, time, causality, the division of the world into permanent objects (one of which is himself), the notion of permanent substance, permanent numbers of objects, etc., etc. All of these notions are interwoven into the fabric of perception, in the sense that they help shape the structure of what appears in the "inner show" that is present in our awareness. So while we are able to "attune" ourselves to new kinds of structures when we meet something new, there seem to be certain general structural features, of the kind described above, which were first learned in childhood, and which are present in all that we perceive.

The over-all or general structure of our total perceptual process can be regarded not only from the standpoint of its development from infancy but can also be investigated directly in the adult. Such studies have been made by Hebb and his group,[1] by isolating individuals in environments in which there was little or nothing to be perceived. The extreme cases of such isolation involved putting people in tanks of water at a comfortable temperature, with nothing to be seen or heard, and with hands covered in such a way that nothing could be felt. Those individuals who were hardy enough to volunteer for such treatment found that after a while the structure of the perceptual field began to change. Hallucinations and other self-induced perceptions, as well as distortions of awareness of time, became more and more frequent. Finally, when these people emerged from isolation, it was found that they had undergone a considerable degree of general disorientation, not only in their emotions but also in their ability to perceive. For example, they often found themselves unable to see the shapes of objects clearly, or even to see their forms as fixed. They saw changing colors which were not there, etc. etc. (In time, normal perception was, of course, regained.)

The results of these experiments were rather difficult to understand in detail, but their over-all implication was that the general structural "attunements," built into the brain since early childhood, tend to disintegrate when there is no appropriately structured environment for them to work on. If we compare these attunements to some kinds of skills, needed in meeting our typical environment, then perhaps it is not entirely unexpected that they should decay when they are not used. But what is still surprising is the extremely great speed with which such "skills" built up over a lifetime can deteriorate. To explain this it has been proposed that when there is no external environment for the brain to work on it starts to operate on the internal environment, i.e., on the impulses produced spontaneously on the nervous system itself. But these impulses do not seem actually to have a well-defined structure that is comprehensible to us. So in the active effort to "attune" to a structure that is either nonexistent or else incomprehensible to the people who actually did the experiment, the older adjustments, built up over a lifetime, are mixed up and broken down.

[1] See survey by R. Held and S. J. Freedmon, *Science*, **142**, 455 (1963); also the Symposium on Sensory Deprivation, *The Journal of Nervous and Mental Diseases*, No. 1, January 1961.

The above hypothesis has to some extent been confirmed by experiments in which people looked for a long time at a television screen containing a changing random (unstructured) pattern of spots. A disorientation of perception resulted which was similar to that obtained in the experiments in which subjects were isolated. Thus it could be argued that in the effort to adjust to a nonexistent or incomprehensible structure in its general environment, the brain began to break down the older structural "attunement" that was appropriate to the normal environment in which people generally live.

The implications of these experiments are so far reaching as to be rather disturbing. Nevertheless, it can be seen that, on the whole, they tend to carry further what is already suggested in the work of Piaget and in the results that have been summarized in this section. For in all of this we have seen that in perception there is present an outgoing nervous impulse producing a movement, in response to which there is a coordinated incoming set of sensations. The ability to abstract an invariant relationship in these nervous impulses seems to be what is at the basis of intelligent perception. For the structure that is present in the "inner show" is determined by the need to account for what is invariant in the relationship of the outgoing movements and the incoming sensations. In this way the percipient is not only always learning about his environment but is also *changing himself*. That is, some reflection of the general structure of his environment is being built into his nervous system. As long as his general environment is not too different in structure from what has already thus been built into his nervous system he can make adjustments by "attuning" to the new features of the environment. But in an environment without such a perceptible structure, it seems that there is a tendency for this attunement to be lost, in the search for a structure which either does not exist or which has features that are beyond the ability of the percipient to grasp if it does exist.

These results lead us back to the old question first formulated by Kant, as to whether our general mode of apprehending the world as ordered and structured in space and time and through causal relationships, etc., is objectively inherent in the nature of the world, or whether it is *imposed* by our own minds. Kant proposed that these general principles constituted a kind of *a priori* knowledge, built into the mind, which was a necessary precondition for any recognizable experience at all, but which may not be a characteristic of "things in themselves." It would seem that Kant's proposal was right in some respects but basically wrong in that he had considered the problem in too narrow a framework. It is certainly true that at any given moment we meet new experience with a particular structural "attunement" in the brain that is a necessary condition for perception of recognizable aspects of the world. This "attunement" is responsible for our ability to see a more or less fixed set of things at each moment, organized in space, causally related, changing in a simply ordered time sequence, etc. When this "attunement" is broken down by long isolation from perception or by perception of an environment without visible structure, then the experiments cited above do indeed show that the process of recognizable experiencing of an environment is seriously interfered with.

On the other hand, a broader view of this problem shows that an adult's attunement to the general structure of the world has been built up in a development, starting with infancy. In the beginning of this development the child must *discover* the structure of his environment in a long process in which he *experiments* with it, operates on it, etc. His procedure in doing this is perhaps not basically different from that used in scientific research. He is *interested* in his environment, probing it, testing it, observing it, etc., and, as it were, always developing new perceptual "hypotheses" in the "inner show" that explain his experiences better. In doing this he is "attuning" himself to his environment, developing the right responses to perceive its structure adequately. As he gets older this whole process tends to fall into the domain of habit. But whenever he meets something strange and unexpected, he is able to abstract new structural features, by a continuation of the kind of interested experimentation and observation that is characteristic of early childhood.

Of course, a person finds it hard to change *very general* structural features, such as the organization of all experience in terms of space, time, causality, etc. Yet the experiments cited above suggest that there seems to be no inherent need to continue any particular structure, and that the brain probably is capable of abstracting a very wide variety of kinds of structural features that may be actually present in the part of the environment that is available to his senses, provided that there is appropriate interest, leading to the proper kind of experimentation, probing, etc. At any given moment the structure that we already know depends on past experiences, habits, etc.; this in turn is dictated in part by the general environment that people have actually lived in, and in part by the interests that determine to which structural features people will have payed a great deal of attention. So we do in fact approach new experiences, as Kant suggested, with some kind of already given general structural principles. Yet the experiments cited here suggest that Kant was wrong in regarding any particular set of principles of this kind as *inevitably* following *a priori* from the very nature of the human mind. Rather, along the lines suggested by Gibson, it would seem that a person might become "attuned" to any structural features of his environment to which his nervous system could respond, and in which he was sufficiently interested.

In terms of the notions described above we can see that while our perceptions do have a subjective side, dependent on the particular background and conditioning of each person, as well as on the general background and conditioning of the whole of humanity, they also have a kind of objective content, which can go beyond this particular and limited background. For the *general* structure of our perceptions (resulting from this background) can be regarded as a kind of *hypothesis*, with the aid of which we approach subsequent experiences in which things have changed not only of their own accord, but also because of our own movements, actions, and probings, which alter our own relationships to our environments. To the extent that the new experiences fit into the continuation of the old structure without contradictions, these hypotheses are effectively confirmed. But if we are alert, we will sense contradictions which they arise (as we have already seen, in numerous examples discussed earlier). When this happens the brain is sensitive to the discovery of new relationships, leading spontaneously to further hypotheses, which are embodied in the appearance of new structures in the "inner show." Anyone can see this happening as he approaches a distant object that is unknown to him, or as he approaches something unknown in the obscure light, for example, of the moon. He will see various forms, shapes, objects, etc., which appear and then disappear, because they are not compatible with further experiences resulting from his movements, probings, etc. So there is a continual process of "trial and error" in which what is shown to be false is continually being set aside, while new structures are continually being put forth for "criticism." Eventually there develops in this way a perception which stands up to further movements, probings, etc., in the sense that its predictive implications are actually borne out in such experiences. (Of course, even this is always tentative, in the sense that it can be contradicted later.)

The objective content of our perceptions is then implicit in the process of falsification and confirmation described above. Indeed, the very fact that our vision of the world can be falsified as a result of further movement, observation, probing, etc., implies that there is more in the world than what we have perceived and known. That is to say, we do not actually create the world. In fact, we only create an "inner show" of the world in response to our movements and sensations. It is, however, the possibility of confirmation of the "inner show" which demonstrates that there is more in it than merely a summary of past experiences. For this "inner show" is based on the abstraction of the *general structure* of these past experiences, the structure having predictive inferences for later experiences. For example, as we approach the front of an object such as a house, we (largely unconsciously) predict a great many structural features of the parts of the object that are not yet visible. Thus, on seeing the front and one side of the house, along with parts of its roof, we infer that it has other sides, that these have certain parallel lines, certain angles, etc. These inferences may come *partially* from memory, having gone round similar houses previously. But in large part they come, not from the simple recall of earlier experiences themselves, but from the general structural principles that have been abstracted from a very wide range of such experiences (e.g., the three dimensionality of space, the existence of straight lines, parallel lines, and right angles, all of which together imply a certain general field of possibilities for the unseen sides of an object, independent of the particular memories of similar objects that we may possess).

A little reflection shows that there is an enormous number of cases in which the above-described kinds of predictive inferences based on the general structure of our perceptions have turned out to be correct. That is to say, the "world" that we see in immediate perception has, at a given moment, a *general* structure, which has withstood a long series of tests, in the observations that have led up to the moment in question. And as a rule it happens that the natural projection of this structure in accordance with the known state of movement of the observer and of what is in the field of perception will continue to be more or less in accord with later observations in a great many respects. This means that the general structure of our perceptions has a certain similarity to the general structure of what is actually in our environment. Yet, the similarity is not perfect, as is evidenced by the appearance of contradictions, unexpected events, etc., which necessitate continual changes in what is "constructed" in the field of perception, and are not merely the result of the natural projection from what was perceived earlier. In this way we are continually being confronted with what is not even implicitly contained in our earlier perceptions, thus we are being reminded that there is a reality beyond what we have already perceived, aspects of which are always in the process of being revealed in our further perceptions.

A-4. THE SIMILARITY BETWEEN THE PROCESS OF PERCEPTION AND THE PROCESS BY WHICH SCIENCE INVESTIGATES THE WORLD

In the previous sections of this Appendix we have discussed studies of the development of the process of perception in an individual human being from infancy, as well as direct studies of how this process takes place in adults. What comes out of these studies can be summed up in the statement that in the process of perception we learn about the world mainly by being sensitive to what is invariant in the relationships between our own movements, activities, probings, etc., and the resulting changes in what comes in through our sense organs. These invariant relationships are then presented immediately in our awareness as a kind of "construction" in an "inner show," embodying, in effect, a hypothesis that accounts for the invariant features that have been found in such experiences up to the moment in question. This hypothesis is, however, tentative in the sense that it will be replaced by another one, if in our subsequent movements, probings, etc., we encounter contradictions with the implications of our "constructions."

Throughout this book, however, we have seen that research in physics has shown basic features very similar to those of perception described above, and that with the further development of physics, into its more modern forms (in particular, with the theory of relativity), this similarity has tended to become stronger. Thus, those aspects of Newtonian mechanics which eventually proved to be correct consisted of the discovery of the invariance of certain relationships (Newton's laws of motion), in a wide variety of systems, movements, changes of frames of reference, etc. On the other hand, those features of the theory which were considered to represent absolutes (i.e., absolute space, absolute time, the notion of permanent substances with fixed masses, etc.) were eventually shown to be unnecessary, and indeed important sources of confusion and error, in the effort to extend scientific knowledge of the laws of movement into broader domains. Einstein's major steps were based on setting aside such ideas of an absolute, and on extending into broader domains the notion of the laws of physics as invariant relationships (e.g., so as to include velocities comparable to that of light). In doing this he was led also to drop the notion of fixed quantities of substances, having constant masses. Instead, mass was seen to be only a relatively invariant property, expressing a relationship between energy of a body and its inertial resistance to acceleration, along with its gravitational properties. Further developments in modern physics, including quantum theory and the studies of the transformations of the so-called "elementary" particles (as discussed in Chapter 23) suggest that the notion of permanent entities constituted of substances with unchanging qualitative and quantitative properties may have to be dropped altogether, and that physics will be left with nothing but the study of what is relatively invariant in as wide as possible a variety of movements, transformations of coordinates, changes of perspective, etc.

Moreover (as we saw in Chapter 24), it seems that the notion that science is collecting absolute truths about nature, or even approaching such truths in a convergent fashion, is not in good accord with the facts concerning the actual development of scientific theories thus far, and has indeed also been a major source of confusion in scientific research. Rather, as Professor Popper has emphasized, science actually progresses through the putting forth of falsifiable hypotheses, which are confirmed up to a certain point and thereafter, as a rule, eventually falsified. New hypotheses are then put forth, which are criticized and tested by a process of "trial and error" very similar to that to which our immediate perceptions are continually being subjected.

The interesting point that has emerged from a simultaneous consideration of what has developed in modern science and of what has been disclosed in modern studies of the process of perception is that the new ideas required to understand the both of them are rather similar. In this section we shall give some arguments in favor of the suggestion that this similarity is not accidental but rather has a deep reason behind it. The reason that we are proposing is that scientific investigation is basically a mode of extending our *perception* of the world, and not mainly a mode of obtaining *knowledge* about it. That is to say, while science does involve a search for knowledge, the essential role of this knowledge is that it is an adjunct to an extended perceptual process. And if science is basically such a mode of perception, then, as we shall try to show, it is quite reasonable that certain essential features of scientific research shall be rather similar to corresponding features of immediate perception.[1]

Since science has generally been regarded thus far as *basically* a search for knowledge, it will be necessary to begin by going more deeply into the question of the relationship between knowledge and immediate perception. Now, as we have seen, what appears in immediate perception already embodies a kind of abstraction of the general structure of what has been found to be invariant in an earlier active process of probing the environment that has led up to the perception in question. We propose that knowledge is a *higher-level abstraction*, based on what is found to be invariant in a wide range of experiences involving immediate perception.

We can perhaps explain this notion most directly by first referring to Piaget's account of the development of the child's concept of space (discussed in Section A-2). At first the child discovers a group of operations, such that he can go from one place to another by a certain route, and return invariantly to the same place by a wide range of different routes. Later the child is able to *imagine* (i.e., to produce a mental image) of a space, containing even objects that are no longer in his field of immediate perception, and also an imagined object that corresponds to *himself*. The structure of this mental image faithfully corresponds to what has been found by the child to be invariant in his earlier experiences with groups of movements. This mental image therefore *abstracts* a kind of "higher-order invariant," i.e., something

---

[1] The similarity between scientific research and perception has already been noted by several authors. See N. H. Hanson, *Patterns of Discovery*, Cambridge University Press, New York, 1958, and T. Kuhn, *The Nature of Scientific Revolutions*, University of Chicago Press, Chicago 1963.

that has been invariant in a wide range of immediate perceptions. When we use the words "to abstract" we do not wish to suggest that there is merely a process of induction, or of taking out some kind of summation of what has been experienced earlier. Rather, each abstraction constitutes, as it were, a kind of "hypothesis," put forth to explain what has been found to be invariant in such earlier experiences. Only the abstractions which stand up to further tests and probings will be retained. Eventually, however, these become habitual, and we cease to be aware of their basically hypothetical and tentative character, regarding them instead as inherent and necessary features of all that exists, in every possible domain and field of experiencing and investigation.

Piaget then goes on to describe how with the development of language and logical thinking the child goes on to make still higher level abstractions, in which there are formed structures of words, ideas, concepts, etc., which express the invariant features of the world that he abstractly considers in his perceptions. Evidently there is in principle no limit to this process of abstraction. Thus science and mathematics may be said to form still higher level abstractions (formulated in words, diagrams, and mathematical symbols), expressing the invariant features of what has been found in experiments and observations (which latter are carried out in terms of the ordinary abstractions of everyday language and common sense). Thus all knowledge is a structure of abstractions, the ultimate test of the validity of which is, however, in the process of coming into contact with the world that takes place in immediate perception.

It can be seen that a crucial state in this over-all process of abstraction is the setting aside of certain parts of what appears in the "inner show" as not *directly* representing immediate perception. These are what we *imagine*, conceive, symbolize, think about, etc. These parts are then seen to be related to immediate perception as abstractions, representing the general structural features of this perception, much as a map represents the terrain of which it is a map.[1] However, as has been pointed out in Section A–2, a young child does not readily distinguish between what has been imagined and what is seen in response to immediate perception. In this way, there arises the habit of confusing our abstract conceptual "maps" with reality itself, and of not noticing that

[1] See also Chapter 29, where a similar role has been suggested for the Minkowski diagram in physics.

they are only maps. When the child grows older he is able to avoid this confusion in superficial problems, but when it comes to fundamental concepts, such as space, time, causality, etc., it is much more difficult to do so. As a result, the adult continues the habit of looking, as it were, at his comparatively abstract conceptual maps, and seeing them as if they were inherent in the nature of things, rather than understanding that they are higher-level abstractions, having only a kind of structural similarity to what has been found to be invariant in lower levels. It is this confusion, based on habits of very long standing, which makes a clear discussion of such fundamental problems so difficult.

We can perhaps best illustrate these notions with the aid of a simple example. Suppose that we are looking at a circular disk. Now its immediate appearance to our eyes will be that of an ellipse, corresponding to its projection on the retina of the eyes (as would, for example, be portrayed by an artist, who was trying to draw it in perspective). Nevertheless, we *know* that it is really a circle. What is the basis of this knowledge?

What actually happens is, as we have indicated earlier, that the eye, the head, the body, etc., are always moving. In these movements the appearance of the disk is always changing, undergoing in fact a series of *projective transformations* that are related in a definite way to the movements in question. By various means (some of which are discussed in Section A–3) the brain is able to abstract what is invariant in all this movement, change of perspective, etc. This abstraction, expressed in terms of the notion that a circular object accounts for all the changing views of it, is the basis of the "construction" of it that we perceive in the "inner show." The "hypothesis" that this object is really a circle is then further probed and tested in subsequent ways of coming in contact with it perceptually, and it is retained as long as it stands up to such probing and testing.

But the realization that the perceived object is a circle depends also on knowledge going beyond the level of immediate perception. Thus from early childhood a person has learned to *imagine* looking straight at the object in a perpendicular direction, and seeing its circular shape (as well as feeling it to be circular when his hands grasp it). He may also have learned further to imagine himself represented as a point on a diagram, and to follow the course of the light rays from the circle to his point of perspective, thus being able to see how the circular shape is transformed into an elliptical appearance. If he has been further educated, he can go to a still higher level of abstraction, by mathematically calculating the correct shape of the disk, from a knowledge of its appearance in several views and from a knowledge of the relationship of the observer to the disk in all of these views (distance, etc.). In carrying out this calculation he will do consciously on a higher level of abstraction what his brain does spontaneously on a lower level, i.e., to find a single structure that accounts for what is invariant in our changing relationships with the object under discussion.

We see then that there is no *sharp* break between the abstractions of immediate perception and those which constitute our knowledge, even if we carry this knowledge to the highest levels reached by science and mathematics. From the very first, our immediate perceptions express a "construction" in an "inner show," based on a preconscious abstraction of what is invariant in, or active process of coming into contact with, our environment. Each higher level of abstraction repeats a similar process of discovery of what is invariant in lower levels, which is then represented in the form of a picture, an image, a symbolic structure of words and formulas, etc. These higher-level abstractions then contribute to shaping the general structure of those at lower levels, even coming down to that of immediate perception. So between all the levels of abstraction there is a continual two-way interaction.

Consider, for example, the experience of looking out at the night sky. Ancient man abstracted from the stars the patterns of animals, men, and gods, and thereafter was unable to look at the sky without seeing such entities in it. Modern man knows that what is really behind this view is an immeasurable universe of stars, galaxies, galaxies of galaxies, etc., and that each person, having a particular place in this universe, obtains a certain perspective on it, which is what is seen in the night sky. Such a man does not see animals, gods, etc., in the sky, but he sees an immense universe there. But even the view of modern science is probably true only in a certain domain. So future man may form a very different notion of the invariant totality that is behind our view of the night sky, in which present notions will perhaps be seen as a simplification, approximation, and limiting case, but actually very far from being completely true. Can we not say then that at every stage man was extending his perception of the night sky, going from one level of abstraction to another, and in each stage thus being led to hypotheses on what is invariant, which are able to stand up better to further tests, probings, etc.? But if this is the case, then the most abstract and general scientific investigations are natural extensions of the very same process by which the young child learns to come into perceptual contact with his environment.

As we have pointed out on several occasions (e.g., in the discussion of Piaget's work in Section A-2 and of the perception of movement in Section A-3) one of the basic problems that has to be solved in every act of perception is that of taking into account the special point of view and perspective of the observer. The solution of this problem depends essentially on the use of a number of levels of abstraction, all properly related to each other. Thus a person not only perceives the immediate elliptical appearance of the disk in front of him. He can also perceive the changes in appearance of the disk, which result from certain movements which he himself actively undertakes. From these changes his brain is able to abstract information about his relationship to the disk (e.g., how far away it is). The essential point here is that through many levels of abstraction, all going on simultaneously in the mind, it is possible to perceive not only a projection of the object of interest but also the relationship of the observer to the object in question. From this it is always possible in principle to obtain an invariant notion as to what is actually going on. This is represented in a higher level of abstraction, for example, by *imagining* space containing the disk and the observer himself, in which both are represented in their proper relationships. When a person says that the object is *really* circular, he is then evidently not referring to an immediate sensation of the shape of the object but to this extended process of abstraction, the essential results of which are represented in this imagined space, containing both the object and himself.

A very similar problem arises in science. Here, the hands, body, and sense organs of the observer are generally, in effect, extended by means of suitable instruments, which are in *certain ways* more sensitive, more powerful, more accurate, as well as capable of new modes of making contact with the world. But in the essential point that the observer is *actively* probing and testing his environment, the situation is very similar to what it is in immediate perception, unaided by such instruments.

In such tests there is always some observable response to this probing and testing; and it is the relationship of variations in this response to known variations in the state of the instruments that constitutes the relevant information in what is observed (just as happens directly with the sense organs themselves).

As in the case of immediate perception, however, such an observation has very little significance until one knows the relationship of the instrument to the field that is under observation. It is possible to know this relationship with the aid of a series of abstractions. Thus in any experiment one not only knows the observed result; one knows the structure of the instrument, its mode of functioning, etc., all of which has been found out with the aid of earlier observations and actions of many kinds. In other words, in each process of observation there is always implicit an observation of the observing instrument itself, carried out in terms of different levels of conceptual abstractions. But to *understand* the observation one always needs certain modes of thinking about the problem, in which the instrument and what is observed are represented together, so that one can see "a total picture" in which an invariant field of what is being studied stands in a certain relationship to the instrument, this relationship determining, as it were, how what is in the field "projects" into some observable response of the instrument.

In Chapter 29 we have already called attention to a special case of the problem discussed above. Thus, in the theory of relativity one uses the Minkowski diagram, in which one can in principle represent all the events that happen in the whole of space-time. However, each example of such a diagram must contain a line corresponding to the world line of the observer whose results are under discussion. This is usually represented by the axis of the diagram. Then, if we wish to discuss the results of another observer, we must include in the diagram a representation of *his* world line. In a similar way we must choose a point to represent the place and time which determine the perspective of a given observation. By taking all of this into account we are able, from the response of the observing instruments (which is *relative* to their speed, time and place of functioning, etc.), to calculate the invariant properties of what is observed, in such a way that the different results of different observers are explained by their differing *relationships* to the process under investigation. It can be seen then that relativity theory approaches the universe in a way very similar to that in which a person approaches his environment in immediate perception. In both these fields all that is observed is based on the abstraction of what is invariant as seen in various movements, from various points of view, perspectives, frames of reference, etc. And in both the invariant is finally understood with the aid of various hypotheses, expressed in terms of higher levels of abstraction, which serve as a kind of "map," having an order, pattern, and structure similar to that of what is being observed.

The tendency for the use of such maps to become habitual is also common to scientific investigation and to immediate perception. When this happens a person's thinking is limited to what can fit into such maps, because he thinks that they contain all that can possibly happen, in every condition and domain of experience. For example, the common-sense notion of simultaneity of all that is co-present in our immediate perceptions is abstracted into the Newtonian concept of absolute time, with the result that it seems incomprehensible that two twins who are accelerated in different ways and then meet may experience different amounts of time (see Chapter 28). But in Section A–3, we saw that the notion of a single unique time order does not seem to apply without confusion in the field of our immediate perceptions either. The main reason that this has been so little noticed is probably our habit of taking seriously only what fits into our habitual perception of all that happens, both inwardly and outwardly, as being in such a unique and universal time order.

It may be remarked in passing that in the quantum theory the point of view described above is carried even further. The reason is basically the indivisibility of the quantum of action, which implies that when we observe something very precisely at the atomic level, it is found that there must be an irreducible disturbance of the observed system by the quanta needed for such an observation (the fact behind the derivation of Heisenberg's famous uncertainty principle). On the large-scale level the effects of these quanta can be neglected. Therefore, although the observer must engage in active movements and probings in order to perceive anything whatsoever, he can in principle (at least in large-scale optical perception) refrain from significantly disturbing what he is looking at. At the quantum level of accuracy, however, the situation is different. Here, the light quanta may be compared to a blind man's fingers, which can give information about an object only if they move and disturb the latter. The blind man is nevertheless able to abstract certain invariant properties of the object (e.g., size and shape), but in doing this, his brain spontaneously *takes into account* the movement which his perceptual operations impart to the object. Similarly, the physicist is still able to abstract certain invariant properties of atoms, electrons, protons, etc. (e.g., charge, mass, spin, etc.); but in so doing he must consciously take into account the *operations* involved in his observation process in a similar way. (To discuss this point in detail is, of course, beyond the scope of the present work; but these questions will be treated in subsequent publications.)

A-5. THE ROLE OF PERCEPTION IN SCIENTIFIC RESEARCH

In the previous discussion we have seen the close similarity between our modes of immediate perception of the world and our modes of approach to it in modern scientific investigations. We shall now go on to consider directly the centrally perceptual character of scientific research, which we suggested at the beginning of Section A-4.

While man's scientific instruments do constitute, as we have seen, an effective extension of his body and his sense organs, there are no comparable *external* structures that substitute for the *inward* side of the perceptive process (in which the invariant features of what has been experienced are presented in the "inner show"). Thus, it is up to the *scientist himself* to be aware of contradictions between his hypotheses and what he observes, to be sensitive to new relationships in what he observes, and to put forth conjectures or hypotheses, which explain the known facts, embodying these new relationships, and have additional implications with regard to what is as yet unknown, so that they can be tested in further experiments and observations. So there is always finally a stage where an *essentially perceptual process* is needed in scientific research—a process taking place within the scientist himself.

The importance of the perceptual stage tends to be underemphasized, however, because scientists pay attention mostly to the next stage, in which hypotheses that have withstood a number of tests are incorporated into the body of currently accepted scientific knowledge. In effect they are thus led to suppose the essential activity of the scientist is as the *accumulation of verified knowledge*, toward which goal all other activities of the scientist are ultimately directed.

If such knowledge could constitute a set of absolute truths, then it would make at least some kind of sense to regard its accumulation as the main purpose of science. As we have seen, however, it is the fate of all theories eventually to be falsified, so that they are relative truths, adequate in certain domains, including what has already been observed, along with some as yet further unknown region that can be delimited, to some extent at least, in future experiments and observations. But if this is the case then the accumulation of knowledge cannot be regarded as the *essential* purpose of scientific research, simply because the validity of all knowledge is relative to something that is not in the knowledge itself. So one will not be able to see what scientific research is really about without taking into account what it is to which even established and well-tested scientific knowledge must continually be further related, if we are to be able to discuss its (necessarily incompletely known) domain of validity.

There is also a similar relative validity of the knowledge that we gain in immediate perception. But in this field the reason for this is fairly evident. Indeed, the world is so vast and has so much that is unknown within it that we are not tempted to suppose that what we learn from immediate perception is a set of absolute truths, the implications of which could be expected to be valid in unlimited domains of future experience. Rather, we realize that immediate perception is actually a means of remaining in a kind of contact with a certain segment of the world, in such a way that we can be aware of the general structure of that segment, from moment to moment, if we carry out the process of perception properly. In this contact we are satisfied if we are able to keep up with what we see and perhaps, in some respects, get a little ahead of it (e.g., in driving an automobile, we can, to a certain extent, anticipate the movements of other automobiles, people, the turns in the road, etc.). Thus, in the process of immediate perception, one obtains a kind of knowledge, the *implications* of which are valid in the moment of contact and for some unpredictable period beyond this moment. The major significance of past knowledge of this kind is then in its *implications* for present and future perceptions, rather than in the accumulation of a store of truths, considered to be absolute.

Thus our knowledge of what happened yesterday is *in itself* of little significance because yesterday is gone and will never return. This knowledge will be significant, however, to the extent that its implications and the inferences that can be drawn from it may be valid today or at some later date.

Of course, scientific theories evidently have much broader domains of validity of their predictive inferences than do the "hypotheses" that arise in immediate perception (these broader domains being purchased, however, at the expense of the need to operate only at very high levels of abstraction). Because the domain of validity is so broad, it often takes a long time to demonstrate its limits. Nevertheless, what happens in scientific research is, in regard to the problem under discussion, not *fundamentally* different from what happens in immediate perception. For in science too the totality of the universe is too much to be grasped definitively in *any* form of knowledge, not only because it is so vast and immeasurable, but even more because in its many levels, domains, and aspects it contains an inexhaustible variety of structures, which escape any given conceptual "net" that we may use in trying to express their order and pattern. Therefore, as in the field of immediate perception, our knowledge is adequate for an original domain of contact with the world, extending in an unpredictable way into some further domains. Since the goal of obtaining absolutely valid knowledge has no relevance in such a situation, we are led to suggest that scientific research is basically to be regarded as a mode of extending man's perceptual contact with the world, and that the main significance of scientific *knowledge* is (as happens in immediate perception) that it is an adjunct to this process.

The basically perceptual character of scientific research shows up most strongly when the time comes to *understand* new facts, as distinct from merely accumulating further knowledge. Everyone has experienced such a process on various occasions in his life. Suppose something unfamiliar is being explained (e.g., a theorem in geometry). At first a person is able to take in only various bits of knowledge, the relationship of which is not yet clear. But at a certain stage, in a very rapid process often described as "click" or as a "flash," he *understands* what is being explained. When this happens he says "I see," indicating the basically *perceptual* character of such a process. (Of course, he does not see with optical vision but rather, as it were, with the "mind's eye.") But what is it that he sees? What he perceives is a new total structure in terms of which the older items of knowledge all fall into their proper places, naturally related, while many new and unsuspected relationships suddenly come into view. Later, to preserve this understanding, to communicate it to other people, to apply it, or to test its validity, he may translate it into words, formulas, diagrams, etc. But initially it seems to be a single *act*, in which older structures are set aside and a new structure comes into being in the mind.

When the need arises to develop new theories, the basically new step is generally an act or a series of acts of understanding. Previous to such understanding, scientists are facing a set of problems, to which the older theories give rise, when applied in new domains. This process eventually leads to an awareness of contradictions, confusions, and ambiguities in the older theories, when applied in the new problems. Then if the scientist is ready to set aside older notions his mind may become sensitive to new relationships in terms of which facts, both old and new, may be seen. Out of this sensitivity develops a new understanding, i.e., the expression of the old facts in terms of a new structure, having further implications going beyond those of the older points of view.

Of course, we must not suppose that all such acts of understanding lead immediately to correct theories. Far from it, many of them are found to be incapable of solving the basic problems under consideration. Hence each such understanding must be tested to see what the domain of validity actually is. To do this, it is necessary logically to work out the implications of the new structure of ideas that has emerged into the mind. Nevertheless, as important as these latter steps are, they all depend on the essentially creative acts of understanding, without which science would eventually either stop developing or else stagnate in a bounded domain that never went beyond some limited circle of ideas.

There seems to be no limit to the possibility of the human mind for developing new structures in the way described above. And it is this possibility that seems to be behind our ability to put forth new theories and concepts, which lead to knowledge that goes beyond the facts that are accessible at the time when the theories are first developed. It should be recalled that this possibility exists as much in immediate perception as in scientific research, since very often what is constructed in the "inner show" leads, as we have seen earlier, to many correct predictive inferences for future perceptions. It is evident that such an ability cannot be due merely to some sort of mechanism that randomly puts forth "hypotheses" until one of them is confirmed. Rather, for reasons that are as yet not known, the human mind in its general process of perception, whether on the immediate level or on the highest level involved in understanding, can create structures that have *if we sweep the Twin Paradox under the rug.*

a remarkably good chance of being correct in domains going beyond that on which the evidence for them is founded. On the basis of this possibility, the process of "trial and error" can efficiently weed out those structures that are inappropriate. At the same time it can help provide material, the criticism of which leads to a fresh act of understanding or perception, in which yet newer structures are put forth which are generally likely to have a broader domain of validity and better correspondence to the facts than the earlier ones had.

To sum up, the essential point is that through perception we are always in a process of coming into contact with the world, in such a way that we can be aware of the general structure of the segment with which we have been in contact. Science may then be regarded as a means of establishing new kinds of contacts with the world, in new domains, in new levels, with the aid of different instruments, etc. But these contacts would mean very little without the act of understanding, which corresponds on a very high level to that process by which what has been invariant is presented in terms of structure in the "inner show" of immediate perception. It need then no longer be puzzling that science does not lead to knowledge of an absolute truth. For the knowledge supplied by science is (like all other knowledge) basically an expression of the structure that has been revealed in our process of coming from moment to moment into contact with a world the totality of which is beyond our ability to grasp in terms of any given sets of percepts, ideas, concepts, notions, etc. Nevertheless, we can obtain a fairly good grasp of that with which we have thus far been in contact, which is also valid in some domain, either large or small, beyond what is based on this contact. By remaining alert to contradictions and sensitive to new relationships, thus permitting the growth of a fresh understanding, we can keep up with our contact with the world, and in some ways we can anticipate what is coming later.

In science this process takes place at a very high level of abstraction, on a scale of time involving years. In immediate perception it occurs on a lower level of abstraction, and it is very rapid. In science the process depends strongly on collective work, involving contributions of many people, and in immediate perception it is largely individual. But fundamentally both can be regarded as limiting cases of one over-all process, of a generalized kind of perception, in which no absolute knowledge is to be encountered.

INDEX

Aberration of light, 18
Absolute time and space, 48–49
  (*see also* Time)
Absolute truth (*see* Truth)
Abstraction in perception,
  219–223
Addition of velocities, Galilean
  law, 66
  relativistic law, 67
Annihilation and creation of
  particles, 111
Aristotle, doctrines of, 4
  principles of, 5
Atomic constitution of matter and
  the ether (*see* Ether)
Atomic theory, 111

Causality
  compatible with relativity, 156
  definition of, 155–156
  impossible with signals faster
    than light, 156–166
  irrelevant for events in absolute
    elsewhere, 159
Chronological order, 50
Clock rates, relativity of, 59–60

Clock rates according to
  Lorentz transformation
  (*see* Lorentz)
Conception of mass, origin of
  (*see* Mass)
Concepts as maps expressing
  relative invariance, 195
Conservation
  of energy, 82, 92, 100
  of mass, 82, 100
  of matter, concept of, 195
  of momentum, 82
  of number of objects, concept
    of, 193–196
Contraction according to
  Lorentz transformation,
  (*see* Lorentz)
Coordinates, relational notion of,
  48–51
Copernican theory, 6

Decay of mesons as natural clocks,
  76–77 (*see also* Time)
Ditchburn, 198–199
Domains of truth of theories
  (*see* Theories)

Doppler shift of light emitted by
    a moving body, 77–80
  relativistic, 80
Double star observations, 20

Effective mass of radiant energy
    (see Mass)
Einstein
  basic hypothesis of, 55
  point of departure for theories
    of, 54–55
  railway train experiment, 55–57
Electrical forces as states of
    stress and strain in the ether
    (see Ether)
Elementary particles, structure of,
    119–120
Energy
  conservation in a collection of
    bodies, 92, 100
  deduction of relativistic
    formula, 84–90
  equivalence with mass, 91, 93,
    108, 110
  of inward and outward move-
    ment, 116
  kinetic, 92
  rest, 92
  transformations, 115
Equivalence of mass and energy
    (see Mass and Energy)
Ether
  according to Lorentz theory, 23
  and atomic constitution of
    matter, 24
  drag, 18
  hypothesis of, 11, 14, 17
  and stresses and strains
      representing electrical
      forces, 24

Events, geometry of, 146–150
  and processes replacing objects
    in relativity theory 148
    (see also Minkowski
    diagram)
Experimental confirmation of
    relativity theory (see
    Relativity)

Falsifiability of theories
    (see Theories)
Falsification and confirmation of
    theories (see Theories)
Fizeau's method of measuring the
    speed of light, 12, 19, 107
Frames of reference
  for expression of space and time
    concepts, 42–47
  inertial, 7
  space, 44–46
  space and time, 48
  time, 46–47

Galileo, laws of, 6
  transformation of, 8
    (see also Laws)
Gibson, 197, 201, 204, 207
Gravitational mass (see Mass)

Hebb, 212
Held, 201
Hubel, 199, 200
Hyperbolic rotations in relativity,
    149

Identification of things, 112
Inertia, law of (see Laws)
"Inertial frame" of coordinates
    (see Frames of reference)
Inertial mass (see Mass)

Invariance of speed of light under
Lorentz transformation (*see*
Lorentz)

Kant, 213–214
K calculus, 133–145
Lorentz transformation in, 141

Laws
of addition of velocities in
relativity, 67
Copernican, 6
of Galileo, 6
of inertia, 7
of Lorentz, 23–26
of Maxwell, 11
of Newton, relativistic, 100–105
of Newton in terms of
momentum, 81
relational conception of, 4–9
Laws of physics
failure of in Newton's
equations, 72
invariance of, 71
in relation to light cones,
150–154
relational concept of, 4–9
Length, relativity of, 58–59
Light (*see* Speed of light)
Lodge's experiment, 18
Lorentz
contraction, 25, 64, 106
equations, invariance of, 108
theory of clocks, 26–30, 64
theory of electrons, 23–26
theory of ether, 23
theory of invariance of speed of
light, 38, 62
theory of simultaneity, 31
theory of synchronization of
clocks, 32

Lorentz—*continued*
transformation, 36–39, 106
transformation in Einstein's
theory, 61–63
transformation in K calculus,
141
transformation in vector
notation, 69

Mapping of percepts in concepts
in young children, 192
Mass
conservation of, 82, 100
effective, 27
electromagnetic, 29
as energy of inward and
outward movement,
116–117
and equivalence with energy,
91, 93, 108, 110
as explained by internal movement, 93, 117
gravitational aspect of, 113–114
inertial aspect of, 112–113
mechanical, 27
observed, 27
origin of conception of,
110–114
of radiation, effective, 95
relativistic formula for, 84–90
at rest, as equal to zero at
speed of light, 118
rest, invariance of, 98
Maxwell, equations of (*see* Laws)
Measurements
in Lorentz theory, 40–41
as relationships of phenomena
to instruments, 54
with rulers, 43
of time, 44

Michelson and Morley
  experiment, 14, 25, 107
Minkowski diagram, 131–133
  events in, 131
  as a map of events, 180–184
  not a kind of arena, 173–175
  principle of relativity in terms
    of K calculus, 133–145
  as a reconstruction, 174–180
  and the role of the observer,
    182–184
  world line in, 132
Momentum, conservation of, 82
  deduction of relativistic
    formula, 88

Newton's laws of motion, 6, 7
  relativistic form, 160
  (*see also* Laws)
Newton's laws in terms of the
    momentum, 81
  (*see also* Laws)
Nuclear transformations, 93

Observer as part of universe, 177

Paradox of "twins" in relativity,
    165–167
Particles, annihilation of, 93
Perception
  and abstraction, 219–223
  as active process, 197–207
  as attunement, 210–212
  breakdown of, 212–213
  as construction, 203
  as construction of hypotheses,
    215–217
  as extended by science,
    223–224, 230
  as mapping, 225
  optical, 198–207

Perception—*continued*
  role of in scientific research,
    226–227
  and its similarity to scientific
    research, 218–226
  tactile, 197–198
  in terms of structure, 207–
    215
  of time, 208–211
  and understanding in science,
    228–229
Piaget's observations on
    intelligence of children,
    187–197
Platt, 199
Popper's thesis (*see* Falsifiability
    of theories)
Principle of relativity (*see*
    Relativity)
Principle of relativity in
    Minkowski diagram (*see*
    Minkowski diagram)
Proper time (*see* Time)
Ptolemaic theory, 5

Recognition, process of, 188–189
Reflexes
  circular, 188
  coordination of, 188–189
  functional, 187–188
Relational conception of the
    laws of physics
  (*see* Laws of physics)
Relationships of physical
    phenomena to suitable
    measuring instruments
  (*see* Measurements)
Relative invariance
  domain of 121
  instead of permanence of
    things, 111–112

Relative invariance—*continued*
  in physics, 185–186
  in perception, 186
  of properties of matter,
    120–122
Relative truth of theories
  (*see* Theories)
Relativity
  of chronological time compared
    with psychological time,
    172
  confirmation of theory of,
    106–109
  and conservation laws, 89
  in electrodynamics, 70
  general, 55, 166–170
  in laws of electrodynamics and
    optics, 10
  in older laws of physics, 70
  in pre-Einsteinian laws of
    physics, 1, 4–10
  principle of, 8, 73–74, 106, 133
  special, 55
Rest mass explained as inward
  movement, 117
  (*see also* Mass)
Rest mass, invariance of (*see* Mass)

Science, as an essentially
  perceptual process, 226
  as an extension of perception,
    223–224, 230
Signal velocity, speed of light as
  limit on, 57
Simultaneity
  ambiguity of in relativity, 107
  its ambiguity in Lorentz
    theory, 32, 52
  failure of intuitive notions of,
    167–169

Simultaneity—*continued*
  meaning of, 53
  as nonabsolute in Einstein's
    theory, 57
  nonequivalence with
    co-presence, 54
Space
  absolute, 8, 48
  in common sense, 49
  coordinates as relationships, 61
  infants notions of, 190–191
  in Kant's view, 214–215
  measurements, 43
  new concepts of, 44–50
  relativity of, 58–59
  and time as continuum, 150
  unification with time in
    relativity, 149
Speed of light
  as effectively infinite, 47
  as finite, 47
  invariance of, 62
  invariance in Lorentz theory,
    38
  as limit on signal velocity,
    57, 68
  measured by Fizeau's method,
    12, 19, 107
  in running water, 75
Speed of light as maximum
  possible velocity of motion
  of objects, 68, 155–162
"System velocity," general, 83–84

Theories
  domains of truth of, 126
  falsifiability of, 123–125, 218
  falsification and confirmation
    of, 128 (*see also* Truth)
  relative truth of, 127

Time
    absolute, 9, 48, 50
    ambiguity in notions of, 54
    concept of, 50
    coordinates as relationships, 61
    differences, 139
    frame of reference, 46–47
    infants notions of, 190–191
    in Kant's view, 214–215
    measured by meson decay,
        76–77
    measured by moving clock, 107
    measurements, 44
    perception of, 208–211
    proper, 163–164
    relativity of, 59–60
    unification with space in
        relativity, 149
Transformation
    between systems of space
        coordinates, 45
    Galilean, 8
    laws for electric and magnetic
        fields, 104

Transformation—*continued*
    laws for energy and
        momentum, 96–99
    nuclear, 93
Truth, absolute, 125–130
    dynamic apprehension of, 130

Understanding in science as a
    form of perception
    (*see* Perception)
Unification of coordinates in
    geometry, 148
    of space and time in
        relativity, 149

Velocity of light in running
    water (*see* Light)

Wiesel, 199, 200
World line in Minkowski
    diagram (*see* Minkowski
    diagram)

Zero rest mass, 118 (*see also* Mass)